DIARMUID LYNCH

A FORGOTTEN IRISH PATRIOT

EILEEN McGOUGH

MERCIER PRESS

IRISH PUBLISHER – IRISH STORY

MERCIER PRESS

Cork

www.mercierpress.ie

ISBN: 978 1 78117 137 0

10 9 8 7 6 5 4 3 2 1

Printed and bound in the EU.

Contents

'It seemed to me that the men and women of 1916 were not merely rebels but people of vision. What they desired was not simply a government in Dublin, a green flag over Dublin Castle, and a harp on the coinage. These men and women were calling for a cultural revolution, for a transformation of both public and personal reality.'

From Robert Ballagh, '1916 and All That – a Personal Memoir', paper presented at a conference in Trinity College Dublin, 21–22 April 2006, organised by The Ireland Institute and Dublin University Historical Society.

Acknowledgements

Though I have lived in the Tracton area since 1971, it was only in recent times that I became aware that the grand-uncle of those Lynch boys, whom I had taught in the local Knocknamanagh National School, was a man of national significance. A cutting from *The Cork Examiner* was given to me. It was the column written by Pádraig Ó Maidín, County Cork Librarian, to mark the ninety-ninth anniversary of the birth of Diarmuid Lynch. It appeared on 7 January 1977 and gave a brief account of the life of Lynch.

Intrigued, I asked the Lynch family members still resident in the farmhouse where Diarmuid was born for further information, which they readily provided. Since 2007 I have been fully committed to the purpose of making Diarmuid Lynch's work for Ireland better known.

I thank Mary Lynch, who has been the custodian of Diarmuid Lynch's papers for over half a century; Mary's son Ruairí organised the papers in a user-friendly archive. I thank them both for their constant support and steady belief that I would do justice to his remarkable life. Both Diarmuid's niece and grand-niece, Bríd Duggan and Duibhne Daly, generously loaned relevant and precious documents they had in their possession. Another niece, Dolores Lynch, holds the unique distinction of being the only family member who personally knew Diarmuid and she was a source of everyday information on her uncle's life in his later years.

I was encouraged and supported at all times by the following persons whom I thank most sincerely: my husband, Michael Collins, and our extended family; my daughter, Emma, who proof-read; other meticulous proof-readers were neighbours and friends, Niall and Susan Marron and Lynda O'Flaherty; Doctor Michael Doorley, who, having produced a history of the FOIF in 2005, was in the position of knowing precisely what I should research and concentrate on and who generously gave all the help in his power; Gabriel Doherty, my tutor on the MA degree course at UCC, was ever a cheerful and most encouraging reference. I thank Daniel Breen at the Cork Museum and the museum photographer, Dara McGrath; Brian McGee and staff at the Cork City and County Archives; James Harte and other staff members at the National Library; personnel at the Boole Library at UCC; and Michael Mahoney, who obligingly carried out some research for me at the British National Archives at Kew, Richmond, Surrey.

I am grateful for the friendly enthusiasm of Mary Feehan of Mercier Press who, from the start, showed great heart for the project of bringing Diarmuid Lynch to public notice. Mary's late father, Captain Seán Feehan produced the only book which incorporates some of Lynch's reports, *The I.R.B. and the 1916 Insurrection* (1957).

I thank the staff of the American-Irish Historical Society headquarters in New York, who were cheerfully obliging in providing ready access to the crucial documents archived there. I pay tribute to John Fitzpatrick of Fitzpatrick's Hotel, Lexington Avenue, New York, who provided affordable, handsome and friendly lodgings for my week of research in 2011. I thank our New York-based friend, Frank Thompson, who undertook several successful researches in American archives; in one example of that research, Frank tracked down the sailing records of Diarmuid Lynch's many voyages to and from the USA.

Introduction

At a meeting of the Cork City branch of Cumann na nGaedheal on 31 August 1927, those present were considering potential candidates for the forthcoming by-election. An enquiry as to the possibility of inviting Diarmuid Lynch home from New York to contest the seat was met with the query, 'Who is Diarmuid Lynch?' This incurred a wrathful reply from Máire Bean Mhic Giolla Phóil, a sister of the late Michael Collins: '1916 is of course forgotten and so are all those who ever did anything in the fighting days.'[1]

Lynch was a native of Cork county, a member of the Supreme Council of the Irish Republican Brotherhood (IRB) at the time of the Easter Rising, a captain under the command of James Connolly in the GPO for the duration of Easter Week 1916, an elected member of the Dáil in 1918 and a dynamic activist in Ireland and in America after his release from prison in June 1917. Michael Collins was the only other nationalist apart from Lynch to hold power simultaneously in the three groups, the IRB, the Volunteers and Sinn Féin – but who has heard of Diarmuid Lynch?[2] How did he become an unknown in the heart of Cork just ten years after his release from Lewes Prison?

Lynch remains unknown today, despite much published material and media coverage about the IRB, the Easter Rising and the establishment of the Free State. The point was made by Dermot Keogh and Gabriel Doherty: 'Beyond Mick and Dev, what was known about other nationalist leaders … of the revolutionary generation? What was known, for example, about Harry Boland's political ideas and his political formation? The same question may be asked about scores of other leading revolutionaries of the time.'[3] Regarding his obliteration from the popular history of 1916, a relative of Lynch concluded wryly, 'Diarmuid's problem was that he lived, he was not executed.'[4]

Only the briefest autobiographical sketch of Lynch exists, in the book *The I.R.B. and the 1916 Insurrection.*[5] This book will show that Lynch was an unrepentant IRB man for life, an ardent and effective Gaelic League worker and an idealistic and leading nationalist. Adopting many roles successfully, he was envoy, courier, operative, strategist, IRB recruiter, fund-raiser, communicator, editor, researcher, secretary and drillmaster. In meeting the demands of his many roles, he was intelligent, cool, adaptable, dedicated and courageous. He deserves recognition as one of the main architects of the Rising of 1916 and as a crucial link between Ireland and Irish America in the lead-up to the Rising. He had lived in America for eleven years before 1916, thus holding a unique position as a delegate and communicator between the Irish Americans and the IRB in Ireland. There would not have been a Rising but for the monies secreted by Lynch and other couriers as they crossed and re-crossed the Atlantic, bringing the next instalment of cash from the hands of John Devoy and Clan na Gael to equip the Irish Volunteers.

James McGurrin, President-General of the American-Irish Historical Society (AIHS), on hearing of Lynch's death in November 1950, predicted that he would be favourably remembered: 'When the true story of the last forty years of Ireland's struggle for complete national independence is written, few names will shine with as bright a lustre as that of brave, honest, incorruptible Diarmuid Lynch.'[6] His prediction was incorrect. Of those who were in the inner circle of the IRB for the planning and execution of the Easter Rising, none are quite as forgotten as Lynch.

I intend to introduce Diarmuid Lynch to a new generation, to present the life and work of the man who was the last to leave the burning GPO in Easter Week 1916 – a man of integrity who was dedicated to Ireland, who sacrificed his health, career, comfort and financial security to further one cause: the independence of Ireland from Great Britain. I will also consider why he was so swiftly and completely forgotten.

1

'The Child is Father of the Man'[1]

Jeremiah Christopher (Diarmuid) Lynch was born on 10 January 1878 to a comfortable tenant farmer who leased lands overlooking the site where the medieval Cistercian foundation of Tracton Abbey once stood. The Lynchs have been members of the local farming community in south County Cork for generations. Their ancestor Jeremiah was a tenant of the Anglo-Norman landlord of Tracton Abbey, Achilles Daunt.[2] Jeremiah farmed almost 200 acres around his farmhouse in the townland of Granig. As an adult, Jeremiah's grandson and namesake (who used the Irish version, Diarmuid, of his name from early adulthood) took an interest in the ancestral graves in the churchyard of Tracton Abbey, and the record he compiled in 1902 of the several tombs and graves dating back to 1750 is still preserved by the Lynch family.

Tragedy struck early in Diarmuid's life as his mother, Hannah Dunlea of Carrignavar, County Cork, died from bronchial pneumonia on 20 July when he was an infant of six months. His father, Timothy Lynch, was then thirty-five years old and soon married for a second time. His new wife was Margaret Murphy of Ovens, County Cork, who bore him one daughter and four sons.

When writing a biographical essay in 1947 at the behest of Florence (Florrie) O'Donoghue, Lynch was warm in praise of his happy childhood, recalling:

> Our hard-fought hurling matches … Our camans varied from the factory-made to those cut, 'seasoned' and shaped by a few among us, and even to furze 'crooks.' … What competitions we had in running, jumping in all its phases; weight-throwing (nothing less than 28 lb. for us 'men' of 10–12 years!) when we locals adjourned in summer evenings down by Coveney's woollen mills … in spearing the other fellow's peg-top … Marble-playing of our type also called for a high degree of expertness …[3]

He wrote that he was most proud of successfully sewing a handmade *sliotar* (hurling ball) when he was around ten years old.[4]

His initial political education was from his father, who read aloud the speeches of prominent nationalist members of parliament, such as John Dillon and John Redmond. He recalled going with his father to hear Charles Stewart Parnell speak at the Imperial Hotel in Cork city on 21 January 1885, when those stirring words were uttered by Parnell: 'But no man has the right to fix the boundary to the march of a nation. No man has a right to say to his country: "Thus far shalt thou go and no further".' Another political event he attended with his father was a monster Land League meeting in the nearby village of Minane Bridge which was addressed by 'those fiery orators William O'Brien and Dr. Charles Tanner'.[5]

Timothy Lynch died aged forty-five in 1890, leaving his very capable widow with six children to rear and a large farm and its farm labourers to manage. Lynch, as the eldest and a stepson in this bereaved family, felt his responsibility: 'On my father's death when I was 13 years old, the "sling" and the catapult, the "crib" and the snipe snare were discarded, his shot-gun … took their place.'[6] Lynch left school to assist on the home front. He paid tribute to the education he had received while a pupil at Knocknamanagh National School from headmaster Michael McCarthy, an ardent nationalist who shaped the mind of this receptive youth.

Though no official textbook on Irish history then existed, Michael McCarthy taught his pupils about Ireland's past, from early Celtic myths to the era of the Anglo-Normans, who supplanted the Cistercians as lords of Tracton Abbey. Lynch claimed that 'deeper national feelings' were stirred in him by the rendition of patriotic ballads such as 'The Rising of the Moon' at the nearby home of his Ahern cousins. A portrait of Robert Emmet hung in his Granig home with the immortal words Emmet spoke from the dock inscribed thereon: 'When my country takes her place among the nations of the earth then and not 'til then let my epitaph be written.'[7] Apart from night classes in clerical training in Skerry's College in Cork city, Lynch had no further formal education. It was due to his remarkable intellect and self-education that he became a highly effective and accomplished communicator for the organisations of which he was later a member.

At the age of eighteen he passed the state examination for Britain's civil service and was packed off to London to earn his living. He worked as a boy clerk in the Mount Pleasant sorting office of the postal service at a salary of 14 shillings a week. The Mount Pleasant depot employed other fledgling nationalists, including Sam Maguire. Lynch shared lodgings at Duncan Terrace in Islington with another Cork man, Frank Burke, who got Lynch involved in the 'London Gaels' hurling team.[8]

Items from his earliest scrapbook reflect his homesickness. There are copies of poems exhorting the youth of Ireland to stay at home 'in dear old Ireland'. Lynch's copperplate writing of several long poems and ballads pay tribute to the excellent penmanship he was taught at national school. A letter from Michael McCarthy, sent to him at Christmas 1895, declared:

> After such a long silence since I received your last letter I would not be surprised if you thought I had forgotten about you altogether. But no! My dear pupil, I will never forget you, for although I had experience of Ballingarry, Myrtleville and the pupils educated therein in those schools, I must say that you, as a pupil, gave me the most utmost satisfaction.[9]

McCarthy congratulated Lynch on his ongoing study in London of the Irish language 'under a good man'.[10]

Lynch showed his continued political awareness during his exile as he archived and annotated newspaper columns, one of which reported anti-jubilee demonstrations that took place in Dublin in June 1897, protesting against Queen Victoria's Diamond Jubilee. This practice of assembling scrapbooks of newspaper reports, which were often decorated with acerbic comments, became a lifelong habit. On this occasion Lynch wrote, with incredulity, 'Is it possible?' after a sentence in the article claimed that 'The Jubilee was celebrated in almost all parts of Ireland with enthusiasm.'[11]

After some months in London, in 1896 Lynch seized the opportunity to emigrate to America. His maternal uncle and godfather, Cornelius Dunlea, who had emigrated from Carrignavar, County Cork, and was managing director and a partner in the American company of Farquhar & Company, organised this career move for him.

From rural and humble beginnings, Arthur Farquhar had built up a large and very successful company that manufactured agricultural machinery, exporting it to all parts of America and to many overseas markets. Its head office was in York, Pennsylvania, but the shipping office where Cornelius Dunlea worked was in the Cotton Exchange Building, Lower Manhattan, New York. According to *Dun's International Review*, 'The foreign business of A. B. Farquhar & Co. was built up mainly by the late Mr. Cornelius Dunlea, who travelled extensively throughout South America, South Africa, Russia, Cuba, Mexico, etc.'[12]

Correspondence in 1950 between Lynch and Maurice Fitzmahony of Midleton, County Cork, revealed that Maurice's father, Gerald Fitzmahony, 'a good friend of Uncle Corney's', had purchased Lynch's ticket and organised his passage from Queenstown at the behest of Cornelius Dunlea. Lynch spent his last night before sailing at the home of the Fitzmahony family in Midleton and was escorted to the quayside by them.[13] He arrived at Ellis Island in early March 1896.

Life in America delighted Lynch. He acquired a bicycle to save on tram fares and in later years wrote, 'I venture to say I knew the city [New York] better than most native born citizens.' During his first year in Manhattan he 'visited every spot of historical or other interest'.[14] He acquainted himself with the course of American history through a determined study of Bryce's *The American Commonwealth*.[15] He was employed alongside his uncle at the Cotton Exchange Building as a bookkeeper and shipping clerk at a salary of $18 a week. He lodged with a multinational group of tenants at an address in Lennox Avenue, and the first friendships he made in his early days in New York were with German Americans, who celebrated his twenty-first birthday with him in early 1899.[16] His relatives, the Dunleas, lived nearby in West Seventy-Seventh Street, Manhattan, and were supportive as he adapted to living in New York city.

As young Lynch found his way in New York, he searched out organisations that promoted Irish-American interests. He was anxious to continue with the Irish language classes begun in London, but feared that on his meagre salary both texts and fees would be beyond his reach. In the summer of 1897 he attended at the rooms of the Philo-Celtic Society with trepidation, but was relieved to be provided with an Irish language primer which cost a trifling 10 cents.[17]

The Philo-Celtic Society was founded in Boston, Massachusetts, in 1873, and by the 1890s there were several branches of the society in New York city. The society claims that Douglas Hyde founded the Gaelic League in Ireland following a visit to the Philo-Celtic branches in America in 1891, and, as the Gaelic League's revival work in Ireland flourished, it encouraged the Philo-Celtic Society in America, leading to increased membership.

Lynch became an enthusiastic and industrious member, rising to the position of secretary of a branch within a year. Lifelong friendships were forged between Lynch and two other members of the Philo-Celtic Society in New York: Joe McGuinness from County Longford and Richard (Dick) Dalton, a native of County Tipperary, who were dedicated activists for Irish culture and nationalism. On 4 March 1897, he and Dalton travelled to Washington, DC, to witness the inauguration of President William McKinley. He later recalled the deep impression which that day's events made on him, the singing of 'The Star-Spangled Banner', the immense mass of people and the solemn ceremony fronting the magnificent Capitol building.[18]

In 1899, when writing home to 'the boys' (his four half-brothers Dan, Tim, Denis and Michael), Lynch exhibited a new confidence and was campaigning enthusiastically to promote the study and use of the Irish language:

> How are you progressing with the Irish language? As I have said before, you can learn Irish without it in any way interfering with your other lessons. Are you not proud to be Irishmen? This is the time to put the shoulder to the wheel. Are you going to be among those who stand idly by and not lend a helping hand to preserve our beautiful inheritance?[19]

He informed them that he had sent papers about the language revival to Fr Patrick O'Neill, the parish priest of Tracton, who 'evidently did not think the matter worth worrying about'.[20] Lynch informed his brothers that he had circularised several other acquaintances in Ireland with the same promotional material concerning the revival under way in America.[21]

The enthusiasm of young Philo-Celtic Society members such as Lynch led to the society taking an official part for the first time in the St Patrick's Day Parade in 1901. Lynch had been promoted to the vice-presidency of the society, and he and Dalton manufactured large banners for the parade, which proclaimed nationalistic aspirations using the words of popular Gaelic ballads such as, 'Beid Éire Fós ag Cáit Ni Dubuidir [*sic*]' and 'Múscail do Misneach, A Banba'.[22]

The New York branch of the Philo-Celtic Society became politicised when in 1901 it began to oppose any stage production that smacked of the 'Stage Irish'. One protest was against the production of *McFadden's Row of Flats*, which ran at the Fourteenth Street Theatre in the winter of 1901. The play included an Irish male character who sported green whiskers and had a donkey and cart on stage. Lynch and Dalton were at the forefront of the protest, which, at first, consisted of a tame hissing at the actors. Lynch earned a 'black eye' as they were forcibly ejected from the theatre.[23] Further protests in New York, Philadelphia, Buffalo and Boston gained momentum, with *The New York Times* reporting, 'The actors and actresses were pelted with bad vegetables and worse eggs.'[24]

Lynch was proud to acquire American citizenship in 1902 and acknowledged, 'I can say that on first sight of the Statue of Liberty I felt myself to be a good American.'[25]

When Lynch returned to County Cork for a prolonged holiday in 1902, he gave a scrapbook to his childhood friend, Liam De Róiste of nearby Fountainstown, which contained newspaper cuttings describing the protests of the Philo-Celtic Society and other nationalist groups, such as the Ancient Order of Hibernians and Clan na Gael members. He also used his prized camera to take hundreds of photographs which are in the Lynch family archives in the farmhouse in Granig. Representing the Gaelic League in New York, Lynch attended the Ard-Fheis in the Assembly Rooms of the Rotunda in Dublin on Tuesday 20 May and made himself known to the activists in the language revival movement, including several future IRB fellow officers and Irish Volunteers, such as Bulmer Hobson, Eoin MacNeill and Douglas Hyde.

Lynch, with De Róiste, organised an *aeríocht* (outdoor concert) in the village of Minane Bridge in Tracton parish, County Cork, on Sunday 24 August. Lynch had arranged for the Fenian Edward O'Mahony, known as 'The Great American Basso', to perform. Four days later, Lynch and De Róiste attended the Munster Feis in Dunmanway, County Cork.[26] His ability to motivate and to organise, and the whirlwind of activities he undertook that summer, when he was only twenty-four years old, were indications of Lynch's capacity and stamina for work.

On his return to New York, Lynch was elected to the presidency of both the New York State Gaelic League and the Philo-Celtic Society, and he addressed successive meetings of both bodies on the topic of the Irish language revival during 1902 and 1903.

During his presidency, Fr Eugene O'Growney, author of many texts for the teaching of Irish, died in Los Angeles, California, and a decision was made to repatriate his body to Ireland. As president of the League, Lynch was responsible for the reception of the body when the cortège reached New York, en route to embarkation on the SS *Campania* for the final leg of the journey to Ireland. He brashly pestered (he admitted, years later) Daniel F. Cohalan, a high-profile New York lawyer and member of the American-Irish nationalist organisation Clan na Gael, to organise the Clan's Volunteers to provide a guard of honour for the coffin: '… the Guard of Honour materialised [and stood guard during the night in St Patrick's Cathedral].

Not alone that but the I.V. officers had the Regiment under orders to accompany the remains [on the following day] to the SS "Campania".'[27]

Lynch correctly recognised that Cohalan was a political power driver. The oldest child of Timothy Cohalan of Courtmacsherry, County Cork, and Ellen Leary, a native of the nearby village of Lislevane, Cohalan was involved with the Clan na Gael organisation from the 1890s and was district officer for the New York area. He was elected chairman in successive elections in 1902, 1904, 1906 and onwards. He was a member of the board of directors of the Irish-American Athletic Club from 1903 and was also listed as president of the board of directors of *The Gaelic American* newspaper, founded by John Devoy in 1903. Cohalan and his brothers ran a successful law firm in New York. Daniel was known to be chief confidential adviser of Charles F. Murphy, leader of the Tammany Society, a significant political force in New York city.

Cohalan purchased Glandore House in West Cork from Dean Reeves of Rosscarbery as a holiday home, and the Cohalan family stayed there annually. In the extensive gardens surrounding the property there is a 'Pearse Walk', and locals claim that Patrick Pearse stayed here as a guest of the Cohalans.[28]

Lynch's esteem for and loyalty to Cohalan was unwavering. In later years, he wrote of him, 'It is universally acknowledged that in every phase of human endeavour, certain individuals, because of devotion to principle, distinguished service, force of character, ability, experience and general equipment to advance a cause, always attain a commanding influence with their fellow men.'[29]

Lynch recruited Cohalan in 1903 to his cherished cause, the promotion of Irish culture and the revival of the Irish language. Cohalan was guest speaker at a meeting of the Greenpoint Gaelic Society in Brooklyn. Lynch also attended, and the two men shared a cab back to Manhattan.[30] Lynch strove to persuade Cohalan to support the efforts to revive the language, arguing that the revival could and would bolster the work of Clan na Gael. Lynch continued his recruitment campaign another day at the Lawyers' Club in Manhattan when the two men had lunch together. Not long afterwards Cohalan joined the Philo-Celtic Society and a lifelong friendship was forged between the two men.[31]

Around this time, the Philo-Celtic Society established an independent dance organisation, Cumann na Rinncí, to promote jigs, reels and hornpipes. A detailed, handwritten instruction sheet for the four-hand Irish reel is archived in Lynch's papers.

On 9 June 1904, Lynch and Joe McGuinness appeared on stage at the Lexington Opera House in the first Irish-language play ever staged in America, *Ar Son Cáit, a Chéad Grádh*. The play, produced by the Philo-Celtic Society, was based on a Lady Gregory short story and adapted for the stage by Andrew O'Boyle, a member of the society. Lynch also delivered a recitation, 'An Rúaig as Éirinn', and he was one of the four dancers of a reel. The play was a success and received favourable reviews from an American press which was frequently critical of Irish immigrants in the US. It went on to have a Broadway run, playing at the Amsterdam Opera House and the Mendelssohn Hall.

Following the sudden death of his uncle, Cornelius Dunlea, in 1900, Lynch had been working as travelling manager for the Farquhar company in his place. Homesickness caused him to apply for leave in the summer of 1904, which the owner of the Farquhar business reluctantly granted, sensing that the young man's mind was increasingly dwelling on returning to live and work in Ireland. The projected three-week holiday became a lengthy six-week stay because Lynch fell ill on the voyage and was bedbound at the farm in Granig for ten days. According to Lynch, the illness was caused by the 'late hours and continuous rush' involved in issuing a necessary catalogue for Farquhar before his departure.[32] The illness prevented his exploring a business opportunity that might have enabled him to return to live in Ireland.[33] He did attend the public reception in Dublin for a friend, the Irish-American athlete Martin Sheridan, who had competed in the Olympic Games in St Louis, Missouri, that year.

Lynch also spent time with Liam De Róiste. An entry in De Róiste's diary relates, 'Christy Lynch, home from New York, addressed the Celtic Literary Society meeting. Had a walk with him afterwards, 'til midnight.'[34] De Róiste invariably used the familiar 'Christy' when referring to Lynch.

Back in New York, Lynch resumed his work with both

the Gaelic League and the Philo-Celtic Society, in particular preparing for the visit of Douglas Hyde, president of the Gaelic League in Ireland, who hoped to raise funds in a tour of America. There was a succession of letters between Lynch and Hyde from March 1905. Hyde wrote in May from Frenchpark, County Roscommon, 'If I go out in October, how do you think I might go, as a private visitor or as a delegate from our own Coiste Gnótha at home? Who should notify the AOH [Ancient Order of Hibernians] etc., of my intended visit?'[35] Relying on Lynch to smooth the way in New York, he sympathised with him on his recurring ill health.[36] Lynch's physician, Gertrude Kelly (a labour radical and feminist who also espoused Irish independence as a cause) was perturbed by Lynch 'looking so tired, worn and white' at a meeting on 16 May.[37]

A 'splendid and enthusiastic audience in Carnegie Hall' welcomed Hyde on 26 November 1905. Lynch presented him with a colourful scroll designed to mark the occasion. In February 1906, Lynch wrote to all branches of the League requesting financial donations to suitably mark the end of Hyde's tour. The Philo-Celtic Society presented Hyde's play *An Pósadh* at the Lexington Opera House on 28 April, with Lynch playing the part of Antoine Ó Raifteirí, the poet, and Dick Dalton taking the role of the farmer.[38] One of Douglas Hyde's final public appearances, which Diarmuid Lynch helped to organise, was at Madison Square Garden on Friday 11 May.

Lynch and Dalton were back on the offensive in January

1907 at the Hammerstein's Victoria Theatre. The Russell Brothers, who were dramatic directors and actors in the USA, were staging one of their 'Irish Servant Girls' sketches, with the predictable sequence of drunkenness, ribald sayings and simple-minded characters whacking each other with brooms, drinking their employer's booze, breaking china, etc. The show ran to full houses for almost a week before the night of 21 January, when over 300 protestors took over the theatre, pelted the actors with rotten fruit and hurled insults. The show was abandoned.[39] The anti-'Stage Irish' campaign continued vigorously, and in July 1907 Lynch and Dalton protested against another Russell Brothers production which featured Irish burlesque actors at the Opera House and the Orpheum Theatre in Brooklyn. One of their co-protestors was Tom Clarke, who was employed by John Devoy as general manager of *The Gaelic American* weekly newspaper.

By this time, Lynch's homesickness had grown considerably. He later wrote, 'From my earliest connection with the Irish language revival the desire to return permanently to Ireland had grown stronger. By March 1907 I decided that for its fulfilment some drastic step was essential.'[40] Lynch gave formal notice to his employer on 12 March 1907. Farquhar replied immediately, and his regret at losing a most valued employee is evident:

> ... my experience, extended over some fifty years of observation, is that very few who do return [to Ireland] are satisfied. They find the field so much broader in this country that they come back

again, and I fancy it may be the same with you. I honestly believe as your friend, that you would have a better chance of material prosperity, and in the long run, happiness, where you are now and believing this, would it not be well for you to merely take a vacation of a few months?[41]

Lynch sailed for Ireland in July 1907. He later reflected on his reasons for leaving America and the people with whom he had forged strong friendships, people such as Diarmuid O'Donovan Rossa, Dr Thomas Addis Emmet (descended from the family of patriot Robert Emmet) and John Devoy, founder and proprietor of *The Gaelic American* newspaper: 'What an honour and inspiration it was for a young Irishman to have known such living links with Ireland's fight for freedom over the previous century!' In relation to the life he had known in America, he concluded it had been, 'All told, a full life and a happy one – from which I was now about to divorce myself. Well, "the savage loves his native shore." The rest of the answer is that Ireland was the place where "Irish-Ireland" activities were all-important.'[42]

A resolution was unanimously passed at a meeting of the Executive Committee of the Gaelic League, New York, which appeared in *The Cork Examiner*: 'While we regret the loss which this organisation sustains in Mr Lynch's departure, we must congratulate our fellow workers in Ireland on the accession to their ranks of such an exemplary, brilliant and patriotic Gaelic Leaguer.'[43] A friend on the staff of the *New York Herald* wrote:

You did great work here for the Gaelic League, noble work in fact, and what is more you did it modestly. Your part in introducing the Irish drama in New York constitutes in itself an achievement to be proud of. You are bound to meet Douglas Hyde, and won't he welcome you home. There is no fear that he will forget or be unmindful of the part you played in contributing to the success of his great mission two years ago.[44]

A.B. FARQUHAR Co. Limited

York, Pa.

Mar. 13, 1907.

My dear Mr. Lynch:

Your letter of March 12th has just reached me. Yes, I remember that you have several times spoken of your longing for your old home in Ireland. This is natural, and there is no doubt a special attraction there, but my experience, extended over some fifty years of observation, is that very few who do return are satisfied. They find the field so much broader in this country that they come back again, and I fancy it may be the same with you.

A.B. Farquhar Co. Ltd was the company for which Diarmuid Lynch worked from 1896 to 1907. This is part of the letter written to him by Arthur Farquhar attempting to discourage him from returning to Ireland. *Courtesy of Lynch Family Archives*

2

Ireland, 1907–1915

A friend and fellow activist of Diarmuid Lynch, Tom Clarke was also determined to return to Ireland. Clarke was an IRB man and a member of Clan na Gael in New York. His widow Kathleen Clarke later wrote, 'By 1907 Tom was hinting that he would like to go back to Ireland and get things moving' as 'some of the well-informed American journals began to talk of the inevitability of war between England and Germany. The tragedy it would be if Ireland failed to avail herself of such an opportunity to make a bid for freedom.'[1]

Both Clarke and John Devoy, a leading member of Clan na Gael, were aware that the IRB in Ireland was undergoing a shake-up and a renewal, with younger men such as Bulmer Hobson and Denis McCullough coming to the fore of the organisation. McCullough had sworn Hobson into the IRB in 1904. Seán MacDiarmada, Cathal Brugha and Éamonn Ceannt were all sworn in during 1908. The perennial aspiration of the IRB, to win Irish freedom by force of arms, had been resurrected.

Before Clarke left for Ireland in November 1907, Devoy 'promised him all the help in his power, a promise he kept faithfully', according to Kathleen Clarke.[2] He also gave Clarke letters of introduction to the IRB in Ireland, as Tom intended to start his campaign to take advantage of the coming war between England and Germany and 'strike a blow for freedom through the IRB'.[3]

Clan na Gael had signalled its willingness to fund an amalgamation of three existing Irish nationalist groups: the Dungannon Clubs, Arthur Griffith's Sinn Féin party and the Gaelic League. Clarke and Lynch were both aware of this Clan objective, which was achieved in the autumn of 1907. The new entity took the name of one of its component parts, the Sinn Féin party.[4]

As a friend of both Devoy and Clarke, and imbued with the same ambition for Ireland's independence from Britain, when Lynch returned to Ireland in July 1907 he was soon canvassing with Seán MacDiarmada in the North Leitrim by-election on behalf of the Sinn Féin candidate, Charlie Dolan. Not long after his return from America, Fred Allen and P. T. Daly approached him for a 'chat' about the overall situation in America. He claimed that it was later that he learned these men were part of the Supreme Council of the IRB.

Whether Lynch was a member of the IRB, that very secret society, when he first returned to Ireland, is a matter for conjecture. He was always a strong advocate of and adherent to the secrecy practised by the IRB. In his autobiography, he asserted that he was officially approached by Seán T. O'Kelly to join the IRB in 1908 and was then initiated into the Bartholomew Teeling Circle.[5] From 1908 to 1910 Lynch was active in Dublin, attending to both Gaelic League work and IRB clandestine meetings. Men like Hobson, Brugha, MacDiarmada and Ceannt, who were also involved in the Gaelic League or the Sinn Féin party, were now the colleagues and co-activists of Lynch.

Six months after returning to Ireland in 1907 Lynch was still unemployed and Dick Dalton wrote to him from America:

> It's very plain to see that you have been up against it in your efforts to make things go as you wanted them to. Let me now presume on our friendship, and tell you something which perhaps few else can. Don't go ahead and wreck your life. It's too valuable. If Ireland is not ready for you, do not sacrifice yourself for an idea; be a bigger man than you ever were before, and that is saying something, be a bigger man than most of us could be, and come back.[6]

His former employer, A. B. Farquhar, also heard of his fruitless search for employment and wrote to him, 'Sooner or later you will want to come back, and whenever you do you may rest assured you will find the latch string out.' He then offered Lynch re-employment in New York or the option of forging new business for the company in Argentina.[7]

It took almost a year for Lynch to find employment in Dublin. He wrote in his autobiography:

Eventually, in March 1908 I was glad to accept a rather minor post with Thomas McKenzie & Sons, Dublin, – in charge of Feeding Stuffs, Artificial Manure and the Fittings Department … my salary was about one-eighth of that relinquished by me in New York. Even so, I was quite content, busy as I was endeavouring to get a thorough grasp of this retail trade …[8]

In 1910 Lynch relocated to Cork, in a move that was probably planned by the IRB as he immediately became a member of the Cork Circle. He must have impressed, because a year later Seán O'Hegarty (head of the IRB in Cork) notified Lynch that he was 'selected as Divisional Centre for Munster on the Supreme Council'.[9] Lynch wrote in 1947: 'The Circle at Cork City – to which I was transferred about 1910 – was then in its infancy with a small membership which included: Sean O'Hegarty (Centre), Thomas Barry, Tomas MacCurtain, Sean Murphy, Domnall Og O'Callaghan, Diarmaid [*sic*] Fawsitt, Bob Langford, Tadgh Barry, Tommy O'Riordan, Tommy O'Mahony, Sean O'Sullivan, Billy O'Shea.' He added, 'Elsewhere in the County the only Circles I recollect were at Cobh and Millstreet. There were groups at Kinsale, Fermoy, Glanworth, Mitchelstown, Skibbereen and Tracton. I swore in men in some of these places.'[10]

Mick Crowe and Cathal Brugha had done some work in Munster, but Lynch's 'opportunities were more widespread than those of Brugha and Crowe'.[11] Part-time employment as an insurance agent meant that as he travelled the country to

IRB meetings he had a plausible explanation of his journeys for the Royal Irish Constabulary (RIC) and other security personnel. 'I made constant trips through the South as manager in Munster for the Equitable Life Assurance Society of the US.'[12]

Lynch secured further employment with Sutton's of Cork city, merchants for seeds, farm implements and machinery, which also employed Tomás MacCurtain. Tom Clarke wrote to John Devoy in February 1911 and mentioned this new work: 'Jer. Lynch of the Gaelic League, N.Y., at present is in Cork City and is doing well managing the seed and hardware department of the biggest firm in that line in Cork.'[13]

In December 1913, Lynch and Denis McCullough addressed a meeting at the Foresters' Hall, Dublin, to urge members of the IRB to get fully involved in the formation of the new Irish Volunteers, which had been set up in November 1913. Patrick Pearse was present at this meeting, and Lynch thought it was the first IRB meeting Pearse attended.

When Lynch crossed and criss-crossed the country, not only on Equitable Life Assurance Society business, but also on secretive IRB business, he tried to keep his movements hidden from the security forces. Even so, in June 1915 he was ordered by the British government to register as a 'friendly alien' because of his American citizenship. Intelligence sources had by now identified him as a suspicious activist. As a 'friendly alien' he was to report to the RIC on entering and leaving any 'Proclaimed Area' to have his pass stamped.[14] Lynch knew that G-men (plain-clothes detectives) routinely tracked his movements, relaying his position to the security forces at his next destination.

Lynch recorded that he attended Circle meetings in Limerick, Galway, Sligo, Westport and Tipperary. When in Limerick, he never missed an opportunity of calling on John Daly, the Fenian veteran, whose niece, Kathleen, was married to Tom Clarke. An incident at Ennistymon, County Clare, was related to Florrie O'Donoghue in later years:

> At Ennistymon, 1915, I learned from Sean O'Muirthille [*sic*] that the local Irish Volunteers were negotiating with the Redmond Volunteers ... for the purchase of twenty Enfield Rifles, but had not the cash to complete the transaction. I went straight to Dublin and The O'Rahilly gave me the requisite £40. Returning I put up at Sean O'Muirthille's headquarters – a small hotel where Tomas O'Loughlin was also staying at the time. It was agreed that the local IVs [Irish Volunteers] should retain ten rifles. The other ten were to be distributed at my discretion; ... Next morning, I learned that old Tomas on his own initiative ... had remained on guard all night on the stairs outside my room – he having become suspicious of a young R.I.C. man going home on leave who happened to stay at the hotel overnight.[15]

Under Lynch's influence, his brother Michael formed a strong company of the Irish Volunteers in Tracton. Its members included the Nunan brothers of Ballinluig, William and Seán O'Brien of Tubrid, the O'Hallorans of Ballingarry, the

O'Callaghans of Reagrove and another of Lynch's brothers, Tim.[16] The receipt for Michael's Volunteer subscription for 1915 was signed by Bulmer Hobson and Tim's by The O'Rahilly, a founding member of the organisation.

Diarmuid and Michael Lynch attended a Volunteer training camp in County Wicklow in August 1915, under the directorship of J. J. O'Connell of the Cork Volunteers. In early September, the Cork City Volunteers 'marched from the city to Tracton, bivouacked that night at Lynch's, Granig, and after exercises next day, marched back to the city'.[17] Lynch and the curate of Tracton Abbey, Fr Florence O'Mahony, were listed in British Intelligence reports of 1915, where Fr O'Mahony was cited to have been 'present when suspect D. Lynch was drilling thirty young men' on 21 November in Minane Bridge.[18]

Since his return from America in 1907, as well as his work for the IRB and Volunteers, Lynch had continued as an active officer in the Gaelic League. His travelling salesman job for the Equitable Life Assurance Society meant that he could frequently attend Gaelic League meetings in locations around the country. The *Cork County Eagle* reported his presence at one such meeting on 4 May 1913, in Castlehaven, County Cork.

By now, Lynch and other IRB activists had decided to politicise the Gaelic League as they asserted that a 'right wing' had developed in the organisation that supported John Redmond and the Irish Parliamentary Party.[19] Douglas Hyde was president of the League, and he was adamant that politics should not intrude in its affairs, but Lynch challenged him on this principle during the Ard-Fheis in Galway in 1913, querying from the floor, 'An tusa an Ard-Fheis?' – a rhetorical question asking Hyde whether he considered himself the sole decision-maker on the Coiste Gnótha, the steering body of the organisation.

This campaign continued in America during a Gaelic League tour undertaken by Lynch and Thomas Ashe (Tomás Ághas) in 1914. In January of that year, 'Tomas Aghas and myself went on a mission to the United States to raise money for the Gaelic League.'[20] The tour was not a financial success, and in March Lynch wrote from New York to his brother Michael: 'Everybody has the "poor mouth". Money is as hard to get as in Ireland.'[21]

Lynch was in New York on 9 March when Pearse made the 'Emmet Commemoration Speech', which concluded as follows:

> To the grey-haired men whom I see on this platform, to John Devoy and Richard Burke, I bring, then, this message from Ireland, that their seed-sowing of forty years ago has not been without its harvest, that there are young men and boys in Ireland today who remember what they taught and who, with God's blessing, will one day take or make an opportunity of putting their teaching into practice.[22]

In an interview at the time with *The Columbiad*, Lynch declared, 'The Gaelic League is the advance army fighting for Irish nationality.'[23]

The *Irish-American* newspaper reported on a meeting at the Gaelic League of Ireland Headquarters, Madison Avenue, on 9 April. Judge Daniel Cohalan, a member of the Finance Committee of the League, presided. Lynch and Ashe spoke of their progress and planned campaign. Lynch asserted, 'No man of Irish blood with any pretence to patriotism will refuse to subscribe at least $1 to such an all-important national work as the propagation of the Irish language, which is the hallmark of the Irish nation.'[24]

In May the pair of Gaelic League 'missionaries' were in Boston. Lynch and Ashe sometimes dressed in kilts and other recognisably Celtic garments. Lynch explained this dress code in an interview with the *Boston Globe*: 'The Gaels of the Highlands originally emigrated from Ireland taking with them the Gaelic language and Gaelic dress.'[25] The paper also reported him as saying that 'the immediate object of the visit is to enable the Gaelic League in Ireland to increase its field staff of organisers and travelling teachers'.

On 1 June 1914, bolstered by the presence of Pearse, Ashe and Lynch who were all in the USA at that time, Devoy, Richard Burke and others in Clan na Gael set up a new committee, the American Provisional Committee, with the specific aim of raising money for the Irish Volunteers.[26]

With the outbreak of the Great War in August and with little prospect of successfully raising funds for the Gaelic League, Ashe returned to Ireland, but Lynch stayed on as the IRB envoy to the Clan na Gael Biennial Convention at

Atlantic City, New Jersey. Lynch's report on the depleted state of the IRB in Ireland came as an unwelcome shock to the Clan. Roger Casement was one of the speakers to address the convention. Funds were solicited, specifically and publicly at the convention, to arm the Volunteers in Ireland.

Meanwhile, in Ireland John Redmond had announced that the Irish Volunteers would support Great Britain in the war with Germany. Outrage was expressed by speaker after speaker to the convention in progress at Atlantic City at John Redmond's betrayal. Devoy's paper, *The Gaelic American* stated, 'Ireland's interests would be best served by England's defeat in this war. Ireland's sympathies in this war should be with Germany, as her interests undoubtedly are.'[27] The Volunteer organisation split, with the majority of members following Redmond in the National Volunteers, and a depleted Irish Volunteer force left to continue the campaign for Ireland's independence.

In October 1914, after thirty-three weeks in America, Lynch requested his expenses to settle his bills and book his passage home. However, no money was forthcoming from the Gaelic League in Ireland. Lynch received a letter that stated 'Coiste an Airgid [Finance Committee] directs me to say that in the present state of our finances, we are unable to send you a remittance.'[28] He was told to settle his bills from the monies that had been collected.

Lynch sailed for home in November, a draft for $2,000 from Devoy and the Clan concealed on his person – money to arm the Volunteers. He had also purchased an automatic pistol for his own use, which he dutifully declared to the customs officer, who promptly confiscated it. The declaration was a calculated ruse to deflect attention from a more thorough search of his person that might have revealed the hidden money draft.[29] Lynch was instructed to apply to the Home Secretary for the return of his firearm, which he did, and he observed, 'the pistol and ammunition reached me by post; they remained in my possession for "Easter Week".'[30]

In April 1914, Ashe had written to Devoy: 'D. Lynch and I mean to do our utmost to re-model the Gaelic League to get it to preach strong, sterling nationality, and to rid it of some of the old women and of some of the fossils that control it at present.'[31] IRB members who were also members of the Gaelic League wanted to wrest control of the League from the 'right wing' of the organisation. That right wing strove to be apolitical, cooperated with Dublin Castle and was aligned with the Redmonite Party in favour of Home Rule. According to Lynch:

By the summer of 1915, however, when the stage was being secretly set for Insurrection against Britain, the time had come in my opinion when the 'Left Wing' [of the Gaelic League] should control the Coiste Gnotha [Steering Committee] ... Well in advance of the Ard Fheis date I communicated with prominent Gaelic Leaguers – who were also I.R.B. men – urging that delegates favourable to our political views should without fail be selected to attend at Dundalk [for the Gaelic League's Ard-Fheis].[32]

When Seán MacDiarmada and Ernest Blythe (both impris-oned at the time and both IRB men) were the first nomina-tions from the floor for the Coiste Gnótha, Douglas Hyde quickly realised that the Ard-Fheis had been usurped by the IRB faction and resigned as president. Lynch observed, 'had he given that [his resignation] as an ultimatum when the list of nominations was read, we would not have swerved from our plan at that juncture in national affairs.'[33]

The decision of the Supreme Council of the IRB that the war between Germany and Great Britain provided an opportunity to mount an insurrection against British rule in Ireland led to an accelerated programme. Strategic organisational changes were initiated, such as the abolition of an advisory committee and the establishment of a nuclear, three-man military committee.[34] At a meeting of the IRB Executive at the end of May, Lynch moved the motion to have Pearse, Joseph Plunkett and Éamonn Ceannt formally appointed as the IRB's 'Military Committee'.[35]

When Seán MacDiarmada, secretary of the IRB, had been imprisoned in May 1915, Lynch had taken on the duties of secretary in his place.[36] As secretary, he was privy to the agenda planned by Pearse and Clarke, and supervised the divisional elections of the IRB in the west of Ireland.[37] He also deputised for MacDiarmada as business manager of the *Nationality* paper (the Sinn Féin newspaper edited by Arthur Griffith) and, indeed, it was Lynch who oversaw the production of the final edition of *Nationality* on the Saturday of Holy Week, 1916.

The funeral of O'Donovan Rossa in early August 1915 provided the nationalist movement with an excellent opportunity to proclaim its intention to seek independence. Lynch was now a leading member of the small group that was planning an armed uprising. All of the main players in this plan were at the graveside in Glasnevin Cemetery on 1 August, among them Patrick Pearse, Éamonn Ceannt, Tom Clarke, Con Colbert, James Connolly, Major John MacBride, Thomas MacDonagh and Éamon de Valera. At a meeting after the funeral, Pearse, Clarke, Seán MacDiarmada and Patrick McCartan were co-opted to the Supreme Council of the IRB.[38]

Late in August, the IRB sent Robert Monteith (a captain in the Irish Volunteers) to Germany. Lynch and Clarke briefed him in Clarke's tobacconist's shop in Parnell Street, Dublin. Monteith went first to Devoy in New York, then on to Germany to assist Roger Casement in his efforts to recruit German aid for the planned rising.[39]

Confident that Devoy would deliver on the promise of German arms, in September 1915 Pearse planned a trip for Lynch to Kerry to decide on the best landing site. Having completed his official insurance business and undercover IRB business in Cork city, Lynch reported to the RIC station, as required by the British authorities, before leaving the city. In Tralee he met Austin Stack and other Volunteers, and both they and the Dingle IRB Centre were convinced that Fenit was the most advantageous location for the delivery of the cargo of arms.

***

During 1914, John Devoy published a series of articles in *The Gaelic American* written by Roger Casement between 1911 and 1914. The monthly bulletin of the IRB in Dublin, *Irish Freedom*, subsequently republished the articles, and the Supreme Council decided to distribute them in pamphlet form, as *Ireland, Germany and the Freedom of the Seas*.[40] They commissioned Larry de Lacey, editor of the *Enniscorthy Echo*, to print them. (De Lacey and several of his staff were IRB members.) The pamphlet, which included titles such as 'How Ireland Might Help Germany and How Germany Should Help Ireland', was viewed as seditious by a British government preparing for war with Germany.[41] The following extract exemplifies the sentiments expressed in it:

> The day the first German comrade lands in Ireland, the day the first German warship is seen proudly breasting the waves of the Irish Sea, with the flag of Ireland at her prow, that day many Irishmen must die, but they shall die in the sure peace of God that Ireland may live.[42]

When the printing was completed, the pamphlets were stored in de Lacey's home until the time was right. A raid on his house by the RIC did not uncover the criminal printed matter, and the dangerous cargo was moved to a vacant building, Oulartleigh House, near Borelia in County Wexford.

Lynch undertook the job of distribution. As he was employed by Sutton's agricultural merchants in Cork city, he had access to lists of the names and addresses of the recipients of annual bulb and seed catalogues, as well as the postal addresses for county councillors and other professional men who were routinely sent advertising materials in envelopes which were stamped with the logos of a number of Irish agricultural businesses. Sutton's, as a major distributor of such materials, had supplies of these prestamped business envelopes, which Lynch confiscated for the planned distribution of the seditious pamphlet.

In September, Lynch set off from Dublin to retrieve the pamphlets. His companion was Joe Dunn, taxi driver and IRB member. Both men were armed. On the road south to Wexford, while enjoying a brief stop in their journey, a car in which a British naval officer was travelling came into view. Joe quickly pretended to be working on his engine. The driver stopped to ask if they needed help, an offer Joe graciously declined saying that he had 'only a little engine trouble'.[43]

It was late when they set off on the return journey to Dublin, their cargo of pamphlets concealed in burlap potato sacks. A dense fog had descended along the east coast, which slowed them considerably, and it was 2 a.m. when they reached Arklow, County Wicklow. They came to a halt near Kynoch's Munitions Factory, unsure of which direction to take, when a car came up behind them. They hoped that its occupants would be able to direct them correctly, but to their horror it was the same naval officer they had encountered on the outward journey. To compound the danger, while the men were in strained conversation, an armed coastguard jumped over a nearby ditch and approached them.

The coastguard questioned Lynch and Dunn about their destination and the purpose of the journey. He glanced into the back of the car, but the window was fogged up and he did not notice the sacks piled up on the back seat. 'Had that Coastguard opened the door and seen the rear piled with burlap bags containing bulky material, certain it is that further investigation would ensue – with the alternative of shooting our way out.'[44]

The sentry gave them correct directions but Dunn and Lynch were not out of trouble yet, as the naval officer's car followed them for many miles. Dunn tried to shake them off by speeding up, at considerable risk in the deplorable driving conditions, but the official car also quickened its pace, no doubt glad of the guidance of their rear lights in the fog. This continued for a long time, and their dilemma was where to deposit their cargo safely without arousing any suspicion. Fortunately, the other car turned off towards Wicklow town, but it was almost daylight when the IRB men finally reached the outskirts of Dublin and Lynch deemed it too dangerous to approach Anthony Mackey's house on the south side of the city, as had been arranged.

Dunn drove to St Enda's School in Rathfarnham instead, where Pearse lived and worked. They hurriedly hid the sacks in the shrubbery along the avenue, then Lynch went on up to the house to tell Pearse, who promptly came down to see the material for himself. Pearse said that he would inform his caretaker, Micheál Mac Ruadhraí about what was deposited in the shrubbery, and when Lynch wondered aloud if this was prudent, Pearse replied, 'Oh, I must tell Miceal [*sic*]; if he should come across them during the day and realised that I had not trusted him with my knowledge of their whereabouts he'd never forgive me.'[45]

During the following days the pamphlets were safely removed to various houses around Dublin for the final task of putting them into envelopes. Using Lynch's mailing lists, Connolly had already addressed the empty envelopes at Liberty Hall.

The next step in the distribution operation was on Sunday 12 September, when Wexford and Dublin met at Croke Park for the Leinster Senior Football Final. Suitcases of the pamphlets were collected by IRB men 'up for the match' from the provinces. They were instructed to post all of their packages at their respective post offices at precisely 6 p.m. on the following Thursday. The Dublin consignment almost came to grief when the lad charged with posting it arrived minutes too late at the correct postal department, but, having spun a tale of woe about how his job would be in jeopardy if he missed the 6 p.m. postal deadline, an unsuspecting and kindly clerk relented. Denis McCullough told Florrie O'Donoghue that it was his wife, Agnes Ryan, who brought the consignment of pamphlets destined for northern recipients to Belfast and posted them there.[46]

Lynch travelled back to Cork on the Thursday. On Friday morning he took a trip in to Kinsale town from Granig, anxious to see if his plan had worked. When he called to chat to Séamus O'Neill in his shop, O'Neill showed Lynch the extraordinary package he had received that morning, a banned pamphlet of flagrantly anti-British material, purportedly sent out from a leading unionist business in Cork. What was more, he knew that others had received the same materials in the morning post. Leaving a bemused O'Neill, Lynch went home, well satisfied.[47]

Outrage was quickly expressed around the country by those loyal to the British crown and by the seed merchants who had played an involuntary role in the distribution. One Belfast-based company, White, Tomkins & Courage, offered a reward of £100 for any information that would reveal the identity of those who had abused their good name.[48] Messrs Nicholas Hardy & Co. Ltd of Dundalk offered a similar reward. Other companies who unwittingly assisted the widespread distribution were Fennesseys of Waterford, Mackeys of Dublin and the Co-op. Society of Limerick. Another outcome was that the Post Office tightened up its regulations about packages presented for postage. From that day on, all packages had to be opened and inspected before being sent on to recipients.

A month after the successful distribution of the Casement pamphlet, Lynch and Ned Hegarty carried a consignment of arms to the Cork Volunteers from Dublin.[49] Lynch also procured two cases of type in Dublin for the printing press at the Cork headquarters of the Volunteers. Robert Langford, second lieutenant of the Cork City Volunteer Brigade, had lost his job as a printer with *The Cork Examiner* because of his Volunteer activities. When Lynch delivered the type to Cork, Langford was able to resume printing Volunteer publicity material, inflammatory propaganda which no orthodox printer would handle.

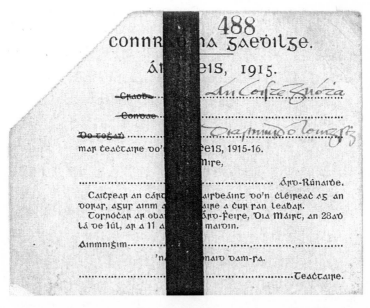

Diarmuid Lynch's delegate card for the Gaelic League Ard-Fheis, 1915. *Courtesy of Lynch Family Archives*

3

1916

Early in January 1916, Pearse and Lynch met at St Enda's School in Rathfarnham. Pearse gave Lynch instructions for the Volunteers in Cork, Kerry, Limerick and Galway. He was to convey the instructions orally to the commandants of the brigades in those counties on his next scheduled journey to the areas. However, before Lynch could carry out that crucial mission he was reclassified by British Intelligence as an 'enemy alien', so he was no longer free to travel outside a five-mile radius of his Dublin address.[1]

When the eleven members of the Supreme Council of the IRB met at Clontarf Town Hall in January 1916, MacDiarmada's motion 'That we fight at the earliest date possible' was accepted by the Council. Lynch observed that the crucial date had already been decided by the Military Committee members, Pearse, Clarke and MacDiarmada, but it was not conveyed to the others at the meeting, a precaution to maintain the secrecy deemed necessary and jealously guarded.

James Connolly of the Irish Citizen Army (ICA) was

made privy to the plans in January and was co-opted onto the Military Committee to circumvent his threat to stage an immediate military coup with the ICA. Subsequently, Connolly was present at a meeting in March with MacDiarmada, Pearse, Ceannt and Plunkett at 77 Amiens Street. Lynch arrived at the house to confer with MacDiarmada. '[Connolly's] look of astonishment at my entry convinced me that he had no notion that any person other than the present colleagues of the Military Committee knew of the existence of such a group.'[2]

In New York the Irish Race Convention, which was convened by Clan na Gael, established a new organisation, the 'Friends of Irish Freedom' (FOIF) on 4 March 1916. The Executive included Cohalan and Dalton, with Devoy attending each meeting until his death in 1928. Four of those attending the convention knew that an insurrection was planned for Easter Sunday, including Devoy and Cohalan, who were involved in the plan to import armaments to Ireland from Germany. Devoy went so far as to attempt to book a passage to Dublin to be present for the realisation of his dream of armed insurrection, but the seventy-four-year-old Fenian veteran was dissuaded from travelling.[3]

At the beginning of April, Lynch formed an ad hoc committee to plan the sabotage of telegraph and telephone lines between Dublin Castle and various barracks in Dublin and other police posts further afield. Lynch jocosely referred to this committee as 'The Committee on Manholes'. Richard Mulcahy and other operatives employed by the Post Office were involved, and manholes covering strategic telephone lines to and from Dublin Castle were identified and mapped. Duplicate keys for the manholes had to be acquired and tools for lifting them were supplied to each appointed operative. The completed plan was presented by Lynch to MacDiarmada on the Monday of Holy Week 1916.

Lynch lunched with MacDiarmada on the Wednesday of Holy Week, and when Seán said to him, 'Diarmuid, I want to tell you something which you should have been informed of earlier, the Rising is fixed for next Sunday', Lynch replied, 'I know that.' MacDiarmada was confounded, as the secret had been closely guarded from all but the very few necessary persons. Lynch allayed the alarm he had caused, saying 'Seán, no one actually told me but ever since the January meeting of the Supreme Council I was satisfied on that point in my own mind.'[4]

Certainly, Lynch was in such close contact with all of the key personnel during the months from January onwards that it would be surprising if he had not come to the correct conclusion.

Lynch and MacDiarmada lunched together again on Friday, at the Red Bank restaurant, and MacDiarmada handed back the sketch maps prepared for the manhole operation to Lynch. Lynch recalls:

> … I was further commissioned to personally deliver the sketches to the respective Commandants and go over the details with them individually. I have a happy recollection of those special meetings

with Daly, Kent [*sic*], de Valera and MacDonagh. Therein also lies one of the sad notes in my memory, as it was the last time I spoke with three of them.[5]

The secrecy upon which the military committee of the IRB insisted in planning the Easter Week Rising meant that the commander-in-chief of the Volunteers, Eoin MacNeill, had no inkling until late on the Wednesday of Holy Week that an insurrection was imminent. Lynch asserted that 'the Military Committee [IRB] aimed at throwing the Volunteers en masse into the proposed Rising.'[6]

Bulmer Hobson overheard a remark at a meeting on the Wednesday evening which led him to believe that something was afoot, and he went straight to MacNeill. Though Hobson had once been a member of the Supreme Council of the IRB, he was now *persona non grata* as he had backed John Redmond's call to the Volunteers to join the British Army in fighting in the Great War.[7]

MacNeill immediately sent J. J. O'Connell to Cork with an instruction to every Volunteer brigade to ignore all orders emanating from Pearse, the Director of Operations in the Volunteer movement. Hobson and MacNeill called to Pearse at St Enda's early the following morning and challenged him. He told them that a Rising was planned for Sunday. MacNeill was adamant that the Rising would not go ahead as it breached the *raison d'être* of the Volunteer organisation, which advocated a defensive, not an aggressive role.

Lynch and Ashe were handed a copy of MacNeill's order on Good Friday and immediately reported to Connolly and Clarke. MacDonagh then arrived and reassured the four men that the crisis was over: he and Pearse had spoken to MacNeill that morning and had informed him of the imminent arrival of the German cargo of arms, whereupon MacNeill had reluctantly agreed that the Rising would go ahead. Then came the chilling news of the arrest of Roger Casement on Good Friday and the scuttling of the *Aud* off the Cork coast on the following day with the loss of the armaments. Again MacNeill sent messengers around the country with the following countermanding order, 'Volunteers completely deceived. All orders for special action are hereby cancelled and on no account will action be taken.'[8]

Lynch was at the crisis meeting at 27 Hardwicke Street on Easter Saturday night with Pearse, MacDiarmada, Plunkett and MacDonagh. MacDiarmada was ill and Lynch described the scene:

> Poor MacDermott [*sic*], whose health had been shattered years before in his work for Ireland and who was physically worn out by the strenuous months of anxiety through which he had just passed, writhed in anguish. All were shocked at the desperate situation which had suddenly been thrust upon them.[9]

A decision was made to meet at Liberty Hall the following morning.

Lynch was there when Clarke, Connolly and Ceannt joined the other members of the Military Committee at Liberty Hall. The decision was made that the Rising would proceed at noon on Easter Monday, come what may. Lynch described how later that day he was in the rooms of the Keating Branch of the Gaelic League in North Frederick Street when Pearse was arranging for the dispatch of his final order, which was ready 'on small slips of paper'.[10]

Despite the confusion caused by the differing orders from MacNeill and Pearse, Lynch wrote of Easter Monday, 24 April, 'there were sufficient men to take possession of each strategic position; ... When the meagre forces in Liberty Hall filed out into the square it was absolutely certain that nothing could stop the fight for an Irish Republic – the hour had come at last.'[11]

There are plenty of dramatic accounts of the scenes in the GPO during Easter Week 1916. In an arresting read, Desmond Ryan stated, 'Dermot Lynch descends to the cellars where he hears some prisoners have been held. Through the roaring flames he makes his way ...'[12] Max Caulfield used language as vivid as Ryan to describe the same event: 'Flames roaring near the head of the ventilator shaft sent sparks floating into the basement where the gelignite and bombs had been lodged for safety when the fires first started. Captain Dermot Lynch led a party into the basement to remove the stuff to a safer place.'[13]

Lynch was an inveterate record-keeper, and he was conscious of the need to record the recollections and experiences of those who took part in the Rising. When he returned to Ireland in 1932 and moved to Dublin in 1935 he immediately set in motion the campaign to collect those vital records. He devised a simple record sheet and dispatched it to hundreds of the known and traceable survivors of the GPO garrison and collated the information provided in the 165 accounts which were returned to him.[14] The next step was a gathering in Dublin of those survivors, who collectively edited and amended the accounts. Lynch revised this draft, and the final edition of forty-four pages was approved in 1937 by another gathering of the survivors. After the Bureau of Military History was inaugurated, Lynch lodged this account in 1947[15] together with a supplementary account which he wrote himself.[16] These two accounts steered clear of the descriptions included in other, more dramatic accounts of Easter Week 1916, and the roaring fires, thunderous noise, fear, hunger, injuries and moans of dying men do not feature.

Lynch's dictum in regard to records was invariably 'the importance of avoiding misstatements of fact, or statements which may lead to the wrong conclusions'.[17] His primary objective was to account truthfully and accurately, not to entertain. The following account of Easter Week unfolding in the GPO is based on Lynch's witness statements.

As one of the insurgent Volunteers who occupied the GPO at noon on Monday 24 April, Lynch set to work, with Clarke, smashing the glass barrier that separated the public office from the primary sorting office, then sandbagging and manning the barricades at all windows fronting on to Sackville Street (now O'Connell Street).

In the afternoon, all remaining Volunteers and their ammunition were transferred from Liberty Hall to the GPO. With George Plunkett (Joseph Plunkett's brother), Lynch commanded a bodyguard squad for Pearse in the early afternoon of Tuesday 25 April, when Pearse read the Proclamation of the Republic to the bemused citizens of Dublin outside the GPO.[18] Immediately afterwards the insurgents opened fire on the British cavalry – the Lancers – who had advanced towards the GPO up Sackville Street.

Clarke and Lynch then examined RIC mail which was pigeonholed in the GPO. Most letters were from district inspectors and contained information on Volunteer strength, armaments and activities in the week before. 'The entire contents of the sorting tables and the pigeon-holes was then dumped into waste paper baskets.'[19]

On Tuesday afternoon, Lynch and George Plunkett were ordered out of the building, this time to quell looting from Lawrence's shop which looters had set ablaze. To deter looters and to enable the Fire Brigade to tackle the blaze, Lynch and Plunkett fired pistol shots over the heads of the crowd.[20]

On Wednesday, Connolly ordered Lynch and a squad of men to tunnel through the south wall of the GPO until they met with Frank Henderson's squad, who were tunnelling through from the Coliseum theatre on Henry Street. Because the tunnelling crossed the Dublin Waxworks, Lynch humorously reported to

Connolly that they had captured three British generals, but that, regretfully, they were only wax models.

Seán MacEntee, a founding member of the Volunteers in Dundalk, had arrived at the GPO on Easter Monday, at the same time as the Maynooth Volunteers. He later recalled:

> They were building new defences and consolidating old ones. The most active of these were some men under the command of Dermot Lynch, the officer responsible for the defence of the ground floor. They were working so hard that I became ashamed of my inactivity and joined in to help them. The task was arduous for it consisted of filling the largest mail sacks we could find with debris of all kinds. All this work had to be done in the yard and then the sacks had to be carried into the front of the building, where they were built into breastworks.[21]

The Maynooth Volunteers were assigned to Lynch's section of the building, the 'right hand ground floor abutting O'Connell and Henry Streets'.[22]

On Wednesday, as numbers increased inside the GPO, Lynch decided to record the names and assign a number to each member of the garrison. When recollecting these events in the 1940s, Lynch regretted the loss of that list and thought that it was burnt in the fire that consumed the GPO on Friday 28 April.

Lynch visited flashpoints within the building on the Wednesday evening. The 'men under Liam Cullen on the second floor overlooking Henry Street' were under sniper fire.[23]

His *Report on Operations, Easter Week 1916* for that day stated, 'The manufacture of bombs continued uninterruptedly.'[24] These improvised armaments were highly unstable so in the early hours of Friday, in anticipation of a bombardment of the roof, Lynch was directed by MacDiarmada to transfer all armaments from the second floor, directly under the roof, to the basement.

At daybreak, Lynch responded to MacDiarmada's request for 'a good man' to get to the corner of Liffey Street and Henry Street and convey an order to the front-line troops holding that position to fall back to the GPO. Lynch recorded, 'One of my happiest recollections of Easter Week is that of Seán MacDermott [*sic*] and Tom Clarke sitting on the edge of the mails platform – beaming satisfaction and expressing their congratulations for the safe retreat of those men to the GPO.'[25]

Following that operation, Lynch recorded, 'For the next three hours I enjoyed my first sleep of the week – on a mattress in the hospital section.' He also permitted himself 'the luxury of a shave'.[26] He breakfasted for the last time in the GPO 'on tea and liberal amounts of bread and margarine'.[27]

Lynch was immediately back in action then, with his men building an L-shaped barricade 'midway on the floor' as a fall-back position should the crumbling façade of the building be rushed from outside. The only material to hand for a barricade was coal, so they filled mail sacks with it.[28]

On Friday, when the decision was taken by Pearse and Connolly to evacuate the building, a new alarm was raised. The fires, which were then out of control throughout the building, were threatening to set alight the volatile armaments which had been stored in the basement, and again Lynch commanded a squad that manually removed the armaments to the Prince's Street side of the building. He also undertook to remove the Volunteers' prisoners to the general sorting office from the now dangerous basement. This group of prisoners included Lieutenant A. D. Chalmers, a British officer who happened to be in the GPO when it was first occupied by the insurgents and who gave hostile evidence against Lynch and others during their courts martial.

Was Lynch the 'last man out' of the GPO? He was aide-de-camp to Commandant James Connolly who was carried out wounded on an improvised stretcher during Friday's evacuation. When Pearse and Connolly made the decision to evacuate, the plan was that, following the departure of women and the wounded escorted by Fr Michael Flanagan, the able-bodied would make a dash through their own barricades at Henry Street into Moore Street. Connolly insisted that he would remain until the evacuation was complete, at which point his stretcher-bearers carried him out.

Those who were removing armaments from the basement remained under orders to complete that job. As Lynch was in command of that task, he was more than likely to have been the last man to leave the building. Some witnesses and historians have accepted that Lynch was the last of the garrison to leave the burning GPO. To quote a recent account, 'Harry [Boland] closely followed by Diarmuid Lynch, narrowly avoided self-immolation by dashing out of the abandoned building at 8.40 p.m. Harry spent his last moments in the GPO helping Lynch to dismantle the remaining bombs and explosives.'[29]

Desmond Ryan's publication, *The Rising*, included a vivid recreation of the week in the GPO which included the statement: 'Dermot Lynch descends to the cellar where he hears some prisoners have been held. Through the roaring flames he makes his way, and reappears with a British Officer whom he sets free.'[30] Ryan's book is replete with dramatic language such as 'fatal incendiary shells bursting over the portico … debris crashed with the giving floors and thick columns of flame and smoke … Boom! Boom! Boom! The great building shakes while the defenders stand behind the barricades of coal sacks improvised within.'[31]

Lynch reviewed Ryan's book and was scathing of his colourful descriptions, but his wrath was directed chiefly at numerous assertions which Ryan made, the accuracy of which Lynch disputed.[32] Lynch was incensed that factual and truthful reporting of the Rising was being eclipsed by accounts designed to primarily hold the attention of readers rather than to accurately record what happened. On p. 154 of his book, Ryan reported, 'Clarke informed his wife at their final interview that he was the last man out. Others believe that Pearse returned alone.' Lynch dealt with this assertion thus: 'It was neither Clarke nor Pearse. See my statement on this.'[33] In a footnote to his 'Report on Operations, Easter Week, 1916', Lynch noted:

My statement is based on reports made by members of the [GPO] Garrison. While Harry Boland and myself were making the bombs and explosives safe from accidental explosion pending evacuation of the G.P.O., the evacuation had actually taken place before we were aware of the fact. Harry left a minute or so before I did. As I ran through the G.P.O. to exit on Henry Street there was not a man in sight in the building. The rearguard was then at the angle of Henry Place, Padraig Pearse commanding.[34]

A controversy arose in newspaper columns in April and May 1938 as to the identity of the last man to leave the GPO, centring on one allegation that it was Clarke who was the last to leave. Lynch wrote in 1945, 'Though I knew who that "last man to leave the GPO" happened to be, I did not take part in the controversy, the matter being of no consequence.'[35] However, in 1938, urged on by his nephew and nieces who lived in County Wicklow, he wrote an account of the sequence of events during the evacuations of the GPO.[36] This account was deposited at the Bureau of Military History by Florrie O'Donoghue in 1947 and the section which deals with Lynch's final minutes in the burning GPO reads:

Meanwhile, the bombs, gelignite, etc., were being placed in a storeroom off the yard abutting Princes Street; each man on depositing his quota (which in the instance of bombs consisted of only two – one in each hand), crossed the Sorting Room to the other basement for another lot. Then, to make assurance dou[b]ly sure, I had other men soak mail bags in water and these I spread over the explosive materials … While so engaged, Harry Boland arrived on the scene and lent me a hand. Just as the covering was almost finished Harry, remarking that they were 'now safe enough', rushed towards the Sorting Room. In a few moments I followed. To my astonishment there was not a man left in that room in which the garrison had been assembled – the evacuation had been completed while I was engaged in the task of averting the danger of a premature explosion. (This is a fact worth remembering in view of the controversy as to who was 'the last man to leave the GPO' – which was a matter of no consequence as I view it.)[37]

When other accounts gave a differing version of the evacuation of the GPO, Lynch invariably repeated his version of the sequence of events, as when commenting on R. M. Fox's *Green Banners* in 1946: 'In my account of the evacuation (written elsewhere) I cite facts to show that Harry Boland left the G.P.O. later than Pearse, etc., and that I left later than Harry B.'[38] Lynch's account continued:

On reaching Henry Street through the exit nearest O'Connell Street on that side of the GPO, and having crossed into Henry Place I saw some of our forces bunched at the angle of the latter where it turns at right angles towards Moore Street … A few paces further on I met Padraic Pearse.[39]

Pearse immediately ordered Lynch to take a half-dozen men, break into O'Brien's shop and cross the roofs to access the shops on Moore Street between Henry Place and Henry Street. This manoeuvre was frustrated as they would have had to run the gauntlet of raking gunshot in an intervening laneway. Lynch decided that they would bore through the houses on the left side of Moore Street until they got to Henry Street. 'Boring with pieces of iron which were entirely unsuitable for the purpose, but the best we could find, our progress through the walls to Henry Street was slow.'[40] In one of the rooms into which they broke, the occupants had fled, leaving their chicken supper on the table. Many years later, Lynch recalled the enjoyment caused by the welcome snack.[41]

At daybreak they sent a report to Pearse, who was pinned down in No. 16 Moore Street. Orders were brought back from Pearse that their group should rejoin the main body of Volunteers, which they did. The wounded Connolly lay on his makeshift stretcher and there seemed no prospect of advancing or retreating further. They were trapped, raging fires menacing their position. Lynch readied a group of some fifty men, armed with bayonets and rifles. He proposed to Pearse and Connolly that he lead a bayonet charge to the sandbag barricades near Parnell Street, creating a diversion that would allow the main body of Volunteers to leave the Moore Street houses. Pearse declined the move as he had already opened negotiations with the British commander, Brigadier-General Lowe.

One of the conditions imposed by the British was that Connolly be given up at once. MacDiarmada asked Lynch to accompany Connolly to the position of the British O/C in

Parnell Street. Discarding his Sam Browne and pistol (the one he had brought from America in 1914), Lynch led the stretcher group, which included Michael Staines and Séamus Devoy (a nephew of John Devoy). When they reached the position indicated, they were searched, the soldiers finding some loose ammunition in Lynch's tunic pocket. Surrounded by a heavily armed guard, they proceeded to the Parnell monument where they were ordered to travel via Capel Street to Dublin Castle.

Lynch walked in front with the British officer in command, who interrogated him about the events of the week. Lynch was unresponsive. On reaching the Upper Castle Yard at Dublin Castle, the stretcher-bearers laid Connolly on the ground. Lynch got down on one knee alongside his commandant and asked if Connolly had any messages to send. He never saw Connolly again.[42]

Lynch and about thirty men were then imprisoned for the night in the guardroom of Ship Street Barracks, adjacent to Dublin Castle. On the afternoon of Sunday 30 April, they were removed to the old wing cells of Kilmainham Gaol. Belligerent wardens rough-handled the prisoners as they filed past, and when Lynch protested he was struck on the jaw with a baton. They were marshalled into the main hall of the prison and an inquisition began in the adjoining room. One of those on guard took a fancy to Lynch's pig-skin gaiters (which he had also brought from America) and requisitioned them. When Lynch realised that names, ranks and other military information were being demanded of each insurgent, he instructed that no one was to divulge his name or any other information. Finding the inquisition a failure, the authorities transferred the prisoners to the disused rooms of the old prison infirmary. Gunshot volleys woke them in the early hours of Wednesday 3 May; the executions had begun.[43]

Though he was in the confidence of the seven-member military committee of the IRB, all signatories of the Proclamation, and though he was present with them at crucial meetings in 17 Hardwicke Street on Saturday 22 April and at Liberty Hall the following morning, Diarmuid Lynch did not meet the same fate. One factor in his favour was that no one identified him until late May. When this happened, it was Second Lieutenant A. D. Chalmers of the 14th Royal Fusiliers who identified Lynch, in Richmond Barracks.

Chalmers had been on sick leave in Dublin on 24 April and had just entered the GPO when the rebels invaded. He was kept a prisoner there from Easter Monday until the following Friday when, according to a statement he made to a reporter afterwards, he was given the choice of being shot immediately or running the gauntlet of British soldiers' fire to draw it away from the escaping rebels. His personal account to the press described a week of frightening experiences and appeared in the *Sinn Féin Rebellion Handbook*.[44]

When the burning GPO was abandoned, Chalmers sustained a serious gunshot wound. The published account described:

Bullets were then coming into the room where Second Lieutenant Chalmers, Second Lieutenant King, RIF, Lieutenant Mahony, IAMS and other captives to the number of sixteen were imprisoned. They crouched under a table, as the roof was falling in, and part of an inside wall had collapsed. Prisoners were led to Henry Place, to be used by the rebels as a screen to facilitate their escape. Lieutenant Chalmers was placed at the head of the line of prisoners. Pointing a Mauser pistol at him one of the rebels told him to run or he would fire. He had not got ten yards when he was shot in the thigh.[45]

Chalmers was not present when the other imprisoned officer, Lieutenant King, gave evidence at the courts martial of Pádraig and Willie Pearse, but was sufficiently recovered by 9 May to be present at the court martial of Connolly.

Lynch was made aware of the hostile witness statement being presented by Chalmers and managed to smuggle a letter to Edward L. Adams, the American Consul in Dublin, asking him to attend at his court martial.[46] (As an American citizen it was his legal entitlement to be represented by the Consul.) Lynch's only contribution to his court martial, which took place at Kilmainham Gaol on 18 May, was a robust denial of the more colourful details of Chalmer's account of the week he spent as a prisoner of the rebels in the GPO. In his *Supplementary Statement on 'Easter Week'*, Lynch said:

Just as the transfer [of live ammunition from the storeroom to the basement] had commenced The O'Rahilly called my attention to the fact that our prisoners (a British officer, some privates, and some D.M.P. [Dublin Metropolitan Police] men) were in a room at the other side of the underground corridor – a storeroom which extended under the interior of the building – to which they had been transferred for safety when the top of the building where they had been located during the week was endangered by the fire. The danger to which our own men were subject threatened the prisoners also. My impulse was to remove them instanter [*sic*], but decided to first report the situation to General Connolly (a matter of a minute or two) and leave him say where they should now be placed. His order was to shift them to the safest point then available; I had them escorted to the rear of the General Sorting Room and left them under guard.

The sequel to this was that at the subsequent courts martial the British officer testified that he and his fellow prisoners had been placed in that room in the basement and 'left to die like rats in a trap'. … The fact, of course, was that their detention in the basement was but temporary pending our evacuation of the GPO, and that just as soon as the danger to the explosives was noted they were promptly transferred therefrom. I took occasion to contradict the officer's wrongful assertion and to state the facts during the course of my court martial – my only statement thereat.[47]

The supplementary statement concludes with a further reference to Lieutenant Chalmers:

As I write it occurs to me to give the name of the 'rat in trap' officer – Second Lieut. A. D. Chalmers – which I recall from reading a statement made by him and published in the 'Irish Times' Handbook. Due to the fact that I was in charge of the squad that shifted the prisoners from the GPO basement on Friday of Easter Week, he was called on to testify to my presence in the GPO as a participant in the Rising – an unnecessary formality on the part of the Court. Prior to the date of my appearance he came into our room in Richmond Barracks accompanied by Detective Inspector Love. We were all ordered to stand up for inspection. That he came to identify some one was evident, but he did not get his man. He was looking for me as we soon learned. Himself and Love retired from the room and returned in a few minutes. We stood again and at a jocose remark by one of our number we all laughed. Then Chalmers pointed to me, saying: 'You're Lynch. I recognise you by your gold tooth.'[48]

Lynch was convinced that it was by his Volunteer uniform, not by his gold tooth, that Chalmers recognised him. The rebels had precious little to laugh about during the time Chalmers was imprisoned in the GPO so he doubted that Chalmers had noticed the gold tooth before the identification in Richmond.

Chalmers intruded on Lynch's consciousness yet again in 1949 when he undertook his dissection of Desmond Ryan's book, *The Rising*. Ryan had written a colourful account of the British officer's capture and stated that Chalmers had 'bandied indignant words with Plunkett, Brennan-Whitmore and Michael Collins outside on the very steps'.[49]

Apart from the mundane reality that there were no steps leading into the GPO, Lynch asserted that Chalmers was already inside the GPO when he was taken prisoner.[50] Lynch's factual account differs from another colourful depiction, that of Desmond Fitzgerald:

> There was a Lieutenant who presumably happened to be there by accident. The Lieutenant held a bottle of brandy, which he was drinking in a state of utter gloom. When I got back to my own part of the building I found that the Lieutenant had finished his brandy and was now very drunk and demanding another bottle.[51]

Later in the week, according to Fitzgerald, Chalmers became more abject and querulous: 'He constantly came to me asking for more brandy.'

Lynch's final pronouncement was:

> Naturally, I bear Chalmers not the slightest illwill for testifying against me, but for his malicious lies in the 'Times' Handbook – which in view of the <u>facts</u>, are ridiculous – he deserved no better treatment than that usually accorded to a 'rat in a trap'. Thank God he and his ilk have passed into the limbo of forgotten things.[52]

4

Court Martial and Imprisonment

On Thursday 18 May 1916, in Richmond Barracks, Dublin, Jeremiah Christopher Lynch was formally charged with treason. The words on the charge sheet read, 'Did an act to wit take part in an armed rebellion and in the waging of war against His Majesty the King, such act being of such a nature as to be calculated to be prejudicial to the Defence of the Realm and being done with the intention and for the purpose of assisting the enemy.'[1]

Though Lynch had requested that the American Consul attend his court martial, and though Consul Edward L. Adams travelled to Richmond Barracks, he was not allowed to be present when Lynch was charged. In his supplementary statement Lynch wrote:

> … while Billy Partridge and myself were awaiting transfer to Kilmainham (after our court martial), I saw him [Adams] drive from the barracks precincts in company with the members of the Court. … That evening, Thursday May 18th, the decision of the Court was announced to me at Kilmainham: sentenced to be shot …[2]

Lynch's brother Denis immediately telegraphed news of the death sentence to Dick Dalton in New York. Dalton and Daniel Cohalan took action and contacted Senator James O'Gorman of New York who urgently approached Joseph Tumulty, the US President's Secretary. President Woodrow Wilson and his wife were at the theatre, so Tumulty and Senator O'Gorman rushed to the theatre in a White House automobile. Calling the president to the rear of his box, Tumulty briefed him on the critical situation. Wilson instructed Tumulty to contact Frank Polk, the Acting Secretary of State, to cable the British Foreign Office to request that Lynch's execution be deferred until the American government could investigate the case.

It was after midnight in New York when Polk dispatched his cable, and, as far as the Americans knew, Lynch was to be shot at 4 a.m., so it is not surprising that his fate was not known with certainty until a few days had elapsed.[3]

The American papers ran screaming headlines on 19 May. Lynch was 'Doomed to Die as Irish Martyr', according to the *New York American*. The front page of the *Evening World* announced 'President Waits Fate of American for Whom He Made Dramatic Plea'. The *Evening Telegraph* led with 'President asks stay from Great Britain of Lynch execution. Pleads for delay in carrying out sentence to shoot naturalized American this morning. Message may have been too late.'

Other American friends and former colleagues made urgent representations on behalf of Lynch. Among them was the proprietor of the famous Waldorf Astoria Hotel in New

York, George C. Boldt, possibly at the behest of Jamie Lee, who was paymaster at the hotel. Lee was a friend of Lynch from his Philo-Celtic days, and Lynch was godfather to Lee's first child.

The decision not to execute Lynch was the result of a very strong reaction against the executions which swept across the world. The fact that he and Éamon de Valera, who had also been condemned to death, were American citizens, had been emphasised to the British authorities by anxious relatives and friends.

Lynch was informed of the commutation of his sentence on Saturday 20 May. He wrote to his brother Denis from Kilmainham, scribbling his note on a torn fragment of a brown paper bag. The note is vividly descriptive and informative because of its content, the very limited material available upon which to write and the hurried nature of the script:

I got my sentence last night; perhaps it is in the papers, death commuted to ten years. I expected something like that from the attitude of the Court at my trial. I requested that the American Consul should be present thereat but they would not wait. They sent for him and allowed him to look over the summary of the evidence as made out by the prosecuting officer. I did not attempt to deny the main charge against me, that I held the rank of Captain in the GPO. Lieutenant E. L. King, whom I released from the cellar when they were in great danger from fire and explosives, was the only witness produced to show that I participated actively in the fight. I believe I go to Mountjoy from here and then on to somewhere in ——? They have one pound and four pence belonged to me and my pipe. Slán libh, Diarmuid.[4]

Consul Adams' account is recorded in the archives of the US Department of State.[5] Owen Dudley Edwards wrote the following account, having examined the Consul's report:

> The affaire de Valera was to Adams almost a routine matter. He was, however, far more affected by a gruesome experience when called on to speak for Jeremiah C. Lynch, better known to his fellow-members of the IRB in the Irish form of the name, 'Diarmuid'. Adams was escorted to a waiting room which overlooked the courtyard. Under his horrified eyes Lynch was 'placed against the high stone wall, the soldiers forming a hollow square about him'.[6]

At this point Adams was removed from the waiting room and escorted from the prison. Two days later he was informed that Lynch had not been shot, that his death sentence had been commuted to ten years of penal servitude. The cruel mock-execution enacted in the courtyard may have been an error, but it was more likely a vengeful hoax to terrorise Lynch and to reprove the American for attempting to lend the weight of his official presence to the British court-martial proceedings.

On the day Lynch was condemned he had a visit in Kilmainham from three women: his half-sister Mary, his sister-in-law Alice and Kathleen (Kit) Quinn, his unofficial fiancée. The request for the visit was addressed to Sir John

Maxwell, the military governor, on 18 May and is in the Lynch Family Archives. It states, 'A Miss Lynch, who has been sent to me by the Bishop of Cork, wishes to see her brothers, Dermot Lynch, Timothy Lynch and Michael Lynch.'[7] The request was sent from the law office at Dublin Castle and continued, 'If there is no military reason to the contrary, I would be obliged if her wish could be acceded to. She says Dermot was in the Rising but the others were not.'[8]

A subsequent letter from Alice to Lynch recalled that visit. To all concerned it was a farewell: 'We often think and speak of that day in Kilmainham; it was great that we got to see you that day and it gave us such consolation for you were so brave.'[9] The visitors brought a change of clothing for Lynch and took away his soiled Volunteer uniform. (The uniform is on permanent display at the Cork Museum along with other items belonging to Diarmuid and Michael Lynch.)[10]

Following the commutation of his sentence, Lynch was moved to Mountjoy Gaol, where records show that he was ill for some time. All those with whom Lynch had lived 'cheek by jowl' in the months and weeks leading up to the insurrection – Pearse, MacDiarmada, Connolly, Clarke, Plunkett, Mac-Donagh and Ned Daly – were dead. Grief, the stress of events and his impaired health all combined to cause this severe illness, while he was a prisoner in Mountjoy during the last days of May 1916. Consul Adams visited him there and undertook to get a certificate from a doctor detailing Lynch's illness, as well as seeking medication. No other visitors were allowed.

On 27 May, Lynch was one of a batch of prisoners embarking at Dublin's North Wall for imprisonment in Britain. He hoped to have a chance to speak to a member of his family, but this was in vain as 'no deportees, even those whose death sentence was commuted to penal service for life, were given the opportunity to meet family or friends before leaving.'[11] Lynch was taken to Dartmoor Prison in Devon. Regulations governing letters and visiting rights were strict, as conveyed to Denis Lynch by Governor Greenway on 25 August:

> Prisoners in their first year of imprisonment are allowed to write and receive a letter and to receive a visit every four months. Letters and visits are privileges which are earned by prisoners by industry and good conduct and are liable to forfeiture for misconduct, etc.[12]

Lynch's first letter from Dartmoor was sent on 29 May 1916, and in it he reassured his sister Mary of his well-being. He said that after the long weeks of incarceration, the bracing voyage to Wales and the subsequent train journey to Dartmoor had been welcome. Sombrely he added, 'Don't forget to pray for Seán [MacDiarmada] and all my dear comrades who died for Ireland during the past month.'[13] In another letter, sent to Denis on 29 August 1916, he detailed the complicated system that would yield the maximum and most effective communication between the limited number of letters and visits allowed to the prisoners.

During his brother Diarmuid's imprisonment, Denis, with Dalton's assistance in the USA, attended to Lynch's insurance business for the American Equitable Life Assurance Society. He also took charge of correspondence. Every letter sent by Lynch was copied and recopied for family and friends. In turn, their replies became 'round robins' with as many as ten correspondents filling the pages of one posting. Every letter had to be timed and juggled with an intended visit; the prisoner could not have both simultaneously.

Visitors were few, as the arduous journey from County Cork to the remote region in Devon discouraged all but the most determined. In October 1916 Lynch did have the comfort of a visit from his sister Mary, accompanied by two female relatives, the Murphys of Grand Parade, Cork.[14] After her visit to Diarmuid in Dartmoor and to her brother Michael, who was being held in Frongoch Prison Camp in Wales, Mary wrote indignantly to the British Home Office on their behalf. In relation to Diarmuid, she wrote:

> Owing to a weak digestion he is unable to eat the food supplied to him at dinner and is obliged to save half the porridge which he receives for breakfast. My brother is an American citizen and has a right to be treated as a prisoner of war instead of which he is treated as a common criminal. I am communicating with the American Ambassador on the subject of his treatment.[15]

A reply from the Home Office refuted all of Mary's claims.[16]

Not satisfied, Mary forwarded a letter to Lynch by another member of the Murphy family of Grand Parade, Dr Thomas Murphy, enclosing a medical certificate. Murphy urged Lynch, in the light of his 'serious stomach trouble in New York' to present it to the prison doctor, adding, 'I feel sure that any doctor learning of this will give you some special diet.'[17]

Maurice Healy, MP, a solicitor based in Cork city, queried the Lynchs' prison conditions in the House of Commons. The reply in December from Mr Herbert Samuel, British Home Secretary, stated that 'an alteration to [Lynch's] diet has been made on the recommendations of the Medical Officer'.[18]

Denis had news for Diarmuid in a letter dated 20 November: 'Brian O'Higgins has a new baby boy and there is another [baby] to your prison companion, de Valera.' His news of Kathleen Clarke (Tom Clarke's widow) was sombre: 'Poor Mrs Clarke has returned to Limerick and is improving in health. Her baby, born in May last, died. Her Uncle John died in July and was buried with military honours.' Denis joked that all the girls Diarmuid knew were being married off. 'If you are not home soon all the girls will be married, but I may be wrong, as it is surprising how "cailíní" friends of yours keep turning up every day, nice girls too!'[19]

The next few months in gaol were spent sewing sandbags, mailbags and harness straps. In October the Irish prisoners began to agitate to have their status as prisoners of war recognised. Lynch wrote to Herbert Samuel, the British Home Secretary:

I am now imprisoned by the British government as an ordinary criminal, against which I protest and claim that I am entitled to the same status and treatment as though taken prisoner while fighting with the Bulgarian or Turkish Allies of Germany on the continent, namely, that of a 'prisoner-of-war.'[20]

At the same time, in New York, Dick Dalton was agitating through official channels to have the status of Lynch and the other Republican prisoners declared political.[21]

A team including Lynch, Larry de Lacey, Gerard Crofts and Robert Brennan managed to get a letter to *The Cork Examiner* out of Dartmoor, an audacious breach of regulations and security. The letter described the poor conditions for the prisoners. Brennan later wrote:

It had been a painstaking and elaborate job. We had to keep it for nearly three weeks until Diarmuid Lynch had a visitor. It was explained to Diarmuid [by the prison authorities] that he would see his visitor in a room but that he was on no account to approach him. Diarmuid was searched as he left the exercise ground for the visit and again before he entered the office. In a corner of his handkerchief which he held aloft during the search, he had the precious letter. As he entered the office and saw his friend, Diarmuid conveniently forgot his instructions and he stepped impulsively forward. 'Why, hello, Séamus!' he cried, as he shook hands with the visitor. The letter was now in safe hands.[22]

When the letter was published it caused a furore in the prison.

According to one prison officer, 'It has never been done before in Dartmoor.'[23]

Urgent questions were asked in parliament on 24 November by Maurice Healy, MP for Cork, concerning the conditions of the Irish prisoners as alleged in the columns of *The Cork Examiner*. In December Denis Lynch was able to inform Dalton that political-prisoner status had been granted and that the Irish rebels in Dartmoor would be moved to Lewes Prison in Sussex.[24] By 18 December the transfer was complete, and Lynch informed his brother Dan, '[Joe] McGuinness and [Piaras] Béaslaí were among the batch from Portland yesterday. Before the end of the week I expect that all the Irish prisoners, including de Valera, etc. will have arrived here, quite a family gathering for Christmas.'[25] Lynch asked for £5 to be forwarded to the prison governor so that a dentist could be brought in to attend to his painful teeth.[26]

Under the more relaxed regime in Lewes, the prisoners were able to pursue their preferred studies. Lynch requested books in German and Irish grammar from Denis. He turned the Irish grammar book *Ceachta Cainnte Gramadaighe* into a rare collection of the autographs of all the 1916 Irish political prisoners in Lewes Prison, asking each of his nationalist co-prisoners to sign the page that corresponded to their convict number. Boland signed on page 90 because he was prisoner Q90; de Valera on page 95, Béaslaí on page 116 and Lynch himself, convict Q192, signed on page 192.[27]

At Lewes in 1917, as much as was possible, the Irish

prisoners established a programme of education, physical exercise and spirited resistance to their incarceration. 'Lewes, like "Frongoch University", provided ample opportunity for crash courses in Irish culture.'[28] In his book, Robert Brennan gives a detailed account of the life of the prisoners in Lewes. During exercise time, Eoin MacNeill lectured on ancient Irish history, and Brennan himself gave talks on beekeeping.[29]

A Saint Patrick's Day postcard sent from Oxford to Lynch read, 'Kind regards to all the boys in Lewes from the following undergraduates at present in Oxford.' It was signed by Darrell Figgis, Dr Patrick McCartan, Seán T. O'Kelly and 'Sceilg' (the writer John J. O'Kelly).[30]

One of the letters Lynch wrote from Lewes was to Madge Daly, niece of John Daly of Limerick. Referring to John, who had died on 1 July 1916, Lynch wrote, 'I am confident that his big, patriotic heart was happy on having lived to see "The Day".'[31]

As the months passed and their expected release did not happen, the Irish prisoners became more mutinous. De Valera was by now the acknowledged leader of the Irish political prisoners in Lewes, and he orchestrated the mutiny. It took the form of refusing to complete prison work until prisoner-of-war status, acknowledging that they were equal combatants in a legitimate war, was granted. After a three-day strike, de Valera, Brennan and some others were moved to Parkhurst Prison on the Isle of Wight, where they continued to disrupt and agitate. Lynch remained in Lewes.

Newspapers were printing leaked stories about prison conditions, and uproar in the prisons must have hastened the decision of the British government, announced in the House of Commons by Bonar Law on 15 June, that all Irish political prisoners were to be released immediately. Transport arrangements were quickly put in place. The men were gathered in Pentonville Prison, London, and were dispatched from there in lorries to the mail steam packet at Holyhead. Dr Patrick McCartan, who was on the Supreme Council of the IRB, joined them there. He used the time on the triumphant voyage home to brief Lynch and other IRB members on the situation in Ireland.

The rebels arrived in Ireland on Monday 18 June 1917. Piaras Béaslaí, who was amongst them, described the scene:

> The prisoners arrived in Dublin and received a tremendous popular ovation. They drove in brakes [horse-drawn carriages] through the streets which were packed with cheering crowds. Little over a year ago they had been marched prisoners through these streets to the boats amid silent or hostile demonstrations. Now they were received as heroes and leaders of the people of Dublin.[32]

Lynch's signature was on a petition compiled on that June day, along with the signatures of other released leaders – Éamon de Valera, Eoin MacNeill, Robert Brennan, Seán McGarry and Thomas Ashe. The petition was for delivery to President Woodrow Wilson of the USA, and it asked for the active support of the American president and of the American government in the Irish struggle for independence. The petition was entrusted to McCartan for presentation to President Wilson himself.[33]

Pages from Lynch's Irish grammar book inscribed by all of his Irish fellow inmates in Lewes, 1917. *Courtesy of Lynch Family Archives*

5

'The Most Senior IRB Leader'

When Lynch disembarked at Westland Row station in Dublin on 18 June 1917, he was returning as one of the heroes, recognised and acknowledged by nationalists as a man who had been and would still be a vital operator in a reinvigorated campaign to get Britain to relinquish its rule in Ireland. Historian John Borgonovo observes: 'Lynch was the most senior IRB leader to survive the Easter Rising.'[1] He had played a courageous role during Easter Week in the GPO and had acted as a leader within the confines of Lewes Prison.

After some days of celebration in Dublin, a group of Corkonians headed for home on Saturday 23 June, to be greeted at the station in Glanmire, County Cork, by an exultant crowd of 10,000 people. 2,000 people escorted the released prisoners to the city and thousands gathered on Grand Parade to hear them speak. Addressing the crowd, Diarmuid Lynch shouted that as a Cork man he was 'glad to return to his native city and to find that it was a Rebel Cork, a Republican Cork and an Irish Cork'. Although most of the crowd dispersed afterwards, trouble broke out on Saturday evening and again on Sunday between Republican supporters and British forces.[2] Lynch had spent the weekend at home in Granig, but was back in the city on Monday to add his name to an appeal for calm on the streets of the city, issued to the newspapers by the other nationalist leaders, Tomás MacCurtain, Terence MacSwiney and J. J. Walsh.[3]

In July Lynch was selected as a counting agent on behalf of de Valera, the Sinn Féin candidate in the East Clare by-election.[4] The outcome was a resounding victory for the Sinn Féiners, a title now applied by the British authorities to all Irish nationalists, although several organisations and groups of differing philosophies were included in the misleading categorisation.

During the following months, Lynch was centrally engaged in tactics, policy and publicity across the spectrum of nationalist organisations. Béaslaí wrote, 'The most frequent companions of Collins at this time were Diarmuid Lynch, Harry Boland, Diarmuid O'Hegarty, Fionán Lynch and I.'[5] According to P. S. O'Hegarty, 'Mrs Clarke, who had kept the threads and contacts of the IRB in her capable hands while the men were in prison, handed them on, on their release, to Diarmuid Lynch, Harry Boland, and these two, with Collins and McGarry and others, took up the threads again and put them together.'[6]

Writing to Béaslaí in August 1925, Lynch noted:

I think I can truthfully say that during the latter months of 1917 and the early part of 1918 there was no man in closer touch with Collins than your humble servant. We collaborated in many, many things, among which I may mention the revision of the Sinn Féin constitution, the revision of the IRB constitution, the reorganisation of the Irish Volunteers, etc.[7]

Two of Lynch's brothers, Michael and Denis, had close friendships with Michael Collins (whom they all referred to invariably as 'Mick') from the 1916 Rising to his untimely and tragic death. Michael Lynch and Michael Collins were imprisoned together in Frongoch Prison Camp in Wales after the Easter Rising and were released just before Christmas 1916. It was Michael who would wrestle with Mick Collins when he arrived to stay overnight in the farmhouse at Granig. In 1919–20 Denis and Alice Lynch were frequently discreet hosts of the fugitive Collins at Distillery House, their home in the grounds of the Dublin Whiskey Distillery in Drumcondra where Denis was manager.

One evening Denis was entertaining business guests and left the table to check on his other, hidden guest. 'What are ye talking about tonight, Denis?' asked the restless Collins.

'Yourself as always, Mick,' came the reply.

In early August 1917, at the IRB Oireachtas in Waterford, those who were determined that the IRB would strengthen its position within the Volunteer and Sinn Féin organisations planned a strategy to achieve that outcome. Michael Collins and 'other hard liners', such as Lynch and McGarry, were elected to the Executive of the Volunteers by large majorities, strengthening the IRB's grip on that organisation.[8]

In that same month, Lynch was involved, along with de Valera, Ashe, Michael Collins and Richard Mulcahy in the reorganisation of the Volunteers. Lynch, Michael Collins, Con Collins and Ashe were also engaged in drawing up a new constitution for the IRB. When Ashe, who was arrested in the same month for sedition, died on hunger strike in September as a result of force-feeding by the Mountjoy authorities, Lynch was a member of the funeral committee. Some objected to Michael Collins being chosen to speak at the graveside, but Lynch supported the choice.[9]

On 26 October, Lynch was elected Director of Communications of the revamped Volunteer movement. He and Collins were also, in time-honoured IRB style, planning a coup at the forthcoming Sinn Féin Ard-Fheis to ensure that IRB men would be voted into key positions. Lynch was elected as a member of the Supreme Executive Council of Sinn Féin. He was also elected Treasurer of the Supreme Council of the IRB.[10]

With Con Collins and Cathal Brugha, Lynch was commissioned by the IRB to investigate the inaction of the Volunteers of Counties Limerick, Kerry and Cork during Easter Week in 1916. Lynch wrote an account for Florrie O'Donoghue of the enquiry procedure which was conducted in Cork 'on the second Saturday of January 1918'.[11] He recounted that Tom Hales, Michael Leahy, Seán O'Sullivan and his brother,

Michael Lynch, were present and that it was held under cover of a Gaelic League dance. With the passing of almost thirty years, Lynch admitted that he could not remember if the location was An Grianán in Queen Street or the Capuchin Hall. He was also puzzled as to why Seán O'Hegarty, as leader of the Cork IRB, was not present.[12] Lynch's conclusion to the investigation was that due to MacNeill's countermanding orders and because the German arms ship was lost, the insurgents in the southern counties had no choice but to abandon their plans.[13] In 1922, in reply to a query from O'Donoghue, Cathal Brugha had said, 'No blame attaches to the Brigade officers.'[14]

It was at this time of renewal and acceleration of activity in 1917 that a divergence of opinion as to strategy became apparent between de Valera and the revitalised IRB. Éamon de Valera was a reluctant secret society member, and he now distanced himself from his former comrades in the IRB, arguing that the organisation was no longer needed in the campaign for national independence. In contrast Lynch was adamant, as was Michael Collins, that the IRB campaign had to continue and that it was only through IRB methods that independence would be achieved.[15]

As a member of the Supreme Executive Council of Sinn Féin, Lynch had been appointed as Director for Food at the Ard-Fheis of October 1917. Consistent with the intention of this new Sinn Féin administration, to bypass the British government or its agents in Ireland and to become, in effect, the Provisional Government of an independent Irish State, Lynch initiated a survey of food supplies. Acting in the interests of Irish food producers he began a campaign to have food exports from Ireland to England stopped.[16] Food scarcity was an issue in Ireland, a result of increasing exports to England because of its war with Germany, and Lynch railed against the wholesale exporting of native foodstuffs.[17] In a letter to the *Irish Independent* of 17 January 1918 he complained that '100,000 barrels of oats, lying at the southern ports, have been commandeered by the military'.

On 21 February 1918, he took the campaign a step further when he masterminded, on behalf of the citizens of Dublin, the seizure of a herd of pigs being driven from the market at North Circular Road to the North Wall for export. They were seized in Dorset Street by a team of twenty-four men led by Lynch and brought to a depot belonging to the Corporation Cleansing Department. The gates were secured against any intrusion. Waiting butchers slaughtered the pigs, and the meat was sold to local consumers. The owners were repaid for their animals by the Sinn Féin administration.

Charlie Dalton was a schoolboy when he took part in this Sinn Féin operation. In *With the Dublin Brigade (1917–1921)*, he gives a vivid account.[18] Charlie's role was to brush the blood of the slaughtered pigs into the channels, from where it was hosed away. The crowd that had gathered outside the gates exclaimed, in true Dubliner style, 'Ah! isn't it a terrible shame to be wasting all that blood which would make grand black puddings!'

When writing his recollections of this particular episode in later years, Darrell Figgis recorded:

> The noise this exploit made was astonishing. Both Irish and English newspapers made it the event of the hour. It indicated at once a care for the home people and a deliberate, calculated defiance of British Administration. So strong was the feeling in the country that, under this Department [Lynch's] local Sinn Féin markets were created for the sale of Irish foodstuffs to the poor at reasonable prices.[19]

Lynch was arrested on 23 February and detained at Mountjoy. When he appeared at the Southern Police Courts in Dublin on 8 March before Magistrate Swifte, his brother Denis was there, with his wife Alice, their sister Mary and Kit Quinn. He was charged that 'he took part in unlawful assembly and in an unlawful conspiracy to seize pigs and other animals from their lawful owners so as to prevent the export of such animals'.[20] Lynch made a ringing political declaration at his trial, saying, 'I stand by the inalienable right of the Irish Republic as enunciated by the gallant men murdered by England in 1916.'[21] Mr Devitt for the Crown, as reported in *The Cork Examiner* of 9 March, described the pig-seizure offence as 'a startling and unparalleled outrage'.[22]

Lynch refused to recognise the authority of the court and also refused bail, forcing the British government to imprison him, a publicity exercise that was widely reported in Irish, English and American papers. Lynch was sentenced to two months' imprisonment and was returned to Mountjoy Gaol where he joined the action of the hunger-striking nationalists who were demanding to be treated as prisoners of war. A letter from Mountjoy to his sister Mary, only days later, informed her that Austin Stack had called off the hunger strike as agreement had been reached with the British government as to prison conditions.[23] Restrictions were consequently relaxed and Denis and Kit Quinn were able to visit him. In the same letter to Mary, Lynch confided about his fiancée Kit: 'We have all sorts of glorious plans to take effect soon after my sojourn here is ended.'[24]

Lynch was moved to Dundalk Gaol on 20 March to serve the remainder of his sentence. At forty years of age, he was by then a seasoned inmate of His Majesty's prisons, having been imprisoned in eight different establishments because of his nationalist activities.

The regime in Dundalk was more relaxed. Friends were allowed to provide him with a new bed, mattress and pillow, while the local Cumann na mBan (Women's Volunteers Corps) were permitted to supply the inmates with seventeen dozen eggs to celebrate Easter.[25] For company, his co-prisoners were Ernest Blythe, Frank Thornton, Dick McKee and Terence MacSwiney.

Sometime in April, a deportation order was served on Lynch. As an American citizen he was to be sent back to America. Expecting this development, he had applied to the prison governor for temporary parole so he could marry his fiancée. This would mean, in the event of deportation, that Kit would be able to enter America as his wife. Parole was refused. Lynch then asked permission to marry her in prison; however, he did not wait for the outcome to this request but made his own discreet arrangements instead.

The consensus within the family is that Lynch met Kit in 1915 at a social gathering at the home of the Kennedy family in Dundrum, County Dublin. Mrs Hanora Kennedy (née Dalton) was an aunt of Dick Dalton, Lynch's American friend, and also an aunt of Alice Wyatt, the wife of Denis Lynch.[26] Kit had written to Diarmuid when he was imprisoned in Kilmainham, Dartmoor and Lewes. One of her messages was scribbled on a ten-shilling note which she managed to pass to him in Kilmainham. Lynch wrote an explanatory note on the reverse of the currency note: 'I revered this note from Kit, which I got in Kilmainham Gaol and kept by me on my person during my stay in Dartmoor, Lewes, Portland and Pentonville Prisons, 1916–1917.'[27]

On 24 April 1918, Kit, her half-sister Carmel and the Capuchin priest, Fr Aloysius Travers, presented themselves at the prison, having filed a request to visit three named inmates: Diarmuid Lynch, Frank Henderson and Michael Brennan. During the short visit, at noon, Kit and Lynch were married, with Henderson and Brennan as their witnesses. Lynch had arranged for his marriage to take place on the same date and at the same time as the Easter Rising had commenced in 1916.

Several descriptions of the brief wedding ceremony were

recorded. Henderson's, filed at the Bureau of Military History, reads as follows:

One of the imprisoned Republicans was Diarmuid Lynch. He had been condemned to death in 1916 for the part he took in the Rising but the death sentence was not carried out owing to the fact that he was an American citizen. After the Rising it is believed that he became Head Centre of the Irish Republican Brotherhood. He was regarded by the British Government as a dangerous man. On the other hand the Volunteers held him in great esteem – and justly so – for he was a determined, unflinching soldier and an Irishman of clear vision and of great probity, forthright in his views with a certain stubbornness at times. The British authorities informed Diarmuid Lynch … that they were about to take him from Dundalk and transport him to America. He asked that he be given facilities while still in Ireland to marry his fiancée so that she could rejoin him on his arrival in America … The facilities were refused. Arrangements were then made, unknown to the British authorities, for the marriage ceremony to take place inside the prison. Ecclesiastical permission was obtained by a Dublin priest and, in due course, he arrived at the prison accompanied by the bride, Miss Quinn, and her sister and requested a visit to Michael Brennan and myself whom they did not know. I received intimation of this about twenty minutes before the visit, and was given instructions to put my back against the door of the visiting room, carry on a pretended conversation with the bride's sister, and if the warder, who was always present during visits, attempted to convey to the Governor what was taking place to prevent him by force from doing so. The marriage ceremony was carried out without a hitch and in the presence of the necessary number of witnesses.[28]

The visiting room was divided by a counter to keep visitors and prisoners apart, but clearly it was not an efficient obstacle in this case.[29] Ernest Blythe described how the priest drew the couple aside for a confidential 'chat' during which the essential words were spoken by the necessary parties.[30]

Later that day Lynch announced his marriage to his co-prisoners, and word filtered swiftly to the governor, with the result that Lynch was immediately removed from his cell and put on a train for Dublin under the supervision of two armed detectives, Patrick Smith and Daniel Hoey. Coincidentally, his bride Kit, Carmel Quinn and Fr Aloysius were returning to Dublin on the same train, so the couple spent the first hours of their married life in the same compartment under the watchful eyes of the armed detectives.

Demonstrating the effectiveness of the IRB grapevine, by the time the train arrived at Amiens Street Station it was met by a horde of well-wishers, including de Valera and Collins. Years later, when he was campaigning for his service pension, Lynch described the scene that developed at Amiens Street on that April evening:

Word was immediately telephoned to Dublin with the result that a company of Volunteers, mustered that day for a special occasion, proceeded to Amiens Street Station and awaited my arrival. The police authorities being notified of their presence dispatched a large force of armed constables to the station. On our exit from the train Harry Boland informed me that the Volunteers were prepared to attempt my rescue. With the large force of police in evidence at one point and the rest of the space packed with Volunteers and civilians, I told Harry that the attempt would most likely fail, that many men would most certainly be shot. I negatived the proposal. Harry acquiesced. As I entered the Black Maria, my wife and friends joined me, Éamon De Valera completing the party en route to the Bridewell. The detectives were too inhibited by the crowd to object to this unusual procedure. The assembled Volunteers, headed by Harry Boland and Michael Collins, marched in front of the Black Maria along the quays to the Bridewell, where Collins and myself were, strange to say, permitted to hold a private conversation away from the police and those friends of ours who were also there.[31]

It was the last time that three of the key personalities of the Irish independence struggle, Collins, de Valera and Lynch, met together.

A colourful account of the wedding drama appeared in *The Gaelic American*, which reported that de Valera shouted to Lynch as the Black Maria sped away, 'Diarmuid, you have set a new style in weddings by taking your bride to the Bridewell.'[32]

The following morning Collins again joined Kit and Diarmuid Lynch with their G-men escort on the train to Kingstown. Lynch was dispatched on the next mail boat sailing to Liverpool, and Kit sailed to Liverpool with him, hoping that she would be allowed to travel onwards to the US with Diarmuid. Smith and Hoey handed their prisoner over to the Lime Street Bridewell in Liverpool, and Lynch spent the night in custody there. Kit had a rougher night as she was repeatedly questioned and was dubbed an 'enemy alien'. The two Dublin detectives spoke up for her but to no avail. Kit was kept in custody until the following morning when she was escorted to the boat train by four detectives, then put in the charge of the guard, who, in turn, handed her over to a custom officer for her voyage back to Dublin.

> They allowed me to walk with Diarmuid to the Bridewell but refused to let me see or speak with him after that and when I stated that I was his wife they put me under arrest as an alien and being in a prohibited area without being registered and informed me that I had committed a grave offence against the Defence of the Realm and was liable to six months imprisonment.[33]

Meanwhile, Lynch was escorted under armed guard on board the SS *New York*. Before his armed escort disembarked, they informed Lynch that the cost of his passage to the USA had been deducted from his own cash (which had been confiscated) and that the ship's purser would restore the balance to him when they berthed in New York.

After returning to Dublin, Kit then planned to sail to New York with the Dublin Lord Mayor, Laurence O'Neill, who had been imprisoned with Lynch in Richmond Barracks in 1916, but a delay in acquiring their marriage certificate prevented this. After an appeal to the Cardinal of Armagh, Michael Logue, by her new brother-in-law, Denis, the marriage certificate was finally obtained.[34] Kit eventually sailed for New York on 1 June 1918. The first officer of the ship, T. J. Gill, sent a letter to Mary Lynch to reassure the family that Kit had arrived safely after a good passage, despite the perils of a wartime Atlantic crossing.[35]

Lynch wrote to Denis and apologised roguishly for his delay in putting pen to paper, explaining, 'I wanted Kit here before I could get myself to write and finally when I had her – Well!'[36] Kit was equally exuberant when writing to Alice, 'What an age it seems since the morning of 1 June and how wonderful life has become since then!'[37] The couple stayed with Dick Dalton and his wife at first, but they soon began to search for their own apartment. In October Lynch wrote cheerfully to his siblings in Granig: 'Here we are in "our own" apartment. We had some job in getting it; it's nothing wonderful of course, but considering our resources we did very well.'[38] The apartment, at 2366 Grand Concourse in the Bronx was, as Lynch explained to his sister, 'about eight miles from my office and on the outskirts of the city. It takes me about an hour to get there.'[39]

Despite their bliss, both expressed regret at leaving Ireland. Lynch observed, 'Kit and myself are very happy, but only wish we could have a honeymoon in Ireland among all the old friends.' Kit added in the same letter, 'I don't let my thoughts dwell too long at a time on home or on all my dear friends but just keep thinking of the time when we shall all be together again.'[40]

In May 1919, Patrick Lee delivered a silver-plated, inscribed tray to Kit and Diarmuid Lynch, a gift from Lynch's fellow prisoners in Dundalk Gaol. The tray is still displayed in the Granig farmhouse where Lynch was born. The inscription reads, 'Souvenir of the marriage of Diarmuid and Caitlín Lynch in Dundalk Jail on the 24th April 1918. Presented to them by the Irish Republican Prisoners then in Dundalk as a mark of their friendship and esteem and a tribute to Diarmuid's distinguished services to the Irish Republic.'

Silver-plated tray presented to Diarmuid and Kit Lynch to commemorate their wedding in Dundalk Gaol, 24 April 1918, by Lynch's fellow inmates.
Courtesy of Lynch family; photographed by Adrian O'Herlihy

6

America: Setting the Scene

When Patrick McCartan arrived in America with the petition for President Wilson which the IRB leaders had signed in Fleming's Hotel in Dublin on 18 June 1917, he was initially employed by Joseph McGarrity and was later appointed editor of McGarrity's *Irish Press*. McGarrity was a wealthy Irish-American businessman based in Philadelphia. He was a Clan na Gael veteran and a member of the FOIF Executive (the American-Irish foundation established in March 1916). He founded the Philadelphia newspaper the *Irish Press* in 1918 specifically to further the cause of Irish independence.

McGarrity, McCartan and their associate, Dr William Maloney, disagreed fundamentally with three of the key members of the FOIF, Cohalan, Dalton and Devoy, as to what approach should be adopted by Irish-American lobbyists towards the American government. They did not want money and time wasted on fighting President Wilson's 'League of Nations' concept. In addition, McGarrity's group argued vehemently that all money collected by the FOIF should be sent to Ireland.

With the passing into American law of the Espionage Act in June 1917, new and intrusive restrictions had been applied to publications, meetings, speeches and lobbying of politicians – all activities which had been key tools in the campaign of the FOIF and Clan na Gael. Furthermore, with America's entry to the First World War, the close relationship fostered since 1914 between German Americans and Irish Americans was viewed with cold suspicion by the authorities.

Former US President Theodore Roosevelt suggested in January 1918 that leading Irish Americans should be imprisoned as 'enemy aliens'. Until the Great War ended, Lynch was routinely followed from his home to the FOIF office in Broadway, where he worked, and back:

> For months, I was, day by day, shadowed by at least two secret service men (who were occasionally relieved by relays) all the way from my residence to my office or to any address at which I had an appointment, and back again to my home, a matter of twelve miles, more or less, in each direction. If and when I made evening calls, the same procedure held.[1]

A recent release of British Intelligence records reveals that British Intelligence shared information on Lynch with its American counterpart during 1918 when the American State Department was considering revoking his American citizenship.[2] A report in 1919 informed them that 'Diarmuid Lynch is Director-in-Chief in America' (of the IRB).[3]

On 8 April 1918, Daniel Cohalan told a gathering of Irish Americans at Carnegie Hall that they would be loyal to the USA, but that they would equally hold President Wilson to his declaration: 'We shall fight … for the rights and liberties of small nations'.[4] The FOIF was determined that this statement must apply to the small nation of Ireland.

In his closing speech to the Race Convention in May of that year, Cohalan reiterated the 'Americanism' of the Irish in America, emphasising repeatedly that Irish immigrants had always loyally supported the USA, had fought in the American War of Independence against Britain and had become steadfast citizens in their adherence to American ideals. He used the occasion to highlight the effective use the British government made of propaganda against the nationalist movement in Ireland and against Irish Americans, pointing out the necessity of counterbalancing that damaging propaganda by acquainting the American people with the facts concerning British misrule in Ireland: 'If you leave to the enemies of Ireland the supplying of the information by which American public opinion is to be convinced, you will have nobody but yourselves to blame, if upon the misinformation which may be furnished, the case goes against you in that matter.'[5]

Cohalan had been appointed a judge of the Supreme Court in New York in 1912 and was a politician of significant influence. He had himself been the target of a calculated attack by intelligence agencies in September 1917, when documentary evidence was simultaneously published by both the British and

Americans that revealed his involvement with Roger Casement's attempt to smuggle German armaments into Ireland
for the 1916 insurrection.

When Devoy and the Clan castigated the alignment of
America with Great Britain in successive issues of *The Gaelic
American* and vehemently opposed the intention of the British
government to introduce conscription in Ireland, a government
ban meant that *The Gaelic American* could no longer be posted
to its many recipients in the US and abroad using the US mail
system.[6]

During May and June 1918, intelligence sources in Britain
and in the USA released reports of an alleged 'German Plot'
in Ireland, which led to the mass arrest and imprisonment
of hundreds of nationalists. The reports were reproduced
in newspapers on both sides of the Atlantic, leading to
even greater levels of public hostility to the Irish-American
population. The Espionage Act was followed in 1918 by the
more repressive measures of the Sedition Act. The FOIF
operated a muted campaign until the war ended, and that did
not sit well with some of its members. McGarrity's group was
deeply exasperated by the measured programme followed by
the organisation.

Liam Mellows, a prominent member of the Irish Volunteers
who had led the 1916 insurgents in Galway, was also frustrated
by the attitude of the FOIF. Mellows had been sent to the
USA by the IRB as a mouthpiece for its nationalist cause after
months spent in hiding in Ireland following the Rising. After

he arrived in New York in December 1916, Devoy had given him a job on the staff of *The Gaelic American*.

Mellows was well aware that the propaganda war in the US by British Intelligence was a menacing threat to the cause of Irish nationalists. He wrote to his brother Barney in November 1917 and complained of the propaganda directed at Irish-American activists. 'English "airgead" [money] is like water here. Press largely owned or controlled by Northcliffe, hence violently pro-E [English] and bitterly anti-Irish.'[7] In February 1919 he addressed the Irish Race Convention at Philadelphia and referred to the hostile propaganda campaign: 'There has been a propaganda war carried out seditiously and vindictively, not alone among the people of Ireland but against the Irish Race the world over. That propaganda has been started for the purpose and maintained for the purpose of defeating the aspirations of the Irish people.'[8]

As time passed Mellows became increasingly infuriated by the muted campaign for Irish self-determination which the FOIF was pursuing while the Great War lasted. Mellows' sympathies were now on the side of those calling for more strident action: Joe McGarrity, Dr Patrick McCartan and Dr William Maloney.

Following the end of the war, President Woodrow Wilson was determined that the question of Irish self-determination would not intrude at the Paris Peace Conference. He did not want to antagonise Britain, as he needed its support for his cherished project, the League of Nations. As 1919 progressed,

Devoy and Cohalan mounted an intensive publicity campaign against this League. The long-standing animosity between Woodrow Wilson and Cohalan, the recognised spokesman for the Irish-American lobby, worsened as the clamorous campaign of the FOIF against the League of Nations escalated.

***

When Diarmuid Lynch disembarked at Ellis Island on 6 May 1918, he was a man of notoriety: an American citizen who had played a key role in the 1916 insurrection against the British government, America's ally in the Great War. He had survived the death penalty and had served time in eight British prisons. As a member of the Supreme Council of the IRB, Director of Communications for the Volunteers and Sinn Féin Director for Food, he left Ireland in a blaze of popular support and publicity.

The America he was returning to was a country markedly more hostile towards immigrant groups, such as the Irish Americans, than it had previously been, because of its alignment with Great Britain in the Great War. In a telegram to his wife on 14 May, Lynch wrote, 'Tell Mick that friends here consider it not advisable to have Harry [Boland] come, pending further advice.'[9]

Lynch's return was fêted by sections of the Irish-American community, and he was taken instantly to the heart of the FOIF. His closest friends in America, Cohalan and Dalton, were its executive officers, and Devoy had been a founding member. Proposed by Dalton and seconded by Gertrude Kelly, Lynch's selection for the post of National Secretary of the FOIF on 19 May at the second Irish Race Convention was almost uncontested.

When Lynch was introduced to the capacity crowd by the chairman, Revd T. J. Hurton, according to the report published in a May issue of *The Gaelic American*, 'The whole Convention stood up and cheered him to the echo, remaining standing for several minutes.' In a long speech peppered with prolonged applause by the audience, Lynch threw down the gauntlet to those who impeded the realisation of Irish independence: 'The Ireland of today is not the Ireland of 1914. It knows exactly what it wants.' Lynch refuted the accusations then rife in the American and British press, of a continuing German Plot.[10] At the Annual Convention of the New York Gaelic League, Lynch again received a standing ovation and was thanked warmly for 'representing the executive of that organisation on the Coiste Gnótha in Ireland for several years past'.[11]

Under Lynch's secretaryship, the FOIF moved headquarters from 1482 Broadway to larger and more central premises which he secured at the Sun Building, 280 Broadway. Liam Mellows noted Lynch's changes over the three months from June to September 1918. Writing to Peter Golden in August, he observed, 'Diarmuid Lynch is making a big effort to pull the FOIF together and appears to be doing well.'[12]

Discovering that the organisation was handicapped by

having only one named contact for each branch, Lynch mounted an ambitious campaign to record the names and addresses of every member of all branches of the FOIF in America. From his meticulous records it is clear that a phenomenal growth in membership was achieved in the months that followed. The organisation burgeoned from just eighteen affiliated regular branches in January 1918 to eighty-eight branches, and from fifteen affiliated associate branches to two hundred and five by the date of the Philadelphia Convention, 22 February 1919. A random example taken from the minutes of meetings in New York shows, for example, an attendance of over seventy at the meeting of 14 April 1919, compared to a habitual seven or eight attendees during 1917.

Mellows, Lynch and McCartan were all elected to Dáil Éireann in the November 1918 'Sinn Féin' elections. Lynch was elected to represent the South-East Constituency in Cork with a total vote of 17,419 in his favour. At a celebratory gathering in Cohalan's New York home on 29 December, McCartan and William Maloney urged that the FOIF should immediately declare for the Republic of Ireland. However, Fr Peter Magennis, Chairman of the FOIF, disagreed with this proposal, as did Cohalan, Lynch and Dalton, concluding that they must await guidance from the newly elected Dáil in Dublin before going public with any announcement. This angered McCartan, Maloney, McGarrity and Mellows. McCartan went ahead, without sanction, and sent a note to the US Secretary of State Robert Lansing and to foreign diplomats, announcing that 'The United Kingdom of Great Britain and Ireland is at an end'.[13]

With Congressional elections imminent, the FOIF mounted a pressure campaign on the electoral candidates in the form of a questionnaire which was designed to clarify for voters the positions those candidates were adopting on the question of Irish self-determination. The questionnaire demanded explicit support for the objectives of the FOIF in relation to Ireland and requested that Ireland's case be presented at the forthcoming Peace Conference in Paris.[14] During November, Lynch, Mellows and Dalton drafted a proclamation directed at President Wilson requesting that the forthcoming Peace Conference 'take cognisance of Ireland's national status'.[15] Copies of the demand were sent to the ambassadors and consuls in the USA of twenty other countries.[16]

When the Committee on Foreign Affairs of the US Congress granted the FOIF's request for a hearing, to take place on 12 and 13 December, Lynch sent a circular to all FOIF branches urging them to have a delegation in Washington on the days of the hearings. As well as rallying the FOIF faithful, Lynch organised twenty-eight public meetings to take place simultaneously in cities around America to copperfasten the public perception that Ireland's call for independence was widely supported and legitimately within the ambit of President Wilson's stated aim of fighting for 'the rights and liberties of small nations'.[17]

As part of the build-up to the Congressional hearing,

the FOIF organised a 'Self-Determination for Ireland' week in cities around the USA. The highlight was an address by Boston's Cardinal William Henry O'Connell to a capacity audience at Madison Square Garden in New York on 10 December. In direct reference to the cause being pursued by the FOIF, and pointedly using the terminology of President Wilson, O'Connell stated, 'This war we are told, was for justice for all and for the inviolable rights of small nations. The war can be justified only by the universal application of those principles. Let that application begin with Ireland.'[18]

Lynch hurried from the Madison Square Garden meeting to Washington to address the Congressional hearing. This extract from his presentation shows his attitude towards the government of Ireland by Britain:

> Ireland has suffered at the hands of England the suspension of the exercise of her sovereign will, which she has never surrendered, the domination of her people by military and naval force, the burdens of over taxation, the tragic wiping out of her population, the crushing of her industries, the suppression of her merchant marine, the campaign of calumny to which she has been subjected, the falsification of her history, her ideals and her aspirations.[19]

One of the resolutions presented by Congressman William E. Mason sought that 'an appropriation be made out of the treasury of the United States to provide for salaries for a minister and consuls to the Republic of Ireland'.[20] If this resolution had been successful, it would have amounted to the tacit recognition of the Irish state and its nominated representatives by an important section of the American government. A second resolution, presented by Senator Thomas Gallagher in 1919, was more explicit, calling for 'the right of Ireland to freedom, independence and self-determination' to be an item on the agenda at the Peace Conference in Paris.[21] A massive majority passed the Gallagher Resolution in the US Congress on 4 March 1919.[22]

In September 1918 Lynch had reported that there was a paltry $410 available for the work of the FOIF. By April 1919, with the massive increase in numbers, this financial situation had improved and the organisation now had a balance of $8,080.[23] The FOIF had launched a major fund-raising drive at the Philadelphia Convention in February 1919. Lynch had dispatched an appeal during January and February, as well as invitations and requests for delegates to the Convention. 'Approximately 14,500 appeal letters were mailed by the national secretary to the branches of the FOIF, to members of all Irish organisations in the United States and to a large number of Catholic clergy with Irish names.'[24]

The Philadelphia Convention was held in the Second Regiment Armoury on 22 and 23 February. Over 5,000 delegates, representing all eighty-eight branches of the FOIF, were present, as well as delegates from disparate groups, such as the Ancient Order of Hibernians, the National Foresters and Clan na Gael clubs. The clergy was also strongly represented.

At the convention Lynch distributed 50,000 copies of a 140-page pamphlet: *The Irish Republic, Why?* Written by Lawrence Ginnell while a prisoner in Mountjoy Gaol, it promoted the idea of a republic in Ireland. It had been smuggled out of Ireland into Lynch's hands in America for publication and distribution.[25]

The Irish Victory Fund, first proposed by the FOIF in January, was endorsed at the convention. Its stated objective was to raise $1 million for the work of the FOIF. With continuing hostility to the Irish-American agenda, the FOIF decided that their American credentials must henceforth be a prominent feature of their manifesto. The three main articles in the FOIF Constitution were revised during the conference and now not only reiterated the organisation's commitment to do all in its power to achieve independence for Ireland, but was also more emphatic in its commitment to America and an American-based agenda. This emphasis on the Americanness of the FOIF reflected the increased influence of Cohalan in the formation of official policy. However, it was seen as an abandonment of principle by the Philadelphia group led by McGarrity.

The keynote address at the convention was delivered by a churchman of prestige, Cardinal James Gibbons, whose script reflected the official policy of the FOIF, a call for self-determination for Ireland. The text deliberately quoted the declaration which President Wilson had made to Congress on 11 February 1918: 'National aspirations must be respected;

peoples may now be dominated and governed only by their consent. "Self-Determination" is not a mere phrase.'

The Philadelphia Convention was regarded as the most successful gathering of Irish Americans ever. Cohalan closed the final session with the words, 'There never was a gathering which will be most result-full for the cause of the Independence of Ireland and for the welfare and good of America.'[26] The FOIF was at the height of its power and effectiveness.

Immediately after the convention, Cohalan led a delegation to Washington to present the adopted resolutions to the president. Cohalan had first earned the enmity of Woodrow Wilson when he had opposed his selection as the Democratic presidential candidate in 1912. With bitter animosity, Wilson refused to see the delegation unless Cohalan withdrew, which, in the interest of the FOIF mission, the judge did.[27]

On 7 May 1919, Lynch was the guest of honour at the Annual Banquet of the Maynooth Alumni Association at the Hotel Astor, New York. It was the first time that a layman had attended this exclusive event, and Lynch was referred to glowingly. 'Diarmuid Lynch, the National Secretary of the Friends of Irish Freedom was hailed as the true champion of the vindication of America's honour and as the representative of the Gael.'[28]

In September Lynch was appointed Secretary of the Board of Trustees of the FOIF. The report of the 7 October meeting of the combined FOIF National Executive and National Council gives an indication of his heavy workload. He was to mail circulars, address envelopes, contact the Kerrymen's Association and the New York Local Council and attend to the propaganda literature. Following a resolution which had been adopted at the February convention, Lynch was also assigned the task of effecting the purchase of St Enda's, Pearse's school in Rathfarnham, County Dublin. The school was insolvent and under threat of eviction. The FOIF resolution was that the building would be purchased and presented to the Irish nation in memory of the Pearse brothers who had been executed after the Easter Rising.

There were also more contentious matters to attend to: some individuals in New York had formed a new association calling themselves 'American Sons of Irish Freedom'. In July 1919 Lynch was charged with the task of setting in motion the incorporation of the FOIF for the protection of its title. This was no small task, as all branches had to be incorporated under their own separate state legislature. Lynch was responsible for all documentation and correspondence regarding this operation, which dragged on for some years.[29]

As donations towards the Victory Fund began to trickle in, Lynch implemented a strict accounting of all monies and funds, as evidenced by a congratulatory letter from Richard Wolfe of Chicago, one of the Board of Trustees:

I am very happy indeed to know that you are taking definite steps towards the proper handling of the funds. It is unpardonable negligence that this was not done at the very outset. There is danger and ground for just criticism in the loose handling of funds. I frankly confess that I feel ashamed that we did not have the business sense to adopt at the outset the simple method of business in handling our funds.[30]

Reports from Dáil Éireann were regularly received, printed and distributed from the National Secretary's office. The *Irish Bulletin* printed news of raids and arrests in Ireland and was routinely sent from Dublin to Lynch. In turn, Robert Brennan, Sinn Féin's Director of Publicity, solicited information and ideas from Lynch for inclusion in the *Bulletin*.[31] Other nationalist literature was organised from Lynch's office, such as Lawrence Ginnell's second pamphlet, *English Atrocities in Ireland, 1917–1918*, which Harry Boland brought from Ireland in June 1919.

During the first six months of 1919 the Executive of the Provisional Government in Ireland was relying on Lynch to further the cause of Irish independence in the US and was seeking desperately needed funds. Letters from Ireland written by Michael Collins, Cathal Brugha and Arthur Griffith were all addressed to Diarmuid Lynch with urgent and repeated requests for funds and political action.[32]

At the same time, Lynch did not ignore the fine detail, sending a donation of £168 16s 10d from FOIF funds to the Presentation Convent in Rathmore, County Kerry, to rebuild the convent and school after it had burned down.[33]

Parallel to the campaign to have Ireland's case presented at the Peace Conference in Paris, the FOIF mounted a relentless effort in 1919 to defeat President Wilson's cherished project, the League of Nations. Cohalan believed that the proposed League would mean the defeat of the aim to have Ireland recognised as a separate nation. He thought it was not in America's interest to agree to a binding league with Britain. At weekly meetings in East Coast venues he spoke vehemently against the proposal. During 1919 a flood of pamphlets, maps and newsletters opposing the League flowed from Lynch's office to senators, politicians and the officers of numerous targeted organisations. The League proposal was resoundingly defeated in the Senate on 6 November 1919.

Influential politicians who favoured the Irish case, such as Senator William Borah and Senator Henry Lodge, were courted by the FOIF. When it was learned that Senator Joseph Sherman Frelinghuysen of New Jersey was wavering in his opposition to the League, the Advertising Committee, comprising Lynch, Dalton and Cohalan, organised a deluge of postcards from his voters.[34]

The Irish National Bureau in Washington had been set up by the Irish Progressive League (an American-Irish organisation) to disseminate information on Irish affairs. The League became an associate member of the FOIF in 1919 and in July of that year the FOIF took over the functions of the Bureau. Full use was made of its proximity to the seat of government to push the Irish-American agenda in Congress. Lynch was responsible for regular weekly mailings of the Bureau's newsletter to members of Congress, to all embassies, to the governors of all states, to editors of all the daily newspapers in New York, and Catholic and Irish newspapers in America, and to newspapers abroad, to libraries, to presidents of universities, colleges and schools, and to officers of all Irish-American societies.[35]

As well as being responsible for the printing and distribution of all promotional literature from the FOIF office in New York and from the National Bureau in Washington, Lynch also managed the funds of the National Bureau.[36] In the period 1919–20, thirty-one pamphlets on separate issues were distributed from the Bureau's offices at Washington. Recollecting this period of intense campaigning, Daniel T. O'Connell, Director of the Bureau, wrote, 'My superior [at the Bureau in Washington] was Diarmuid Lynch, our national secretary, and Ireland can never repay Lynch for the work he has done for her.'[37]

With the frenetic pace of Lynch's life, ill-health again intruded and he used the brief 'time off' to write home to his family in Cork: 'I can never count on anything. Just so surely as I make an appointment, I eventually have to cancel it. Important matters continually turn up day-by-day which must be attended to.' A more exact description of the effects of his hectic schedule was added to the letter by his wife:

Diarmuid is feeling A1 again and can take his food as well as ever. He would need all his strength now because he is working as he has never worked before and that is saying a great deal, but you know it's now or never with us, both here and at home presently and nothing that's possible will be left undone.[38]

During 1919 the FOIF became increasingly influential in political terms. The Victory Fund had realised over $1 million by August 1919. Each week brought confirmation of new branches being formed. Membership records show a growth from 6,000 members in February 1919 to over 70,000 in December 1919. With single-minded attention, Lynch had succeeded in the ambition he declared in January 1919, to 'enrol into one, militant, disciplined organisation the increasing but unattached supporters of the cause'.[39] He added:

> … what is going to count is Organisation – an organisation that you can get working at the touch of a button, an organisation through which, by the sending of telegrams or one series of letters, you can line up inside a week or less every man and woman of the blood in this country … Unless we are able to do that the politicians will sneer at us, and the British propagandists who are working day and night will sneer at us also – and they will be right.[40]

Lynch was in a powerful and central position, and he was esteemed by his colleagues in the FOIF. J. J. Splain of New Haven, Connecticut, wrote:

> Endowed with remarkable executive and administrative powers, trained to the very last in business details, and with a profound knowledge of Irish affairs gained from actual contact and an extensive course of reading, Lynch brought to his post just the qualities that made him the man of the hour. At once he made

his office a clearing house of detail; the remarkable system of organisation he initiated and developed will long stand as a model of thoroughness.[41]

OFFICE OF NATIONAL SECRETARY

Friends of Irish Freedom

FITZGERALD BUILDING, 1482 BROADWAY

NEW YORK CITY

August 20th, 1918.

A Chara:

   Together with the foregoing letter from our National President, I now have much pleasure in enclosing copy of revised Constitution and By-Laws of the Friends of Irish Freedom. Please read same carefully, especially clauses relating to membership.

   To secure your National Membership card it is essential that I receive your full name and address on enclosed application form, together with $1.00. I prefer that these should come with others through your Branch Financial Secretary—in case you are on such a roll. However, if forwarding through this channel should result in any considerable delay, please send them direct to me at once. Without the possession of a National Membership card no member will in future be considered in good standing.

   The National Council and National Executive aim at promptly building up the Organization on a definite basis, and to enable us to carry out our program, funds are wanted urgently. While we at Headquarters are doing our part to combine all lovers of Irish Freedom into one compact body, our success depends mainly upon individual workers, who will explain the objects of our Organization and bring new members into the ranks.

   How many new members can YOU secure—not next year but during the next few weeks? I will forward application cards on hearing from you. If you wish me to send these cards direct to your friends, please furnish names and addresses on enclosed form.

   If you belong to any other Society whose members sympathize with the objects of the Friends of Irish Freedom, you are urged to attend its next meeting and secure the affiliation of such Society as an Associate Branch.

   In memory of my dear dead comrades of Easter Week, 1916—Clarke, McDermott, Pearse, Connolly, Plunkett, Kent, McDonagh and Ashe—I add a personal plea that all lovers of Freedom, and those of the Irish Race especially, will act promptly towards the accomplishment of the ideal for which they fought and died. The critical moment, when our influence can be used to secure justice and liberty for Ireland, may come unexpectedly and find us but imperfectly organized. Unpreparedness and procrastination lost Ireland many a golden opportunity. Let us profit by the experience of history and get together and act together NOW.

   Is mise, le meas mor,

Diarmuid Lynch

National Secretary.

As National Secretary of the FOIF, Diarmuid Lynch exhorts members to strive to build up the strong organisation he aspired to in 1918. *Courtesy of Lynch Family Archives*

7

The Slide towards Destruction

At the Philadelphia Convention in February 1919, the approach and priorities of the FOIF had been debated and changes in policy adopted. The deliberately pragmatic strategy infuriated some members who saw self-determination as being much less than independence and who were insistent that an Irish republic had already been established by the will of the Irish people in the 1918 elections.

Patrick McCartan, editor of the *Irish Press* in Philadelphia, favoured the more direct approach advocated by Joseph McGarrity, the paper's founder. Liam Mellows resigned his post at *The Gaelic American* newspaper in 1919 having been infuriated by the lack of action, as he saw it, by the FOIF, including his employer, John Devoy. He described to Peter Golden how Lynch had preached the need for 'discipline and obedience' to him.[1] Mellows, disenchanted with this softly-softly approach, now allied himself with the 'Philadelphia trio' of McGarrity, McCartan and William Maloney.[2]

When the FOIF established a board of national trustees

in March 1919, electing Lynch its secretary, McGarrity was one of the eight nominated and elected to the board, reflecting not only the strong support he had within the organisation but also the tactical awareness of Devoy and Cohalan that he should be kept on side if possible. The FOIF Executive was confident that their organisation was on the right course to achieve self-determination for Ireland and that it was equipped to negotiate the necessary political routes towards that end.

Across the Atlantic, in February 1919 Collins had helped facilitate the escape of de Valera, who had been arrested in 1918 as part of the German Plot round-ups, from Lincoln Gaol. Having shipped de Valera safely across the Irish Sea, Collins lodged him in Denis Lynch's home in Drumcondra, the trusted house where he himself often went to ground. Strolling in the grounds of the distillery, de Valera and Harry Boland laid plans for Boland's forthcoming mission to America to prepare for de Valera's own arrival there:

> About 11th May, 1919, Harry Boland arrived in New York …
> On arrival in New York, he went straight to Diarmuid Lynch.
> They were old friends. In a long discussion Diarmuid gave him
> an account of the position in America, including the differences
> of opinion which had arisen between a few of the leaders on
> some matters of policy. On the self-determination issue, Boland
> characterised the fuss which had been raised as 'a tempest in
> a teapot' … Diarmuid proposed to him that he should call a
> conference of Devoy, Cohalan, McCartan, Dalton and five or six
> other men prominent in the movement …[3]

However, this conference did not happen. When he arrived in New York in June 1919, de Valera, accompanied by Harry Boland, paid a brief visit to the FOIF headquarters at 280 Broadway, where a council meeting was in session. He was then brought to Mellows' apartment. Mellows gave voice to his strong disgust with the FOIF's nuanced approach to the crucial Irish question. From there de Valera went to McGarrity's home in Philadelphia, where he stayed for a week and where he was further briefed by the 'Philadelphia trio' on their escalating grievances with the FOIF's current policy.

Lynch, Devoy, Cohalan and Dalton gathered at the Waldorf Astoria Hotel in New York on 23 June 1919 to welcome de Valera on his first public appearance in the US. De Valera was flanked by Joe McGarrity, Liam Mellows and Patrick McCartan – but also by Lynch, Cohalan and Devoy. He told the gathered press and supporters that the purpose of his visit to the USA was twofold: to seek American recognition for Ireland as a nation and to gather much-needed funds for the impoverished Dáil in Ireland. He planned to sell Irish bonds in America.

The welcoming celebrations in the Waldorf Astoria went on for hours, and at 4 a.m. Devoy made his way home to his $1.50-a-night lodgings at the Ennis Hotel on Forty-Second Street. Lynch began the trek home to 2366 Grand Concourse in the Bronx. De Valera, the 'President of Ireland' settled into the luxury of the Waldorf Astoria's presidential suite with members of his entourage, which included Boland.

It was likely that Lynch himself secured the lavish accommodation through his friendship with the Lee brothers, Jamie and Patrick. Jamie was paymaster at the Waldorf Astoria, and both brothers were members of the Philo-Celtic Society and of the FOIF. The proprietor of the hotel, George C. Boldt, was one of those who had pleaded for Lynch's life when he had been condemned to death in May 1916.

The lawyers on the FOIF Executive advised de Valera that a sale of bonds was impossible as it would contravene America's Blue Sky Laws.[4] This advice was interpreted by McGarrity and others as an attempt by the FOIF to delay the bond campaign launch so that the Irish Victory Fund, then gaining momentum, could continue to make money for the FOIF.

Plans for the bond drive went ahead and to make way for the drive, at de Valera's request, the Irish Victory Fund was closed on 31 August 1919, having raised over $1 million. The FOIF was active in the preparation for the launch of the bond drive, and a committee, which included Dalton and former National Secretary, John Moore, was appointed. The expectation of the FOIF was that, having wound up its own Victory Fund campaign, its appointees would handle the bond campaign. The headquarters for the bond drive was accommodated initially within the FOIF rented rooms in the Sun Building on Broadway. 'The Secretary reported having granted the use of room 404 to the American Commission on Irish Independence for the purpose of handling President de Valera's tour and the business connected with the Irish Bond-Certificate drive. His action was approved.'[5]

Lynch observed, 'de Valera was compelled by the legal facts of the situation to abandon the idea of floating "bonds".'[6] In August, Boland, speaking for de Valera, informed the FOIF that the 'American Commission on Irish Independence' would manage a bond-certificate drive under the chairmanship of Frank P. Walsh (one of the three delegates to the Paris Peace Conference).[7] In September, separate headquarters for the bond-certificate drive were established on Fifth Avenue, New York. James O'Mara, an astute businessman, was brought out from Ireland by de Valera to head the team.

Pressure was exerted on Lynch to resign the secretaryship of the FOIF and to join the staff at bond-cert headquarters. Lynch declined on the grounds that the organising of the FOIF and the extension of membership, on the lines to which he had been adhering, was vital to the success of every phase of the movement, including the sale of bond certificates.[8] Subsequently, Lynch handed over his lists of the names and addresses of all 70,000 FOIF members to facilitate the bond-cert team. He then mailed 70,000 sets of bond-cert literature, together with maps of Ireland showing the results in every constituency in the 1918 election in Ireland. The FOIF National Council meeting of 3 October approved a recommendation by the national trustees to loan de Valera $100,000 to kick-start the bond-cert drive. After a delay of five months, in January 1920 the sale of bond certificates was launched.

By late 1919 de Valera's fund-raising tour, now well under way, was heralded by the FOIF in its October newsletter:

'President De Valera's Tour Will Live in History!'[9] McGarrity's *Irish Press* headlined, 'Irish President Is the Moral Leader of the World!'[10] The tour, entirely funded by the FOIF, was an overwhelming publicity success. Lynch described the commitment of the FOIF to de Valera's mission:

> Additional FOIF organisers were appointed; the office space and staff of National Headquarters were doubled; accommodation was provided for the First Consulate of the Irish Republic under Diarmuid Fawsitt. Ten thousand dollars had been furnished to defray President de Valera's initial trip to the Coast. Later over $16,700 was given towards financing his principal tour of the country, the itinerary of which was arranged by his representative consulting with Diarmuid Lynch who provided the names and addresses of men in each of the cities to be visited, who could be relied upon to play a leading part in organising the necessary meetings.[11]

At that time, some 20 million American citizens claimed Irish descent. The novelty of seeing and hearing the 'president' of the home country drew huge crowds at every venue on de Valera's itinerary. 'In ecstasy 25,000 Chicagoans of Irish birth bade him welcome. For thirty-one minutes they cheered. For more than two hours they sang songs of Irish freedom.'[12] Boland reported to Arthur Griffith, 'The President has been received with wonderful enthusiasm. Proclamations are pouring in from all the cities and towns in the country craving a visit.'[13] Lynch's office channelled hundreds of those invitations onwards to Boland.[14]

However, all was not well behind the scenes. In September Devoy wrote a protesting letter to Harry Boland in which he stated:

> The situation is becoming dangerous because the majority who really control things here are treated as if they were unfriendly and the suggestion of a very insignificant minority who can deliver nothing are apparently dictating your actions. ...
>
> Every man who comes here from Ireland not alone misunderstands America, but is filled with preconceived notions that are wholly without foundation, as well as a belief that he knows America better than those who have spent most of their lives in the country or were born in it.[15]

At one meeting of the FOIF, Dalton questioned the retention by the National Council of Philadelphia of $25,000 of the now closed Victory Fund, monies which should have been forwarded to the national treasurer in New York.[16] Likewise, Lynch wrote to James O'Mara wanting an explanation of reports that O'Mara had approved the Chicago branches' retaining of funds.[17] McGarrity presented the FOIF with a postal bill for mailing 10,000 copies of his Philadelphia *Irish Press*, without consultation or prior approval.[18] The issue, dated 10 January 1920, included the text of a pamphlet, *Irish Issues*, by Maloney, which aimed to boost the sale of the bond certificates.[19]

A letter to Lynch from one of his fellow inmates in Dundalk Gaol in 1918, Terence MacSwiney, sent in December 1919, illustrates the wildly incorrect perception of the situation in America held by nationalists in Ireland at the time: 'Though I wouldn't want to leave Ireland at this moment for anything, I envy you all the rousing times and doings you can enjoy uninterrupted in America. In Ireland the Republic is proclaimed, in America you seem to have it pretty much established.'[20]

In America, de Valera continued to speak out on behalf of Ireland without consulting the FOIF policy-makers, which further incensed them. That November, following a meeting with the FOIF, Boland wrote disparagingly in his diary, 'Have a free-for-all row and find everything ends well. Lynch went off like a soda water bottle.'[21]

At the National Council meeting on 10 December, Devoy demanded an explanation of the rumour of de Valera's intention to set up another body that would manage not only his tour of America but also the bond-cert drive and the fight against anti-Irish propaganda. To Devoy this was a radical proposal that threatened to usurp some of the established programmes of Clan na Gael and the FOIF. De Valera scotched the reports, stating publicly that Devoy and Cohalan had given him every assistance in their power, that there was no truth in rumours of a rival organisation.[22] However, de Valera's messages to Arthur Griffith conveyed a radically different position to the one he stated publicly at the 10 December meeting:

Now as to differences here, Dr McCartan can explain them in full. A deadly attempt to ruin our chances for the bonds and for everything we came here to accomplish is being made. If I am asked for the ulterior motives I can only guess that they are to drive me home, jealousy, envy, resentment of a rival, some devilish cause I do not know what prompts.[23]

De Valera also wrote to Collins to condemn Lynch: 'I am sorry to say that Diarmuid supports the Judge's stand with the result that we cannot secure from the FOIF proper co-operation as Lynch is the Executive Secretary and he refuses absolutely to do anything with which the Judge may disagree.'[24]

Devoy formed a poor opinion of de Valera's reaction to the tumultuous reception he had received. 'He is filled with the idea that the great ovations he got here were for him personally and practically gave him a mandate to do as he pleases. His head is turned to a greater extent than any man I have met in more than half a century.'[25]

From the time of de Valera's arrival in June 1919, regular meetings with FOIF officers including Lynch had been held at the Waldorf Astoria Hotel when de Valera was in residence. In January 1920 these meetings ceased.

In February 1920 Joe McGuinness, Lynch's long-time associate from the New York Philo-Celtic Society and by this point a member of Dáil Éireann, wrote:

How are you able to stick it so long over there at the pace I know you are going? It must be taking a great deal out of you for I know how you work and worry. We are delighted with how things are moving there and it has often been mentioned how your work was the great factor in the wonderful change.[26]

A very public row broke out between de Valera and the FOIF in February after the *Westminster Gazette* printed an interview in which de Valera quoted the 'Platt Amendment' between the USA and Cuba as a possible model for the future relationship between Ireland and Great Britain.[27] If implemented, it would mean that Great Britain would retain certain rights in Ireland and it would allow the British navy to expand its role at sea. McCartan was sent home to Ireland by de Valera to explain his proposal to Collins and the Dáil. Though some of the Dáil members disagreed with de Valera's public statement on the Platt Amendment, Collins and Griffith decided that their only possible course of action at that moment in time, and given the distance, was to back de Valera.

Following his interview with the *Westminster Gazette* there was an exchange of angry letters between de Valera and Cohalan. De Valera annotated Cohalan's letter and sent copies of both letters to the Dáil. *The Gaelic American* published de Valera's letter with lengthy and withering comment by Devoy.

The FOIF sought to neutralise de Valera and mustered a mass meeting of members at the Park Avenue Hotel on 19 March 1920 to which he was not invited. However, urged on by McGarrity, de Valera made an appearance. The following eight-hour meeting was fractious, chaotic and turbulent, underlining the deep distrust and hostility on both sides. An

uneasy truce between the warring parties was eventually bro-
kered. A letter from Kit Lynch to Granig reflected the hope of
her husband that a rapprochement had been achieved:

> A very unfortunate position arose which threatened the life of
> the Irish Movement here, but thank God, the men from your
> side awoke before it was too late and realised in time the disaster
> to which they were heading. I never saw anything to worry
> Diarmuid so much as that did, but now all is peace again and
> good feelings prevail all round.[28]

Almost immediately the illusory peace was shattered. When
the Victory Fund had been launched at the February 1919
Convention in Philadelphia, it was explicitly stated that some
of the money raised would be kept in the US to fight anti-
Irish propaganda and to fund the political work in America for
the cause of Irish independence. In April 1920, James O'Mara,
acting for de Valera, demanded an account of the Victory
Fund, claiming that such money had been donated for Ireland
and morally belonged to Ireland.[29] Lynch, acting on a decision
by the FOIF Executive, refused to supply an account.[30] Shortly
afterwards, Boland was sent to Ireland by de Valera to brief
Dáil members on the situation in America.

Articles criticising the FOIF began to appear with
increasing frequency in both American and Irish newspapers,
showing that messages from de Valera and others castigating
Cohalan, Devoy, Lynch and the FOIF were being ferried

across the Atlantic.[31] The perception in Ireland regarding the de Valera–Cohalan power struggle was exemplified by the opinion expressed by Bishop Michael Fogarty of Killaloe, sent to Monsignor James Power, New York: 'One of Ireland's greatest afflictions at this moment is the behaviour of the Cohalan group in America. It is all dished up here in the daily papers.'[32]

Meanwhile, the FOIF was putting in careful diplomatic groundwork to mount a powerful political campaign at the forthcoming American Republican Party Convention in Chicago. Cohalan hoped to 'persuade the Republican Party to adopt a policy "plank" [resolution] in favour of Irish Independence'.[33] There seems to have been a consensus to keep de Valera out of the process of drawing up the strategy for the Convention, although he was briefed.[34] Incensed, de Valera took the initiative. An entourage, which included Seán Nunan (a clerk of the first Dáil who came out to help O'Mara), Mellows and McCartan, arrived in Chicago on 4 June 1920 with much fanfare, 'torchlight parades, marching bands and banners'.[35] Reflecting on the high profile de Valera and his entourage adopted in Chicago, McCartan later admitted ruefully, 'There was no chance of offending America that we did not take.'[36]

Despite being strongly advised by Senator Bourke Cockran and Frank P. Walsh to let Cohalan get on with presenting the resolution for Ireland, de Valera insisted that he alone spoke for Ireland and would formulate and present his own resolution.[37] De Valera's resolution was rejected; Cohalan's was adopted.

But the public display of disunity in such a political arena was a deadly blow. When de Valera publicly disavowed Cohalan's resolution it was removed from the agenda of resolutions to be considered.[38]

De Valera decided to proceed to the Democratic Convention in San Francisco hoping that his resolution would be adopted there, but, considering the sustained aversion of President Wilson and his Democratic supporters to the Irish-American lobby, this was an unrealistic hope.

McGarrity's *Irish Press* castigated Cohalan and the FOIF in its 19 June edition, attributing to Cohalan the failure to have a 'plank' adopted at Chicago. On 26 June the attack continued, with the paper referring to 'those who are resorting to innuendo, to whispering and stabs in the back'.[39]

In June 1920, Count George Noble Plunkett, Minister for Foreign Affairs in Dáil Éireann, condemned Cohalan and Devoy to the assembled members of the Dáil at the Mansion House and his condemnation was written into Dáil records:

> This portion of my Report would be incomplete if it did not refer to the attitude of Supreme Court Judge Daniel F. Cohalan and John Devoy towards the President and his mission. The Ministry learn that these men have never given their whole-hearted support to the President in his campaign. At the very outset, they used their utmost endeavour to prevent the launching of the Bond Drive, and they attempted to force the President into the position of accepting their dictation in all matters of policy connected with his mission. The President has definitely refused to allow his judgement or his

actions to be dictated by these men and the success of his tour and of the Bond Drive are a proof of his wisdom in this matter. The stand taken by the President is that the policy and action of the Irish People must be decided in Ireland.[40]

Until this time, public criticism by both sides was measured and muted, but when William Barry, an Irishman employed on the steamship SS *New York*, was arrested on 1 July at Southampton by British customs officers in possession of ammunitions and guns for delivery to Irish nationalists, five letters in his possession, destined for members of the Dáil, were also confiscated.[41] The content of these letters was released to the British press and was forwarded to the *Philadelphia Ledger* by their London correspondent.[42] The publication of these letters blew any restraint on both sides in the Irish-American power struggle to pieces.

One of the letters was written by Seán Nunan and addressed to Arthur Griffith. It castigated the Dáil member for the Cork South-East Constituency, Diarmuid Lynch:

Lynch, who is Secretary of the FOIF, should be asked to explain his action in connection with this plot against the President. It is inexplicable to me how he can hold his position and represent the people of Cork. His action in retaining the former position and carrying out the instructions of Cohalan makes him in my opinion and in the opinion of other members of the party unworthy to represent any Irish constituency and a grave menace to our cause.[43]

Nunan also addressed a letter to Collins complaining, 'Now Michael, something should be done about Diarmuid. It is absolutely outrageous that he, a member of Dáil Éireann, should be supporting those who are opposing in every way the endeavours of the President.'[44] Another letter from Peter MacSwiney to his brother Terence MacSwiney, Lord Mayor of Cork city, was also condemnatory of Lynch:

> Lynch is the only one who is on the side of Devoy and why he should continue is a mystery to me. It would be very advisable if his constituents in Southeast Cork got together at once and passed a vote of confidence in de Valera and his associates from Ireland.[45]

Reacting to the outcry and in response to the complaints made to the Dáil members in the five letters, the vice-president of the Dáil, Arthur Griffith, wrote to Cohalan and Devoy:

> President de Valera is in the United States vested with the full confidence of the Cabinet and Congress of Ireland to secure explicit recognition by the Government of the United States for the Irish Republic. In such circumstance any word or action which might tend to discredit his office or mission constitutes an affront and an injury to the Irish Republic.[46]

Lynch wrote urgently to Cohalan at his summer residence in Westport, New York State, enclosing the newspaper clipping of the five defamatory letters. His tone was terse:

John Devoy, Dalton and myself think it very advisable that you come down at once to talk over the situation. If you cannot do this J. D. and myself will leave here Thursday early for Westport but it is much preferable that you should come, as others thereby can have a chance to confer. I am writing out my resignation as TD and giving my reasons for not having done so before now, that my actions would have been misconstrued by the enemies of the Irish Republic. Now that the question has been referred to in the press I feel free to act.[47]

On 20 July Lynch resigned his seat in Dáil Éireann.[48] In 1925 he explained to Piaras Béaslaí: 'My resignation was written out on 19 July. Boland had returned from Ireland the day before and had stated to parties in New York that he had a letter in his pocket demanding my resignation from the Dáil.'[49]

Deputy Speaker Richard Mulcahy presented Lynch's resignation letter to the Dáil on 6 August. The letter read as follows:

To the People of South East Cork

A Chairde:

The honour which you conferred on me in my absence from Ireland by electing me, unopposed, as your Representative to Dáil Éireann at the General Election, December, 1918, is one which I shall ever gratefully remember. In being thus honoured by the citizens of my native district, without solicitation or desire for office on my part, I have reason to feel a pardonable pride.

While fully appreciating the confidence which you have

reposed in me, I realised at the time of my election that, the English Government having deported me from Ireland through the exercise of its naval and military power, it would prevent my return thereto until such time as the Irish Republic secured its due recognition.

In full knowledge of how important it was that the Representative for South East Cork should be on the spot in Ireland to attend to the affairs of the Constituency and of the Nation, I seriously considered resigning at that time the position of Teactaire but concluded that my resignation then would have been an embarrassment inasmuch as the Dáil had not yet perfected laws governing such elections.

Differences have arisen since July 1919, between President de Valera and members of Dáil Éireann now in the United States on the one hand and the recognised leaders of the movement here on the other, as to the proper conduct of the campaign in America for the recognition of the Irish Republic. My judgment in this matter, based as it has been upon an intimate knowledge of conditions in America, was generally in agreement with the American leaders. This circumstance has governed my actions as National Secretary of the Friends of Irish Freedom, and has furthered my determination to immediately tender my resignation as a member of Dáil Éireann. The only consideration which deterred me from giving effect to that determination was that my action might have been misconstrued by the enemies of the Irish Republic, and heralded as a break in that splendid unity which has marked the progress of the Republican Government in Ireland.

Now, however, it has become evident from letters apparently written by officials of the Irish Republican Government at present in America, captured by the English Government on the person of a man named Barry and published in the Boston, Philadelphia and Chicago papers, that my resignation may at this time be properly offered without adding to the risk of such misconstruction.

I decline to permit my actions here or the actions of those men who have consistently worked for a generation in America for the establishment in Ireland of a form of government similar to that which prevails in these United States, from being made the subject of controversy and possible dissension in my Constituency. Without acquaintance with conditions in America, you, my friends, cannot possibly understand the American attitude, nor, in particular, the position of those who through the years have borne the brunt of the fight here. It would not be fair to ask you to express an opinion on the merits of the controversy which now diverts the attention of the supporters of the Irish Republic in this country, and it would be unwise to inject it into South East Cork.

The foregoing reasons impel me to hereby resign my position as Teactaire Dáil Éireann representing the Constituency of South East Cork. I am forwarding a duplicate of this resignation to the Speaker of An Dáil Éireann.

In thus definitely severing my official connection with you I desire once more to tender to all my old constituents my sincere thanks for the very great honour conferred on me in my election as your Representative to the first Congress of the Irish Republic, and I beg to assure you of my continued interest in your welfare and in the cause of the entire Irish Nation.

No matter what vicissitudes the future may have in store for me, I shall always cherish with pride the part which I had the honour to fulfil in the councils of those who made 'Easter Week' possible and solidified the foundations of the Irish Republic. It is permissible for me now to speak with a certain amount of freedom in these matters, and it may interest you to learn that during those eventful years prior to 'Easter Week' I was one of the selected few in whose hands lay the destiny of the Irish Republic; that my unalterable belief in the necessity of re-baptising the ideals of Emmet, Tone and Mitchel in the blood of men strong in the faith of Irish Republicanism in order to preserve the National Soul of Ireland, guided me to the right course of action; that my voice and influence were invariably in favour of the Irish Nation reasserting itself in arms before the existing favourable opportunity had passed. Results have justified my judgment and I am happy in this knowledge.

I now feel more free to continue my efforts here for the recognition of the Irish Republic on lines which long and practical experience in America have shown me to be for the best interests of the Irish Cause.

I pray God to preserve the unity and magnificent courage of those who in Ireland are battling against the brutal militarism of England; may He give light to those citizens of the Irish Republic who are as yet irresponsive to the Proclamation of 'Easter Week' that 'The Republic guarantees religious and civil liberty, equal rights, and equal opportunities to all its citizens, and declares its resolve to pursue the happiness and prosperity of the whole nation and of all its parts, cherishing all the children of the nation equally and oblivious of the differences carefully fostered by an alien government which have divided a minority from a majority in the past.'

With renewed assurance of my esteem and my interest in your welfare, and a special word of grateful remembrance to those splendid comrades in South East Cork who in less enlightened days stood unflinchingly for the principle of Irish Republicanism.

Is mise, le meas mor,

Diarmuid Lynch.[50]

Among those attending the Dáil session at Fleming's Hotel that morning were many who had engaged with Lynch on nationalist matters since his repatriation in 1907 or who had been in Lewes Prison with him three short years before. Some were trusted friends, such as Joe McGuinness, Alec McCabe, Frank Fahy, Charlie Dolan (for whom Lynch had canvassed in the constituency of Leitrim in the 1907 election), Terence MacSwiney and even Lynch's childhood friend Liam De Róiste. Yet the only deputy present who expressed unease at Lynch's resignation was J. J. Walsh of Cork, who asked for further information.

Lynch had already sent a formal letter to the Waldorf Astoria Hotel informing de Valera of his decision to resign, adding, 'Speaking to you personally permit me to say that, in my opinion the present situation in America, if continued, can only lead to disaster for the cause of Ireland.'[51]

Kit Lynch wrote to the family at Granig on 28 July, and her words gave an indication of Lynch's viewpoint and anguish at the turn of events:

What makes things more heartbreaking still is the unfortunate and unhappy way things have been going along here among our own people in US. The President and other men from home, acting on the advice of a number of men, have completely ignored the men who have been working for Ireland's freedom all their life and are allowing men such as John Devoy, Judge Cohalan, Diarmuid and others who have served the cause just as faithfully to be hounded through the country by certain Irish-American Newspapers (who profess to be champions of President Dev and the Irish Republic). Dev could put a stop to this disgraceful work by just a raise of his hand but instead he and H. Boland, etc. encourage it by their silence.[52]

When Lynch was compiling the draft history of the FOIF in the 1930s, he admitted (writing in the third person):

By the extreme step which his resignation connoted, Lynch hoped to rouse the Dáil to a realisation of the deplorable situation so largely developed here by procedure which it [the Dáil] on 30 June expressed 'complete satisfaction' with and that it might, even at this late day, endeavour to prevent the dissension in America from running its full course.[53]

Lynch's quote of 'complete satisfaction' was from a cablegram sent by Griffith to de Valera in July 1920:

Dáil Éireann assembled in full session in Dublin today unanimously affirmed the allegiance of the citizens of Ireland to your policy, expresses complete satisfaction with the work you have performed and relies with confidence upon the great American nation to accord recognition to the Republic of Ireland now in fact and in law established.[54]

To the harried members of Dáil Éireann in Ireland, it was incomprehensible that their five colleagues in the USA (de Valera, Boland, Lynch, McCartan and Mellows) were not united in a common purpose to assist those at home.

Collins' response to Lynch's resignation, in a cablegram to Boland, was undoubtedly conveyed to Lynch at the first opportunity: 'He should have remained steadfast to the Dáil and to Ireland and have dropped the FOIF.'[55] Collins instructed Griffith to cease sending the *Irish Bulletin* to Lynch, who habitually included material from it in the newsletters of the FOIF. 'I wonder if you have stopped the *Bulletin* going to him. I think it is absolutely essential. It will give them a power out there to use against the President.'[56]

The verbal battles between those who supported Cohalan, Lynch and Devoy and those who opposed them were played out in public, in the pages of newspapers both in the US and in Ireland during 1920 and 1921. Traditionally, the *Irish World* newspaper, founded in the 1870s by immigrant Patrick Ford as an aid to the Land League movement, had been in harmony with the FOIF, but that ended with the death of editor Robert Ford, Patrick's son and a staunch FOIF member, in January 1920. Ford's brother Austin took over. Hostile to Devoy and Cohalan, he weighed in behind de Valera in the subsequent differences. In July 1920, the paper urged members of the

FOIF to break away from the organisation and what it labelled derisively as 'Cohalan Americans'.

The Cork Examiner reproduced a critical article written by McCartan in the Philadelphia *Irish Press*: 'Great things could have been accomplished if the machinery of the FOIF had been used for the purpose for which it was intended.'[57] The same issue of *The Cork Examiner* underlined the contrast between the political infighting among the opponents in the US with the life and death struggle in Ireland and published reports of the catastrophic breakdown of law and order in the latter. Cork had a nightly curfew imposed from 10 p.m. until 3 a.m., stories of courts martial featured alongside reports of parallel Republican courts, Michael Collins was pursuing guerrilla warfare against the RIC and the British Army, and in March 1920 the Black and Tans had arrived. Reacting angrily to yet another report of friction in America, Collins wrote to Boland, 'There always seems to be something depressing coming from the USA.'[58]

At branch meetings of the FOIF organisation, confusion increasingly reigned. Protests were voiced against the executive members of the FOIF and in favour of de Valera. The Michael Mallon Branch issued a statement on 4 July about 'the malicious and groundless attacks made upon the honesty and integrity of Éamon de Valera, President of the Irish Republic'.[59] A resolution adopted at the Pádraig Pearse Branch in Rochester pledged 'loyal support to Éamon de Valera, President of the Republic of Ireland. It resented and repudiated any movement which will undermine his influence or hamper his usefulness.'[60] The John F. Armstrong Branch in Augusta, Georgia, 'learned with much concern that some of the national officers of this organisation have seen fit to differ with President de Valera'.[61]

Not only did branch after branch of the FOIF question the leadership of Cohalan, Devoy and Lynch, but other organisations, such as the Ancient Order of Hibernians, 'repudiated the attempts to discredit de Valera'.[62] At the annual convention of the Knights of Columbanus on 4 August, 'A communication from Mr Éamon de Valera, President of Ireland, was read amid tremendous applause.'[63] The Philadelphia branch of Cumann na mBan pledged support for de Valera on 7 August and pointedly instructed 'copies of this pledge be sent to the National Secretary of the FOIF'.[64]

Encouraged by the groundswell of support, in August de Valera presented a demand to Bishop Michael J. Gallagher, newly elected president of the FOIF, that the organisation implement reforms. On 10 August, he wrote directly to Lynch reminding him that he had called for a National Council meeting in a more central location, such as Chicago.[65] This would be a tactical victory as most of the support for the officers of the FOIF was in New York. On 19 August 1920 de Valera repeated his request and demanded a reply.

Lynch wrote to Cohalan, concerned about what response the organisation would make to de Valera's proposal for changes: 'The situation is more confused than it ever was before. When the facts become known, it seems to me that our Detroit friend

[Bishop Gallagher] and many other prominent men will withdraw altogether. Dick [Dalton] says he's through, absolutely.'[66] Lynch further expressed his exasperation that Cohalan and Devoy had neglected to discuss this urgent situation during Devoy's recent visit to the judge at his holiday residence in Westport.[67] He continued, 'Personally I desire our visiting friends to have every concession consistent with the safety of the cause from the American viewpoint, but there's the rub.'[68]

Constitution

OF THE

Friends of Irish Freedom

ARTICLE I.

The name of this organization shall be FRIENDS OF IRISH FREEDOM.

ARTICLE II.

The objects of this organization are:
(a) To uphold Ireland's right to Self-Determination and Complete National Independence, and to inform American public opinion on the justice of Ireland's claims.

(b) To diffuse a more intimate knowledge of Irish History and the history of the Irish Race in America, and stimulate a just pride of Irish ideals and achievements, thus enabling our people to contribute in the highest degree to the enrichment of American culture.

(c) To develop the economic resources of Ireland.

(d) To promote the revival of the Language, Music and Customs of Ireland.

ARTICLE III.

Membership in the Friends of Irish

CONSTITUTION
of the
FRIENDS OF IRISH FREEDOM

ARTICLE I.

The name of this organization shall be FRIENDS OF IRISH FREEDOM.

ARTICLE II.

The objects of this organization are:
(a) To maintain America's position as the world-champion of human freedom, by preserving American ideals of liberty and upholding the principles on which the Government of the United States was founded.

(b) To uphold the right of the Republic of Ireland to international recognition, and to inform the American people to the end that the Government of these United States, applying American principles, shall accord full official recognition to the elected Government of the Republic of Ireland.

(c) To diffuse a more intimate knowledge of Irish history and the history of the Irish Race in America, and stimulate a just pride of Irish ideals and achievements, thus enabling our people to contribute in the highest degree to the enrichment of American culture.

(d) To develop the economic resources of Ireland and to promote direct trade relations between the U. S. and Ireland.

(e) To promote the revival of the Language, Music and Customs of Ireland.

The changed emphasis, towards Americanism, in the stated objectives of the FOIF is apparent between the 1918 Constitution (on the left) and the revised and amended Constitution of 1920. *Courtesy of the Lynch Family Archives*

8

The Fall-out Continues

Turmoil was rife amongst the officers and in the branches of the FOIF in July and August of 1920. James K. McGuire resigned on 16 July, citing the 'inner strife' as a cause.[1] The following day, Devoy informed Cohalan that Fr Peter Magennis 'is out for good'.[2] Lynch wrote to Cohalan:

> The Bishop [Gallagher] urges that everything possible be done to prevent the *Irish World* and *Irish Press* from continuing attacks on him this coming week. That if they do continue, he will 'have outlived his usefulness'. Dick argues that John Devoy does not reply to the *Irish World* attacks this coming week. It is very difficult for him [Devoy] to refrain from denying the statement, with 10,000 copies [of *The Gaelic American*] going to Ireland.[3]

Lynch was referring to Devoy's intention to refute Count Plunkett's condemnatory statement made to the Dáil in June.

As well as attacks on the FOIF organisation, personal attacks on Lynch continued. The Progressive League was an associate branch of the FOIF that supported de Valera and the

Philadelphia group. When the League, without the approval of the FOIF, championed a protest by sixty Irish women outside the British Embassy in Washington over the lack of support from the US president for the Ireland-agenda, it was expelled. When Lynch's letter expelling the Progressive League became public, he was attacked for being against the women's picket. A letter from J. J. O'Leary was quoted in the *Irish World* that severely criticised 'The highly paid official of the Friends of Irish Freedom who denounced the splendid women who picketed the British Embassy in Washington'.[4]

Devoy would brook no criticism of Lynch and robustly defended him in the subsequent edition of *The Gaelic American*:

> A man with Mr Lynch's fine record might, of course, be unfit for certain positions but Mr Lynch's work as national secretary has been superb. There has never been in any Irish organisation in America, and the writer has known them for half a century, a more competent, efficient and trustworthy official or one whose work has brought better results.[5]

Emphasising the divisions which now reigned in many branches of the FOIF, with some members roundly condemning de Valera and others vehemently opposed to the position of Cohalan, Devoy and Lynch, a meeting of the Roger Casement Branch in Chicago ended in uproar. Six of the members were subsequently expelled, with the formal letters of expulsion sent out by Lynch. Immediately the expelled members sued for reinstatement, alleging that the move to incorporate the

FOIF in 1919 was a plot by the New York group to control the Victory Fund. They requested that 'their expulsion be declared null and void'.[6] In his role as National Secretary, Lynch was nominated to deal with the legal preparation for the subsequent court case.

In August 1920, de Valera contacted many of the out-of-state FOIF National Council members, urging them to attend a crucial meeting of the National Council on 17 September at the Waldorf Astoria. One anxious recipient, Edward Dunne of Chicago, wrote to Devoy, perplexed by de Valera's summons. 'President de Valera has wired me rather urgently to be in New York on the 17th of this month to attend a meeting of the Executives of the FOIF at which time he says far-reaching decisions have to be arrived at on the Irish cause.'[7]

De Valera's strategy was to outvote the New York 'clique' of Devoy, Cohalan, Lynch and Dalton, and have the changes implemented to the FOIF governance and constitution which he deemed necessary. As a result of de Valera's invitations, a huge meeting was convened. Lynch's minutes record 168 present, including twenty-three priests and twenty-eight women.[8] What de Valera and his party alleged was filibustering and what the officers of the FOIF insisted was routine procedure for meetings caused de Valera to storm out angrily, followed by Boland, who prompted uproar with the following statement directed against Cohalan: 'One word from the man who sits back holding the strings [Cohalan] while his puppets dance will settle this whole matter differently.'[9]

A deputation was sent to ask de Valera to return to the meeting and state his case. Eventually he returned, but his proposals for reform were voted down, and, as he and his supporters left, Boland shouted an invitation to those present to meet with them the following day when they intended setting up an organisation independent of the FOIF. The minutes reported that Judge Goff urged Boland 'not to do something now which might be regretted all the days of his life. He asked Mr Boland to withdraw the invitation tendered for next day and not to be the first to appear to be a secessionist.'[10]

Boland dealt a further hammer blow in October when he announced that he was authorised by the IRB in Ireland to expel the New York Clan na Gael from the parent body of the Clan based in Dublin. In a letter to Devoy, Boland informed the veteran Fenian: 'Speaking with full authority in the name of the Supreme Council of the Irish Republican Brotherhood, I hereby announce that the Clan-na-Gael organisation is no longer affiliated with the Brotherhood'.[11]

When the Chicago local council of the FOIF instructed branches to withhold all funds from the National Council, it was suspended by the National Executive on 21 October 1920. The list of branches which were thereafter suspended is long: the Edward Fitzgerald branch of Philadelphia, the Thomas Ashe branch in San Diego and, in New York, the Éamonn Ceannt, the St Kevin's and the Joseph Plunkett branches, were among dozens of branches expelled for insubordination to the National Council.[12]

Family and friends at Granig when Diarmuid was home from the US in 1902. Diarmuid is on the right of the back row with his hand on Michael's shoulder. Denis is second from the left end of the second row. Tim is on the extreme right of the second row. Mrs Margaret Lynch is on the extreme left of the front row and Mary (Moll) is fourth from the left in the front row.

Courtesy of the Lynch Family Archives

Diarmuid Lynch pictured in New York, 1918.
Courtesy of the Lynch Family Archives

Kit Lynch, New York, 1918.
Courtesy of the Lynch Family Archives

Dick Dalton as a young man in New York, *c.* 1900.
Courtesy of Bríd Duggan, cousin to Dick and daughter of Denis and Alice Lynch

'The Cuba Five' (*left to right*): John Devoy, Charles Underwood O'Connell, Harry Mulleda, Jeremiah (Diarmuid) O'Donovan Rossa and John McClure. They were all deported together from Great Britain, arriving in the USA on the SS *Cuba* in 1871. *Courtesy of the Lynch Family and Cork Museum; photographed by Dara McGrath*

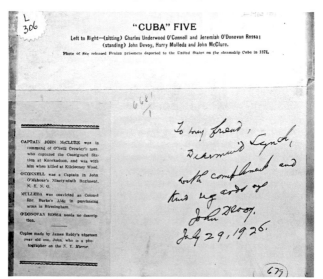

John Devoy was Diarmuid Lynch's revered mentor. He presented this memento of the 'Cuba Five' to Lynch with a personal dedication written on the back. *Courtesy of the Lynch Family and Cork Museum; photographed by Dara McGrath*

An Claidheamh Soluis, published by the Gaelic League, advertised the fund-raising tour of Diarmuid Lynch and Thomas Ashe in 1914.
Courtesy of the Lynch Family Archives

Left to right: Harry Boland, Liam Mellows, Éamon de Valera, John Devoy (seated), Dr Patrick McCartan and Diarmuid Lynch, pictured on the roof of the Waldorf Astoria Hotel, New York, on 23 June 1919.
Courtesy of University College Dublin Archives

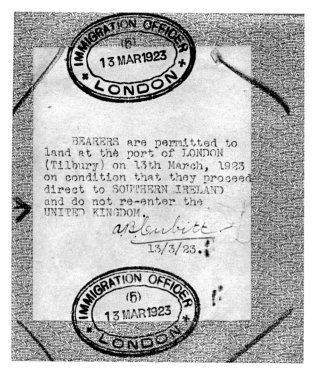

The passport of Diarmuid and Kit Lynch was stamped at Tilbury Docks, London, by the British Immigration Authority in March 1923.
Courtesy of the Lynch Family Archives

Pictured together at Granig in 1923, Seán O'Hegarty, OC Cork No. 1 Brigade, and Diarmuid Lynch. *Courtesy of the National Library of Ireland*

Diarmuid and Kit Lynch at Granig, 1927.
Courtesy of the Lynch Family Archives

President de Valera receiving the Roll of Honour from Diarmuid Lynch,
21 April 1935. *Courtesy of the National Library of Ireland*

(28)

Return to Diarmuid Lynch, 4 Fortfield Drive, Terenure, on or
before May 20th (so that replies may be summarised for the
Special Meeting of the Garrison, Sunday, May 23rd).

G.P.O. AREA - EASTER WEEK.

	Post or subsidiary position	Officer in immediate command.	Duties performed Incidents of special interest recalled.	Hour (approx)
MONDAY	Liberty Hall To G.P.O "Primary Sorting Office"	Gen. Connolly Tom Clarke Gen. Connolly —	Smashed partition to Sorting office on right - of which position I became o/c Connolly Street Lancers came under our fire ...	9 - 11.45 a.m. 11.50 - 12. M. 1.15 p.m
TUES.	Primary Sorting Office G.P.O	Gen. Connolly	Led. Comdt. Barrets bodyguard to b'c street Led squad to stop looters at Lawrence's and prevent spread of fire. Our men assisted in various ways to enable Fire Brigade to close in for operations	12.45 p.m Afternoon.
WED.	Do.	Do.	Took squad to bore walls towards the Coliseum. Soon made contact with Frank Henderson's men who were operating towards us. Inspected post overlooking Henry St of which Liam Cullen was o/c. Inspected other parts of G.P.O.	Morning Midnight
THURS.	Do	Do	(Gen. Connolly wounded)	Afternoon.
THURS. NIGHT	Do.	S Mac Diarmada	Superintended removal of surplus bombs, gelignite (+ powder ?) from upper portion of building + from the Armory in General Sorting office to basement	1.30 - 4.30 a.m.
FRI.	Do.	Do.	Volunteered to carry Mac Diarmada's order for retirement to 3 outposts - O'Neill's (Liffey St + Henry), Lucas's + Independent Ho. (Abbey Street) all men returned safely to G.P.O	6 - 6.15 am
	Do	—	Ordered L shaped interior barricade erected the full length + half width of P.S.O - as secondary line of defence.	Afternoon
	"General Sorting Office"		Removed prisoners from basement when volume of sparks from roof endangered explosives. Ordered transfer of explosives from basement room ("Henry St. side) to storeroom off Princes St yard.	Shortly before Evacuation
	Henry place	C. Gen Pearse	(See Sheet No 2)	

(Signed) _Diarmuid Lynch_

(Address) _____

Note: Any supplementary comment may be written on back of this sheet
or on a separate sheet.

Diarmuid Lynch's original witness statement from the collection
completed in 1937 and now archived at the National Library of Ireland.
Courtesy of the National Library of Ireland

Diarmuid Lynch's coffin is carried from the Sacred Heart Church, Minane Bridge, for burial at Tracton Abbey churchyard, 11 November 1950. Coffin bearers are his half-brother, Michael Lynch, and Michael's son Diarmuid. Dan Lynch (cousin) of Ballyvorane, Nohoval, is on the extreme left. Johnnie Brien, Tubrid, is on the extreme right. Jerome Cronin, Springhill, is seen between two unidentified men on Michael's left. *Courtesy of the* Irish Examiner

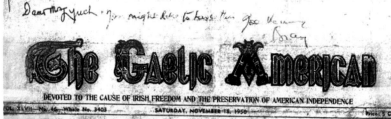

The Gaelic American of 18 November 1950 reports the death of Diarmuid Lynch. *Courtesy of the Lynch Family Archives*

This wall plaque to honour Diarmuid Lynch was unveiled at Granig House by the Cork 1916 Commemorative Committee in 1966 to mark the fiftieth anniversary of the Easter Rising.
Courtesy of the Lynch Family; photographed by Adrian O'Herlihy

On 16 November de Valera's new organisation, the American Association for the Recognition of the Irish Republic (AARIR), was established at the Raleigh Hotel in Washington. John Hearn, who had resigned from the FOIF, was national organiser. Edward Doheny, an Irish-American oil magnate, was de Valera's choice as president. According to McCartan, 'Its origin was due not to the purpose its title proclaimed, but to de Valera's need to form an organisation to supersede Cohalan's'.[13] Membership of the FOIF declined rapidly as branch after branch defected to the AARIR. From over 100,000 regular members in November 1920, FOIF membership had plummeted to 20,000 by the middle of 1921.

Week after week McGarrity's *Irish Press* triumphantly reported the defection of FOIF branches to the AARIR. Lynch's dream of a united organisation, 'an organisation that you can get working at the touch of a button, an organisation through which, by the sending of telegrams or one series of letters, you can line up inside a week or less every man and woman of the blood in this country' was truly shattered.[14]

On 10 December 1920, de Valera left America as secretly as he had arrived eighteen months before.

Various politicians and writers have since apportioned blame to one side or the other for the collapse of the Irish-American political lobby during the eighteen months de Valera spent touring America. Wherever the fault lay, the tour was successful in raising much-needed funds for the emerging Irish state. However, both de Valera and the FOIF failed in their attempt to have the cause of Irish independence championed officially by the US government or to have it listed on the agenda at the Paris Peace conference. Both 'sides' used much of their energy and resources in scoring points against each other in the prolonged struggle, to the detriment of their common cause: to achieve recognition for the state of Ireland from the American government.

From the start of de Valera's tour, the personal antagonism between de Valera and Cohalan had grown to colour all interactions between them. Cohalan was the recognised leader and spokesman for the Irish-American lobby until the arrival of de Valera. The FOIF saw itself as the organisation in America best qualified to formulate and drive forward policy in regard to the American-based campaign for self-determination. However, from the outset, de Valera made it clear that he expected to take on the role of spokesman in America in all matters pertaining to the Irish question. The reorganised and expanded FOIF had plentiful funds following the successful campaign by Lynch and the success of the Victory Fund campaign. But McGarrity, his Philadelphia colleagues and de Valera were incensed that those funds were not passed on in full to Ireland.

Further problems were caused by the radical divergence of opinion between the opposing members of the FOIF – on the one hand Maloney and McGarrity, allied with Dr Patrick McCartan, and on the other Cohalan, Devoy and Lynch – as to what should be demanded of the American government. Self-determination as a goal was not acceptable to the Philadelphia group: they insisted that the Irish Republic had already been established by the 1916 Rising and affirmed by the success of Sinn Féin in the 1918 general election.

Devoy was deeply suspicious of Maloney and ascertained often and publicly that he was a British spy. By this time the 'Sean-Fhear', as Devoy was affectionately called, was deaf and increasingly irascible. His attitude had been shaped in the Fenian years of the 1860s onwards, when spies and subterfuge had consistently undermined the efforts of nationalists to progress the cause of Irish independence.

In Ireland there was bafflement and anger at the tit-for-tat war of words and jockeying for power amongst the protagonists in America, while the people at home were impoverished, hunted and imprisoned. Piaras Béaslaí clarified the prevailing attitude:

> We in Ireland, engaged in a fierce and bloody struggle, were not in a position to study the niceties of American politics. We could only see in the whole controversy an attempt to undermine the influence of the man we had chosen as our representative. In any case it was obviously impossible for us, in the face of the enemy, to 'let down' the man we had elected as President.[15]

To the end of his life, Lynch laid the blame squarely on the Philadelphia camp and on de Valera's 'mistake' in siding with McGarrity, McCartan and Maloney rather than taking the advice and counsel of those seasoned American activists, Devoy and Cohalan. Though he did not explicitly state his agreement with Devoy's belief that Maloney was a secret British agent, when writing the draft history of the FOIF in the 1930s he found much to fault in Maloney's vacillation and deceptions at various times during the critical years of 1919 to 1921. He cited instance after instance where Maloney's 'word was not his bond'. Lynch also laid blame on Devoy and Cohalan for initially bringing Maloney into their confidence, making the FOIF vulnerable when the relationship broke down, because Maloney was privy to many of their confidential discussions.[16]

Lynch was confounded that the organisation he had built up so spectacularly and successfully since his appointment as National Secretary in May 1918 was crushed by May 1921: 'With sorrow and regret Diarmuid Lynch saw, wrecked and broken, the magnificent organisation he had done so much to create.'[17]

The truth was that the organisation of the FOIF left it vulnerable. It declared itself to be a democratic organisation: each branch had its elected officers, every state had its state council, and the National Council existed to coordinate all communications and policy decisions. However, in practice, three men effectively managed the organisation: Cohalan, Devoy and Lynch. This weakness in the structure of the FOIF contributed to its destruction when it was targeted and consistently attacked by McGarrity, Maloney, McCartan and Boland. De Valera criticised the vulnerability and was quoted in the Irish newspapers, stating, 'I had travelled but very little in this country [America] when I observed that the organisation [FOIF] was being greatly handicapped through want of authority in several states to act for themselves and on their own initiative.'[18] The target of de Valera's criticism here was the centralised and controlling authority vested in the trio of Devoy, Cohalan and Lynch.

Regarding de Valera's role in the FOIF's problems, Lynch maintained to the end of his life that de Valera allowed himself to be manipulated: 'Without the misdirected co-operation of President de Valera it would not have been possible for Maloney, McGarrity and McCartan to effect a split. Without the preliminary propaganda and later co-operation of this trio it is inconceivable that de Valera would have attempted it.'[19] It was not an original objective of de Valera's mission to America to reform the FOIF; however, supported by Boland, McGarrity, Maloney and McCartan, this is what he determined to achieve. The methods he employed were instrumental in the destruction of the powerful Irish-American organisation built up by Lynch from May 1918.

After de Valera's departure from America, the public battle of words continued. *The Freeman's Journal* reported a resolution passed by the New York FOIF, calling on de Valera to send the Irish bond-cert money, 'which we understand is idle in American banks in your name' immediately to Ireland, to relieve the distress and to aid in reconstruction.[20] Mary MacSwiney, the sister of Terence, issued a statement protesting against the FOIF allegations about the banked bond-cert money. According to her, the FOIF allegations 'were couched in terms offensive to Ireland's President, an insult to the man of whom we are so proud and who alone is entitled to speak to America with Ireland's voice'.[21]

The Freeman's Journal published Boland's response to the FOIF accusation. Boland alleged that the FOIF was using the Victory Fund to 'undermine the work of President de Valera'.[22] In the *Boston Post* on 21 December, Boland declared, 'The line is clearly drawn. On the one hand Ireland calls you through her official head, President de Valera; on the other the petty, jealous and selfish interest of a group of individuals would deprive Ireland of your aid.'

Devoy's responses in the pages of *The Gaelic American* stoked the fires of resentment. In the 20 December issue he wrote of 'supposedly inspired leaders from Ireland who know as little of American politics as they do of the interior of Patagonia'.[23] In a newsletter signed by Lynch and Bishop Gallagher, and sent to all members of the FOIF in November 1920, the organisation was robustly defended and the tactics of de Valera and those who supported him roundly condemned: 'Our erstwhile friends of a year or more ago vehemently criticised the FOIF for devoting so much of its attention to what they were pleased to call purely American questions. The tactics of our critics were solely for the purpose of defaming the FOIF.'[24] Lynch accused de Valera of 'using a Flying Squadron to destroy the smooth-running organisation which five months earlier, had the enemies of America and Ireland on the run'.[25]

In April 1921, the FOIF issued a detailed statement from Bishop Gallagher, addressing the contents of the contentious letters which had passed between de Valera and Cohalan in February 1920.[26] The statement shows that the public battle of words continued, with each side striving to vindicate its position regarding their differences.

On 9 December 1921, Boland was still venomous in his statements and issued a crushing denunciation of Lynch: 'He can rest assured that those who remained faithful to Dáil Éireann will not now shirk responsibility. When the Irish Free State comes to pass they will not give support or countenance to men who failed miserably to assist the Irish Republic during its life.'[27] Boland expressed the same bitter sentiments in *The New York Times*: 'Failure to aid the Irish Republic while it was fighting England was charged against Daniel F. Cohalan and Diarmuid Lynch this afternoon by Harry J. Boland, former Secretary to Éamonn [*sic*] De Valera.'[28]

Not all nationalists in Ireland discredited Lynch. In October 1920, Terence MacSwiney's wife, Muriel, had written an affectionate letter to Diarmuid and Kit while she was on vigil at her husband's bedside in Brixton Prison:

I have been thinking of you often since the time we were all in Dundalk together. There is little I can say about Terry. I see him every afternoon. He is in great pain at times. I showed him your cable; he was pleased to get it. Le súil go bhfuileann sibh go h-ana-mhaith, le Grádh, ó Múirgheal.[29]

When MacSwiney had been imprisoned and started his hunger strike in August 1920, Lynch had sent an urgent cable to Bainbridge Colby, US Secretary of State:

> As Executive Secretary of the Friends of Irish Freedom, a nation-wide organisation of several hundred thousand American citizens, I respectfully enter a most emphatic protest against the treatment accorded by the British Government to Lord Mayor MacSwiney of Cork, removed from Ireland on a British war-vessel and held by force of military power. We respectfully request you as Secretary of State to immediately make suitable representations to the British Government.[30]

Following her husband's death on 25 October, Muriel was persuaded to travel to America to publicise the treatment he had received during his arrest, imprisonment and death. Lynch, as Secretary of the FOIF, organised her travel arrangements and ensured her welcome in various quarters, such as the Missouri State Council and the FOIF State Convention on 15 December 1920.[31]

That Michael Collins continued in friendship with the Lynch family, despite the public differences which had emerged from the American fiasco, is evidenced by his being photo-graphed alongside his confidante, Gearóid Ó Súilleabháin, in attendance at the wedding of a close relative of Kit Lynch on

22 November 1920. Michael Lynch was the best man at the wedding, and both Denis and Alice were among the seventeen guests, as was Kit's sister Theresa.[32]

During the first six months of 1921, the guerrilla war in Ireland reached a climax, with atrocities on both sides and victory on neither. A truce was signed on 9 July. Negotiations followed in London between Prime Minister David Lloyd George and de Valera about the possible terms of a permanent peace between the two countries and in August Lynch issued a statement from FOIF headquarters: 'The Friends of Irish Freedom are solidly and unalterably behind Dáil Éireann in its refusal to surrender the National Sovereignty of Ireland by entering a conference with the British Cabinet on the basis stipulated by Lloyd George.'[33] He then expressed a personal view:

> Diarmuid Lynch's message reflects the attitude which he has consistently held towards President de Valera, and which has been known to a great many people, namely, that while realising and strongly condemning President de Valera's action in splitting the Friends of Ireland in America at a time when unity was essential to success, Lynch maintained that President de Valera had not parted and would not depart from the position of fighting for the recognition of the established Irish Republic.[34]

Devoy criticised Lynch's confidence in de Valera, observing to Cohalan, 'Diarmuid can't see anything in this but his old friendship with de Valera blinds him.'[35] Lynch's disagreements with Devoy were few, but in 1921 he resigned as a director of *The Gaelic American* because he felt Devoy was exceeding all limits with vituperative, personal attacks on de Valera.

Following months of negotiations, a Treaty was signed in London on 6 December 1921 by the plenipotentiaries appointed by the Dáil and led by Collins. When the terms of the Treaty reached the FOIF, it was reported that Lynch shouted his 'adamant opposition'.[36] A declaration signed by Lynch and by the New York Clan na Gael leader, Laurence Rice, appeared in *The New York Times* on 8 December: 'With Irish coastal fortifications under British control, with an Ireland swearing allegiance to a foreign King, the use of the term "Irish Free State" is an insult to the dead who died fighting for an independent Irish Republic.'[37]

At the National Conference of the FOIF on 11 December, rejection of the Treaty was officially expressed, as was the organisation's disappointment that much less had been achieved than the Republic for which the leaders of 1916 had died. A statement of principle was issued: 'We have given all the moral and material aid within our power, consistent with our duties and responsibilities as American citizens, in support of the Irish Republic. We will continue to give that support to those who carry forward the fight for complete national independence'.[38]

Lynch restated his Republican allegiance in a front-page column of *The New York Times* on 8 January 1922. Speaking on behalf of the FOIF, he declared, 'We pledge to such Republican party in Ireland as may carry forward the traditional struggle for liberty a continuance in full measure of that hearty support we have given in the past.'[39]

However, as 1922 progressed, and when it became clear that those who supported de Valera in his opposition to the Treaty were going to carry on a military campaign for a Republic against the Free State side, the backing of the FOIF was given to those who supported Collins and the pro-Treaty members of Dáil Éireann. Writing to Collins, Devoy did not mince his words:

I am utterly opposed to De Valera's attempt to upset the 'Free State Agreement'. The first blow to the Republic was dealt by him in the Cuban interview. These infamous actions by de Valera were approved or condoned by all of you.[40]

In his reply to Devoy, Collins acknowledged the mistakes made in America. 'Our idea was to have some sort of worldwide, Irish Federation. Unfortunately some of those we sent to America did not understand the vital principle of that idea.'[41]

The FOIF continued to comment on the deteriorating situation in Ireland and blamed de Valera 'for the division in Sinn Féin ranks and accused him of repeating his destructive American tactics'.[42] A declaration was issued in March deploring the dangerous situation developing in Ireland and again laying the blame squarely on de Valera.

The FOIF newsletter of 2 September 1922 led with the news of Collins' death and quoted in full the cable sent by

Lynch on 23 August on behalf of the FOIF to General Richard Mulcahy. The full text of Lynch's cable was also reprinted in *The Cork Examiner* on 25 August:

> What a horrible tragedy! Mick Collins dead, and at the hands of men calling themselves Irish Republicans. Mick, the sincere, genuine republican to whose patriotism, organising genius, resourcefulness, bravery, fearlessness and cheerfulness is due such a very large measure of the credit for the victories since 1916. God rest the noble soul of our dear comrade, Collins, and give you and his other splendid lieutenants the courage and strength to bring order and finally absolute independence out of the present shocking chaos which exists in Ireland.[43]

Reacting to the outbreak of Civil War in Ireland, Diarmuid Lynch, on behalf of the FOIF, arranged for a full-page advertisement to appear in several Irish newspapers. The advertisement's headline was 'A Message from America' and it stated that the FOIF was 'condemning the prolongation of civil war in Ireland against the Government which represented the vast majority of the Irish people.'[44] It deplored the situation in Ireland and urged a ceasefire. It appeared on different dates in various papers during October 1922. The *Irish Independent* gave it full, front-page coverage on 26 October.[45]

A hostile reaction to the exhortations of the FOIF as expressed in the advertisement was immediate. Count Plunkett's scathing response was printed in the *Irish World* (US) and also in the *Irish Independent*:

An advertisement costing about $800 for each insertion appears today in the 'Freeman's Journal' and the 'Independent'. The Irish-Americans and others in the United States can now see the use that is made of American money by the FOIF. Vanity and self-interest cannot prevail against persistent faith and courage. The fight goes on and the Republic is winning.[46]

When Lynch informed Devoy that he intended to travel to Ireland in an effort to broker peace between the Free State side and de Valera's Republicans, *The Gaelic American* reported that 'Devoy exploded to him in one short sentence: "YOU'LL BE SHOT!"'[47] However, Lynch was determined to make an extended visit to Ireland, and in early 1923 he proffered his resignation to the FOIF. He later wrote:

His trip was undertaken solely on his own initiative. He desired to leave the FOIF entirely free for anything he may say or do while away from the US. He stated that while in Ireland he would endeavour to get an accurate perspective of the political situation. He also intimated that he wished to pursue personal business while in Ireland.[48]

Lynch's resignation was not accepted and he was granted a leave of absence with full salary for the period he was away.[49]

It was difficult to obtain a passport from the State Department in Washington because of Lynch's notoriety in intelligence records on both sides of the Atlantic. Nevertheless, in February 1923, Lynch and Kit finally sailed for Ireland on the SS *President Van Buren*.

On arrival at Tilbury Docks, London, the Lynchs were refused entry to England, were held for three days on board and were threatened with deportation back to the USA. An intervention by the Free State government was successful, and Lynch and his wife were allowed to disembark on condition that they 'proceed direct to Southern Ireland and do not re-enter the United Kingdom'.[50]

Lynch explained the reason for his return as follows: 'The prime motive was to personally use my best endeavours towards terminating the civil war then raging in Ireland, through which many of my best comrades of 1916–1918 were losing their lives.' He continued: 'Interesting talks were held with many of my old personal and political friends, both men and women, some of whom were then actively on the Free State side, some who were anti-Treaty, and others who were neutral in the civil war.'[51]

In Cork Lynch liaised with his old IRB comrade Seán O'Hegarty, and the pair crossed the county consulting with those who were in conflict. It is most likely that Lynch and Florrie O'Donoghue (then head of intelligence of the Cork No. 1 Brigade of the IRA) met at this time, as in 1922 and 1923 O'Donoghue worked with O'Hegarty in repeated efforts to broker peace.

9

The National Secretary
Soldiers On

When Lynch resumed his duties as National Secretary of the FOIF after his sojourn in Ireland during 1923, he was charged with downsizing the space rented at 280 Broadway. With a greatly diminished number of members and a shrinking income, the FOIF no longer needed the large premises, and the move to room 625 in the same building saved the organisation some $1,000 per year. Lynch also found a purchaser for the now superfluous office furniture.[1]

Lynch was the main speaker at the IRB Veterans' Banquet at the Hotel Astor, New York, on 9 March 1924. Part of his address lauded Collins:

Were it not for the intimate acquaintance which Collins had with the rank and file in every part of Ireland, his indomitable courage, his tireless energy, his extraordinary grasp of and attention to detail, and above all his marvellous, dynamic power of leadership, the scheme of re-organisation laid down towards the end of 1917, for both the Volunteers and the IRB, could not have attained such wonderful perfection, were it not for him, Collins.[2]

In June 1924, Lynch spoke again, this time at the annual memorial service at the grave of Matilda Tone in Greenwood Cemetery, Brooklyn. Lynch was introduced by the Chairman of Clan na Gael, Laurence Rice, as the 'offspring of Theobald Wolfe Tone and the co-worker of the men of Easter Week'.[3] Lynch reiterated, 'Let us remember that the task which Tone endeavoured to accomplish is not yet complete. The political connection between Ireland and England is not yet broken.'[4]

On 4 July 1924, in a circular letter, Lynch issued a call to all branches of the FOIF for help towards the costs of a visit to Ireland for his mentor, John Devoy. At a subsequent FOIF meeting on 10 July, Lynch was instructed to cable President William Cosgrave in Ireland regarding Devoy's visit.[5] Harry Cunningham, an immigrant from County Donegal, was to be Devoy's designated travelling companion. Lynch himself could not be spared while various FOIF court proceedings were under way. A 'Godspeed Testimonial' ceremony was held for Devoy on 17 July at the Hotel Astor. Attendance was huge, with well-wishers occupying over seventy tables. Lynch, the chief organiser, was on the dais with the other guests of honour: Judge Daniel F. Cohalan, Bishop Michael Gallagher, J. J. Splain and Thomas F. Cooney.[6]

Devoy spent a triumphant six weeks in Ireland, where he

was received at Government Buildings and presided at the Tailteann Games. On his return, Lynch notified each member of the National Council that Devoy would report to the FOIF members on his prolonged visit and explain 'the facts and opinions pertaining to Ireland on which, doubtless, many of our future activities (in regard to Ireland) will be based'.[7]

Hannah Ashe, a sister of Thomas Ashe, wrote to the FOIF from Dingle in November 1924, appealing for financial help. She was ill and unable to pay her doctor's bills. Lynch and Dalton arranged for the transmission of a draft valued at $500 which had been donated to the FOIF by Cumann na mBan.[8] At the same meeting as this was decided, Lynch also procured expenses for Piaras Béaslaí's attempts to have his book on Collins published in America.[9]

There was extensive communication between Lynch and Béaslaí during 1925 and 1926. Lynch contacted and interviewed several publishers in an effort to secure the best publishing rights for Béaslaí.[10] Béaslaí sent the draft of 'The Irish-American Split', the chapter of his book that deals with de Valera's period in America in 1919–20, to Lynch for review.[11] Some of Lynch's letters from this period are addressed from an office in Chambers Street, New York. Lynch explained to Béaslaí that he had once more taken employment as an insurance agent to supplement his income from his now part-time job as National Secretary of the much-diminished FOIF organisation.[12]

When Richard Mulcahy, now a general in the Free State army, visited America in 1925, he was welcomed by Devoy and the 'Old' Clan na Gael, but was attacked viciously in the pages of Austin Ford's *Irish World*. Lynch introduced Mulcahy to the assembled guests at a dinner with the words, 'I deem it a privilege to be here with you to welcome one of Ireland's most distinguished sons, one of her most distinguished soldiers, in the person of one of my old comrades of 1916, General Richard Mulcahy.'[13]

The Lynch household, then at 286 East 206th Street in New York, increased in numbers in late 1925 when Diarmuid's brother Michael, his wife, Carmel (who was Kit's half-sister), and their eldest child, Deirdre, arrived for an extended visit. Carmel was heavily pregnant but had decided to travel with Michael, who was hoping to sell some bloodstock horses in the American market. Their son Diarmuid, who was named after his godfather and uncle, was born in the Union Hospital in the Bronx in February 1926. In Michael's almost daily letters to Carmel from the time he was in Boston looking for buyers, he frequently mentioned the help his brother Diarmuid was providing.[14] Ultimately, Michael's venture was unsuccessful, and the family returned to Ireland before Christmas 1926 with their two children.

Ireland and its affairs were dominant in Lynch's thoughts, and he repeatedly introduced concerns about conditions prevailing in Ireland at successive meetings of the FOIF.[15] Following the formation of de Valera's new party, Fianna Fáil, on 23 March 1926, and in anticipation of a crucial election in Ireland, Lynch informed a meeting of the National Executive in June 1927 that he wanted two months' leave of absence to visit Ireland. Diarmuid wrote to his brother Denis:

> It is also a question as to whether we are very foolish to think of going at all. Because, scraping together every dollar we can, we will have just about enough to pay for the trip, and on our return here, we will not have a blooming cent. Even so, we are in a kind of desperate mood and have decided to go anyway if nothing prevents me from sailing at the end of July.[16]

While in Ireland he found the political situation to be volatile, with two general elections following each other in quick succession:

> As a matter of good policy I have kept out of the political limelight but have not hesitated to express my views and criticism to all and sundry to whom I have privately spoken. The final result [of the second election] will not be known until Tuesday or Wednesday next. I decided to postpone sailing until 15 October. This will allow me to be present at the opening of the Dáil on 11 October to get the views of many men on the situation as they develop.[17]

Lynch may have used his extended leave in Ireland to try to find employment which would enable himself and Kit to return to live in Ireland. The couple's desire to live in Ireland was strong, but their financial circumstances made it impossible until Diarmuid could find employment there.

From 1925 Lynch had to an extent assumed the role of carer of John Devoy. He had been close friends with the now frail 'Sean-Fhear' for almost thirty years. 'I first met John in 1896,' Lynch recalled, 'but I came to know him in 1903.'[18] John Devoy was the leading figure in Clan na Gael when Lynch first arrived in America. As he became active in the Gaelic League in New York, Lynch's relationship with Devoy had developed. *The Gaelic American* had given 'splendid publicity to every phase of the language revival and the members of the Clan were supporters in all our activities'.[19] Lynch revered the elderly Fenian who had been exiled in 1870 to America by the British authorities. He declared in 1921:

> When the Tricolour was planted on the Dublin Post Office and when Pearse marched out to O'Connell Street to read the Declaration of Irish Independence to the citizens, the names of the gallant standard bearers in former generations flashed across our minds, among them John Devoy. I wished that John Devoy was there to witness the sight which would gladden his old heart and repay him for all his years of struggle on behalf of the land of his birth.[20]

Patrick Pearse had appealed to Devoy in 1914 for funds to save his boys school, St Enda's, which was in financial difficulty, and Devoy refinanced the school from Clan resources.[21] Pearse paid homage to Devoy as 'the greatest of the Fenians'.[22]

When Roger Casement determined to go to Germany to solicit armaments and military personnel for the planned

Irish insurrection, the Clan funded him, through Devoy. When returning to Dublin in November 1914, Lynch carried a hidden money draft for $2,000 from Devoy to arm the Irish Volunteers. Working on a draft history of the FOIF in the 1930s, Lynch said of Devoy: 'He never minced words in attacking any man whose words or policy or acts were, in his opinion, either flagrantly unjust or wilfully injurious to the Irish cause; he was content to "let the chips fall where they may".'[23]

Despite the restrictions placed on the American press during the Great War, Devoy continued to print provocative reports, on British suppression in Ireland, of meetings, of political developments; week by week, he poured out relentless, pro-nationalist propaganda. *The Gaelic American* stridently opposed President Woodrow Wilson's ambition to have a 'League of Nations' founded when the war ceased. The FOIF and *The Gaelic American* also vehemently opposed America's alignment with Britain in the Great War.

A confidential letter sent by Lynch to selected people in 1925 alluded to the increasing frailty of the eighty-three-year-old Devoy and the need to provide specific care for him.[24] A private fund was set up, with Lynch, Dalton and Harry Cunningham as trustees. Devoy's friends moved him from his modest room in the Ennis Hotel on Forty-Second Street into more comfortable and suitable lodgings in Harlem with two sisters, Lily Carragher and Alice Comiskey, who liaised with Lynch about his health and welfare. Lynch undertook the handling of Devoy's financial affairs, securing a reduction of some of his debts, and he solicited funds annually from the selected donors until Devoy's death in 1928.[25] Devoy died unaware that his expenses were now met from the secret fund set up by Lynch in 1925.

Lynch had worked with Devoy on his memoirs in his final years, and after Devoy's death he completed the manuscript, which was published in 1929 under the title *Recollections of an Irish Rebel*. Lynch was unanimously elected to represent the FOIF at Devoy's funeral in Glasnevin Cemetery in June 1929. All in all, a fifty-strong contingent accompanied the body to Ireland, including Dalton, Cunningham, Sarah McKelvey and Laurence Rice, all members of the John Devoy Funeral Committee. After the state funeral in Dublin, the American committee arranged for the permanent care of Devoy's grave.[26]

Lynch was one of the executors of Devoy's will, and there was correspondence between him and Devoy's nephew, Peter, during 1928 and 1929.[27] Lynch informed Peter that some of the subscribers to the secret fund were now subsidising the publication of the forthcoming book and that John had died with just $400 to his name. With the consensus of the FOIF members, Lynch organised the purchase and distribution of 500 copies of *Recollections of an Irish Rebel* for colleges, schools and libraries in Ireland.[28]

Lynch's main concern for the 1920s, as National Secretary of the FOIF, was the management of the affairs of that organisation. In his role as National Secretary he was the person responsible for representing the FOIF in court. Yet the most prolonged of the court cases he was involved in did not initially concern the FOIF. The case was brought by the Free State government of Ireland against the nominated trustees of bank accounts set up by de Valera before he left America in December 1920 and concerned the proceeds of the bond-cert fund-raising drive in those bank accounts. John J. Hearn of Westfield, Connecticut, who had left the FOIF to become Treasurer of the AARIR, was one of the trustees, as were Boland, Nunan and McGarrity. The Free State government regarded itself as the lawful inheritor of the bond-cert funds collected in America for the Republic of Ireland and was determined to gain possession of them.

In 1922, when Collins, as Minister of Finance, sought the release of the funds banked in America for use in Ireland, he was stonewalled by de Valera's nominated trustees. Collins sent Professor Timothy Smiddy of University College Cork (UCC) to America to assess the situation and to try to break the deadlock on the funds. Smiddy met with misinformation and resistance, so Collins instructed him to seek a court injunction 'on behalf of the Irish Free State to obtain custody of the funds and securities in the New York banks'.[29]

Proceedings began on 11 August 1922 in the case titled *Irish Free State et al.* v. *Guaranty Safe Deposit Company, et al.* Harry Boland was assassinated just days before the proceedings began and while the case was under way, Collins was assassinated in his native county of Cork. William Cosgrave, who succeeded

Collins as head of the Free State government, continued with the legal action in America.

To complicate matters further, in 1925, while the case was ongoing, John J. Hearn set up a separate committee to claim the funds for the original subscribers on the basis that the money had been collected for an 'Irish Republic' that had not yet been established. Frank P. Walsh, McGarrity and John T. Ryan, an Irish-American activist, were prominent members of the Hearn Committee.[30]

The case went to trial in March 1927, with three able lawyers representing the interests of de Valera and the Republican side: Frank Walsh (who had headed up the bond-cert drive), John Finerty and Martin Conboy. All three were members of the AARIR. Smiddy and the US-based lawyers, Polk, Wardell, Gardiner & Reed, represented the interests of the Free State.

De Valera travelled to America after his release from prison in 1927 to attend the hearing of the case. He wanted to persuade the original subscribers to donate their returned bond certificates to him. His ambition was to establish a daily newspaper in Dublin that would promote his political viewpoint and that of his party.[31]

In June 1927 Judge Curtis Peters decided that all funds collected in the bond-cert drive and retained in the deposit accounts in America must be repaid to the original subscribers.[32] As one of the original subscribers, the FOIF applied for a refund of the $100,000 which it had loaned in 1919 to kick-start the bond-cert drive. The Hearn Committee immediately challenged this in the courts. When Judge Thomas Mahon dismissed the claims of the FOIF in February 1930, the organisation immediately lodged an appeal, which resulted in a retrial. The decision of Judge Townley in June 1931 was in favour of the FOIF, and it was challenged by the Hearn Committee at the Court of Appeals, but their effort to have the decision of Judge Townley reversed was unsuccessful.

Lynch hammered home the victory of the FOIF: 'The *five* sitting judges of the Appellate Division of the Supreme Court unanimously upheld the decision. Said "Hearn Committee" then took the case to the Court of Appeals and the *seven* judges thereof at Albany unanimously affirmed the decision of the Appellate Division.'[33] The FOIF was eventually repaid $73,000, having paid its own legal costs.[34]

In February 1928 de Valera was back in New York to raise funds. On 3 February, he was a guest at the Waldorf Astoria Hotel while the president of the Free State government, William Cosgrave, happened to attend the Emerald Ball in the grand ballroom below – but the two men did not meet. Earlier that day, President Cosgrave had dined with Cohalan, Lynch and other FOIF officers at the Lawyers' Club at the Realty Building on Broadway.

In 1929, McGarrity, Frank P. Walsh and John Ryan of the Hearn Committee started another legal action against the FOIF, claiming that the organisation had misappropriated the Victory Fund. Lynch recorded:

As in the case of the Bond-Certificates, no opportunity was missed either in the complaint or during the subsequent proceedings to exaggerate and misconstrue even minor points. In raking over events of the preceding decade, plaintiff's attorneys introduced eighty-nine 'exhibits' during the examination of Diarmuid Lynch held prior to the trial proper, the majority of which the National Secretary was called on by them to produce from the files of the organisation.[35]

John J. Kirby, who had represented the FOIF so successfully in the bond-cert case, was retained by the FOIF to contest this second case.[36] The pre-trial proceedings continued for six months in 1930. The typescript book of evidence prepared by Lynch on behalf of the FOIF ran to 703 pages.[37] This case, titled *Montague et al.* v. *Cooney et al.,* was conducted in the New York Court over two weeks in June and July 1932. Dalton testified alongside Lynch for the FOIF.

This time, Lynch's integrity came under attack. It was alleged that he had altered the minutes of a crucial meeting held during the Philadelphia Race Convention in February 1919. Lynch was able to show that the alterations had in fact been approved after consultation with Devoy and others, immediately after the convention. Careless typing by an inexperienced stenographer who had been hired for the convention had led to the correction being necessary.[38] Furthermore, McGarrity, Robert Ford and the president of the FOIF, Fr Peter Magennis, had then proof-read and approved the altered minutes in readiness for publication.[39] In dismissing the claim, Supreme

Court Justice Albert Cohn stated in his conclusion, 'The plaintiffs have failed to establish the cause of action alleged in the complaint, or any cause of action against the defendants or any one of them.'[40] Florrie O'Donoghue later wrote:

> It is the unanimous opinion of those who have first hand personal knowledge of Diarmuid's work as National Secretary of the Friends of Irish Freedom that this favourable result would not have been achieved were it not for the extraordinary day-to-day attention he had given to the organisation over the previous years, the excellence, integrity and completeness of his records, and the clarity and honesty of his testimony before the various courts, even under the strain of severe and prolonged cross-examination.[41]

Another onerous undertaking by the National Secretary was the preparation of evidence for yet another court case, this time involving funds donated by the FOIF in 1920 for the purchase of the building that housed St Enda's School – founded by Pearse – in Rathfarnham, Dublin.

When Pearse toured America in 1914, he was given funds by Clan na Gael, via Devoy and Cohalan, to keep St Enda's afloat. After her son's execution, Pearse's mother requested further help from the Clan in America as she intended to act on an option that the premises could be bought out for £6,500. At the Irish Race Convention in May 1918, it was resolved to raise $50,000 to secure St Enda's for the Irish nation, as a memorial to Pearse. Lynch was appointed FOIF correspondent in all matters pertaining to this project.

Two committees were formed, one in Ireland and the second in America, to raise funds for the purchase of the school premises. Donations to the 'Save St Enda's Fund' were banked at the Produce Exchange Bank in New York. Collins wrote to Lynch in July 1919 and listed for him the Irish trustees of the fund. These were Count Plunkett, Joe McGuinness, P. T. McGinley (Cú Uladh), Frank Lawless and the chief trustee, Mrs Margaret Pearse. Collins also requested that the FOIF define exactly the extent of the responsibility of the board of trustees: 'The Ministry consider this question one of far reaching national moment. Hence the necessity of being clear and definite on all details.'[42] American trustees included Joe McGarrity and Mrs Pádraig Colum.[43] A proposal in December 1919 that both sets of trustees combine into one board was not acted upon.

With the option of buying out the building running out, and with favourable exchange rates available in June 1920, Lynch used FOIF funds to purchase a bank draft for the entire £6,500 needed to buy the premises. An agreement was made with the trustees that any monies in the Produce Exchange bank account would be turned over to the treasurer of the FOIF to recompense the organisation for the £6,500 paid from its contingency fund. Patrick Kavanagh of the FOIF Executive delivered the bank draft to Margaret Pearse when he was on holiday in Ireland.

By then relations had soured between McGarrity and the FOIF, and he was adamant that no monies would be paid back to that organisation to reimburse them for the draft handed in good faith to Mrs Pearse. The FOIF sought recourse in the courts, and in June 1924, Supreme Court Justice Guy found in favour of the FOIF. Lynch quoted the words of Justice Guy in the draft history of the FOIF: 'This testimony of Mr Lynch is absolutely un-contradicted.'[44] The case was complicated because Mrs Pearse had retained some of the money received from the FOIF in 1920 for her personal use, but the case was finally settled in 1926, and the FOIF was reimbursed with interest.[45] Lynch concluded:

> The procedure followed in this St Enda's matter by the principal defenders, Austin Ford, Joe McGarrity and Fr. James Power, furnished a striking illustration of the spirit which dominated their whole attitude to the FOIF in connection with the split. They performed an ill-service to St Enda's by their sharp practice.[46]

He noted that the book of evidence he produced for this case ran to 735 pages.[47]

Yet another legal issue regarded the retaining of money subscribed to the Victory Fund in New Jersey. In 1920 Maloney and McGarrity had advised several branches of the FOIF in New Jersey to withhold all funds from the National Treasurer, Michael McGreal. The court action taken by the FOIF against Dr Maloney and Joe McGarrity, *McGreal* v. *Maloney*, was settled in favour of the FOIF in May 1926. From the New

Jersey repayment, at Lynch's suggestion, the FOIF sent £2,000 to Frank Fahy for the Gaelic League in Ireland.

Fahy appealed again to Lynch in 1927: 'You have ever been such a staunch supporter of the Gaelic League that the Coiste Gnótha makes no apologies for once again seeking your advice and assistance. The enclosed brief financial statement, which is sent in strict confidence, will make the position quite clear to you.'[48] The FOIF donated a further $12,000 to the Gaelic League in Ireland, with other sums going to various Irish charities.[49]

At a regular meeting of the National Executive of the FOIF on 16 July 1930, James McGurrin was acting as National Secretary *pro tem* while Lynch's remuneration was considered. The meeting noted that Lynch, the National Secretary of FOIF, had asked for and taken a pay cut from 1 February 1925, to 'devote time to business of a personal nature'. His working hours for the FOIF were reduced and his pay was cut by 10 per cent. Subsequently, the volume of work required of Lynch had actually increased because of the successive court cases. A motion was put and seconded unanimously that he would be paid his full salary backdated to 1 May 1925, excluding those periods of time when he was on leave in Ireland. In addition, his salary was restored to $4,000 per annum.[50]

At a National Council meeting of the FOIF in November 1931, the treasurer, Michael McGreal, emphasised that:

The favourable outcome of the litigation [referring to Judge Townley's favourable decision for the FOIF against the Hearn

Committee in June 1931] pertaining to the aforesaid claim was primarily due to the manner in which the National Secretary had preserved the important records bearing on the prosecution of the case, and to the onerous work which Mr Lynch had performed in the prosecution of the claim. He moved that as a mark of the council's appreciation, a standing vote of thanks be tendered to Diarmuid Lynch.[51]

Lynch's service to the organisation in his meticulous preparation for the various court cases was recognised and rewarded at a meeting of the FOIF Executive on 21 December 1931. Lynch was requested to retire temporarily from the room while a motion to award the National Secretary a sum of $5,000 in recognition of his 'valuable service to this organisation' was approved.[52]

From 1924 onwards, joint action by the FOIF and the American-Irish Historical Society (AIHS) on issues such as the 'Immigration Bill' had become the norm. As many of the personnel belonged to both organisations, eventually, in the 1930s, the FOIF ceased to operate as a separate organisation and its work was continued by the AIHS. FOIF headquarters were moved to the AIHS premises at East Sixteenth Street in May 1933.

10

'We're Home for Good'

Lynch was deported to the USA by the British government in 1918, and it was his intention to return and live in Ireland when it was possible. As the newly married couple had settled into life in New York, Diarmuid had expressed the wish that he and Kit could have spent their honeymoon in Ireland.[1] When the results of the 1918 election in Ireland became known in New York, Kit expressed the couple's disappointment that they were not there to celebrate the Sinn Féin victory. 'It is the regret of our lives that we are missing all the excitement. The Cork people are great.'[2]

In one letter to Béaslaí written in 1925, Lynch observed:

With reference to your inquiry as to when you may see us in Ireland again, I would say that the thought uppermost in our minds is to go there next year 'for good' but this is the same position that we have been in every year since 1918, and from a practical standpoint our hopes are no nearer to realisation now than they have been in the meantime. I may remark that since Mick Collins in a communication to me early in 1922, expressed the wish that we would soon be back in Ireland, you are practically the only individual among all my old comrades who voiced the same thought.[3]

By 1932, Lynch was acknowledged to be the architect of the FOIF success in its several legal actions. He had an esteemed profile in Irish-American affairs but was now mainly remembered in Ireland as one of those who had opposed de Valera. His extraordinary work for the FOIF was unknown in Ireland and deemed irrelevant by the Irish population.

The Lynchs planned to visit Ireland during August and September 1932. At an FOIF meeting before they embarked, a motion was unanimously passed acknowledging Lynch's tendered resignation from the post of National Secretary but suspending its implementation until the ongoing court case concerning the Victory Fund, *Montague et al.* v. *Cooney et al.*, was completed.[4] It was the last meeting of the FOIF Lynch attended.

Before he left, he gave the combination data of the safes in his office to Miss Bridget Kyrens, the office secretary.[5] The two months' holiday became five. Correspondence between Michael McGreal and Lynch in October and November concerned arrangements regarding the organisation's bank accounts and office minutiae. Letters were sent by Lynch from the home of Michael and Carmel Lynch in County Wicklow, and he ended his letter to McGreal with the observation, 'This place where we are staying with my brother is ten miles from

Dublin, so that I am away from the current of politics. I am not sorry.'[6] In December Dick Dalton received a telegram from Kinsale conveying the Lynchs' decision to stay in Ireland.[7]

Diarmuid began work on a draft history of the FOIF. The FOIF had discussed the compilation of a history of the organisation in 1928, but, in Lynch's words, 'legal proceedings in that year stopped any progress.'[8] Before Lynch's departure for Ireland, 'The FOIF agreed to pay $2,000 to Mr Lynch to enable him to prepare the manuscript covering the work of the FOIF since its foundation, which work the Executive Committee tentatively delegated him to do, said work to be completed within one year.'[9] He would be paid in two instalments, the first when he posted the draft manuscript to the New York headquarters and the second when the book was published.

In 1932 Lynch requested various documents to be sent to him from the New York office. Throughout the following year he sought further information and documents from FOIF officers, John Carroll and Dick Dalton, sending each man lengthy pages of queries. James Reidy, who succeeded Devoy as editor of *The Gaelic American*, was also solicited for answers to numerous queries,[10] as was Seán O'Hegarty, who Lynch contacted regarding the Cork Brigades in the 'Tan' war.[11]

In the spring of 1933 Diarmuid and Kit Lynch moved from County Wicklow to a rented house at Goold's Hill in Mallow, County Cork. Lynch's family has no information as to why the couple decided to live in Mallow. A tentative explanation is that he wished seclusion to concentrate on writing his history of the FOIF. Another theory is that he hoped to get employment at the Mallow Sugar Beet Factory which was then under construction, or that the Goold's Hill house was rented to them for a reasonable sum. Kit's brother John wrote from Ohio to ask, 'Has Diarmuid found anything to suit him yet? I hope you won't be very disappointed over there.'[12]

A letter from Lynch to Patrick Lee of the New York branch of the FOIF in October 1934 noted that the manuscript of the draft history had been dispatched to Dalton. Lynch suggested to both Dalton and Lee that outstanding queries should be dealt with by FOIF personnel in New York where the relevant documentation was at hand.

He had written a provisional preface to the draft which clarified his reasons for undertaking the history:

> A compelling reason for what may seem excessive detail is that the opponents of the FOIF in the trial of various lawsuits referred to endeavoured to uphold their ill-founded claims by the selection of numerous issues which, in 1919–1920, were simple, thoroughly-understood phases of procedure and attempted to place a wrong construction on them. Should any similar effort be made in the future this record will be its refutation.[13]

Lynch was clearly impatient to be finished with the matter. In an explanatory letter to Dalton he declared:

The task assigned to me, viz., to prepare the manuscript I have endeavoured to execute as comprehensively and accurately as possible. Were it within my province to edit the narrative for publication I would. I am too close to the subject and in fact too weary of the whole task, to attempt further revision before submitting the MS.[14]

He added, 'Now that the MS is finished we are due to leave Goold's Hill by 31 January next. While under rent to the end of January, we will move out just as soon as I can make definite arrangements for the future, contemplation of which up to this had to be brushed aside.'[15]

It was during his time in Mallow that Lynch began to read the newspaper founded in Dublin by de Valera, *The Irish Press*, and to compile scrapbooks of cuttings on topics of political interest, especially any relating to Easter Week or any that quoted the paper's controlling director and proprietor, de Valera.[16]

Lynch was peeved when, by May 1935, there had been no response or reaction to the first draft of the FOIF history which he had sent to his American ex-colleagues. He was still living at Goold's Hill, and it must be concluded that the promised half of the agreed fee had not been paid which would have enabled him and Kit to move to Dublin as planned.[17] It was August before James McGurrin, then President-General of the AIHS, notified Lynch that the FOIF had been paid the $73,000 due after the decision in their favour in the bond-cert court case. This, McGurrin assured Lynch, would provide for the printing costs of the history. McGurrin was warm in praise of the draft: 'In my opinion it is almost impossible to estimate its value without indulging in what might seem exaggeration and flattery. Every statement you have written you have fortified with documentary evidence which can never be questioned.'[18]

McGurrin relayed the praise which both Dalton and Cohalan had expressed for Lynch's draft at a meeting of the FOIF on 9 August 1935, and a decision was taken at that meeting to form a committee immediately to see to the publication of the history. However, Lynch's manuscript was never published. In 2005 the Four Courts Press in Dublin published a history of the FOIF, *Irish-American Diaspora Nationalism: The Friends of Irish Freedom, 1916–1935*, written by Doctor Michael Doorley, who trawled the extensive files of the FOIF and the Cohalan Papers archived at the AIHS headquarters on Fifth Avenue, New York.

Six months after the FOIF was repaid its bond-cert loan, in February 1936, Dalton wrote hurriedly to Lynch: 'Those cheques have just come in from McGreal,' adding that he was taking the cheques to the SS *Bremen* which was sailing that night, and he would write 'by the next steamer'.[19]

Cheques 230 and 231 from the FOIF account in the Chase National Bank paid Lynch the $2,000 agreed for both the preparation and publication of a history of the FOIF. The second cheque was for a modest £24, the expenses incurred as he travelled to and from Dublin on several occasions, consulting persons and documents in preparing the manuscript.[20]

The long-planned move to Dublin soon followed, and Lynch's note of acknowledgment of monies received was written from his new address at Fortfield Drive, Terenure.[21] By this time Diarmuid was already engaged on other projects. The Easter Week Memorial Committee, under the chairmanship of Peadar Kearney, had asked for his help compiling the GPO Roll of Honour to mark the nineteenth anniversary of the insurrection. Lynch was chosen to present the roll, inscribed with 328 names, to Taoiseach de Valera at a ceremony to be held at Government Buildings on 21 April 1935.[22] The previous evening, Lynch gave an address in the GPO, during which he touched on 'what might have been' had the *Aud* succeeded in landing its cargo of armaments at Fenit as planned.[23]

At noon on Easter Sunday, 21 April 1935, Lynch was one of the veterans present in the GPO at the unveiling of the Cúchulainn statue to commemorate the 1916 Rising. During this gathering of the 1916 activists, Lynch volunteered and was entrusted with the task of organising the collection of reports from survivors of the Rising. He set about establishing the essential facts relating to the Easter Rising as remembered and recounted by those who had been actively engaged in the events. First he devised a record sheet, which was sent to the contactable members of the GPO garrison survivors. One hundred and sixty forms were sent out in 1936, and Lynch received a great response.[24] Not satisfied with some of the particulars, he arranged to meet some of the garrison members at specific flashpoints from the Easter Week action.[25] The final report of forty-four pages was approved at a convened meeting of the surviving garrison members. This report was lodged with the Bureau of Military History in the late 1940s.[26]

At Easter 1936, Lynch was again called upon to present the Roll of Honour to President de Valera, on 24 April. In the letter from the organising committee, sent from Wynn's Hotel, Lynch was asked, 'By the way, would you be good enough to purchase some crepe to drape the Rolls of Honour?' In his meticulous lifelong habit, Lynch recorded that he had purchased a half-yard.[27] In May 1936, Lynch represented the GPO garrison at the annual state tribute at Arbour Hill.

On the insistence of Tom Clarke's widow, Louis N. Le Roux's manuscript on the life of Tom Clarke was submitted to Lynch for proofreading before publication. Among those consulted by Lynch concerning various assertions in Le Roux's draft was Eoin MacNeill, and Lynch urged Le Roux to speak to MacNeill in person to establish the correct information. Lynch took offence to references to Devoy in Chapter 16, which he declared were 'a gratuitous attack on Devoy supported only by misquotations, ridiculous assertions and biased conclusions'.[28] It angered Lynch that upon publication of Le Roux's book in 1936 much of what Lynch had recommended had been ignored in the published work. For example, Le Roux repeated the falsehood that Tom Clarke had been court-martialled by the IRB.[29] Lynch's anger at the erroneous writing of Le Roux was still alive years later when he wrote in 1946 to James McGurrin of the AIHS. Lynch quoted the many errors in

Le Roux's book as a warning to the remaining Clan na Gael personnel in New York, urging them to record accurately their own history while those who had the necessary information were still alive. He explained:

> When Le Roux was writing the Life of Tom Clarke he submitted to me (at the insistence of Mrs Clarke) batches of his manuscript. The story as drafted was so full of errors and of views which I refused to sponsor, that I agreed to co-operate only on condition that my name should not appear among those whom the author may wish to thank. I decided that my safest procedure was to make extracts covering outstanding errors and to comment on these. My work eventually covered 100 foolscap pages of type.[30]

Among those who consulted Lynch on other matters concerning 1916 was Éamonn Dore, who was commissioned to produce a memorial on Sarsfield Bridge in Limerick to honour those who died or were executed in 1916. Lynch assisted Dore with the research, sending letters to still-living participants of the Rising.[31]

In 1937 Lynch initiated a lively exchange of correspondence with Molly Reynolds, Winifred Carney, Desmond Ryan, J. J. Kelly and J. J. O'Connell, to establish the authenticity of Pearse's Valedictory Letter of 28 April 1916.[32] The controversy centred on whether the letter was in Pearse's handwriting, that of his brother Willie, or some other, unknown, writer.

Over the years Lynch also responded comprehensively and

vigorously to articles or letters which appeared in newsprint when they attacked Devoy, the Fenians, the American Clan or the policies of the FOIF.[33]

***

On 29 January 1946, the Referee of the Military Pension Board, Tadhg Mac Firbhisigh, signed a report which stated that Diarmuid Lynch of Tracton, County Cork, was entitled to a military service pension, having served in the Irish Volunteers during the recognised qualifying period from 23 April 1916. For the purpose of ranking, Lynch was deemed to be a quartermaster in the Volunteer Force for the ten years of service acceded to his credit. Therefore, at Rank D, he was awarded the sum of £250 a year for the rest of his days, which were brief, as he passed away in November 1950.[34] Considering that Lynch had first applied for a service pension on 29 November 1934 under the Military Service Pension Act of that year, why did it take almost twelve years to grant this to the veteran nationalist?

With Lynch's record of service in the IRB and Volunteers, and his active involvement in the Rising of Easter Week 1916, there was never a doubt about his qualification for a service pension. At issue was the thorny question of his political life in the USA between May 1918 and July 1921, the cut-off date decided upon by the Pensions Arbitration Board. Again and again he was refused a service pension for any work he did for the Irish state while resident in America, despite an explicit stipulation in the Regulations of the Pensions Act: 'Absence from duty following arrest, imprisonment, internment or deportation shall not be deemed to constitute a breach in the continuity of service'.[35]

From the numerous communications between the Department of Defence and Lynch in the twelve years from 1934 to 1946, it is clear that the Referee and board of assessors were satisfied enough to award Lynch a pension for five of the ten years claimed. This decision was conveyed to him in August 1935, signed by the Referee, J. K. O'Connor. The sum granted was to be £138 7s 1d per annum. The additional pension claimed by Lynch for the period between his deportation in April 1918 to July 1921 was refused. Lynch promptly appealed.

The subsequent prolonged delay and several refusals were because Lynch's work as Secretary of the FOIF in the USA was not recognised as 'service for the Nation of Ireland'.[36] In the 1930s and 1940s, the Referee of the Pensions Board was a member of the judiciary and was appointed by the Minister for Defence. The members of the advisory committee to the Referee were also government appointees and therefore largely supporters of the Fianna Fáil government. For over a decade Lynch showed a dogged determination to have his work in America between May 1918 and July 1921 officially recognised as being in the service of the Irish nation.

A copy of the first pension application form submitted by Lynch from his Mallow address in November 1934 is archived, and it must be acknowledged that he made a mistake by not giving details of his activities in America from May 1918 onwards. In several sections which required him to supply detail, he merely wrote the comment, 'Deportee in USA'.[37]

Following the first rejection, he wrote a detailed letter, at the suggestion of Minister for Defence Frank Aiken, in which he described the circumstances of his deportation from Dublin and the many official communications which had passed between himself, Michael Collins, Cathal Brugha, Éamon de Valera and Arthur Griffith during 1918, 1919 and 1920.[38] Aiken personally presented this letter to the Pensions Board. Other documentary evidence was presented with the letter, including a copy of a letter signed on 29 April 1919 by both de Valera and Collins, which appointed Lynch (with Boland, Mellows and McCartan) to the task of raising an external loan in America for the Irish Republic: 'You are hereby authorised to issue the foregoing prospectus in America, to receive applications for the Certificates described above therein, to receive payment in respect of such applications and generally to act as agents of the Irish Republican government in all matters appertaining to this loan.'[39] The obvious conclusion is that Collins, then Minister for Finance, and de Valera considered Lynch an employee of the declared Irish state.

To support Lynch's claim, Seán T. O'Kelly, whom Lynch had named as a reference in his application, forwarded a copy of a letter which he had received from Griffith in 1919 while he was in Paris as the official Irish envoy to the Peace

Conference. In this letter, Griffith, then acting president of
Dáil Éireann, had urged that Lynch be one of a delegation
sent from America to present Ireland's case at Versailles.[40]

Resident in Dublin from 1935, Lynch was in a position
to personally lobby Dublin-based politicians to support his
pension claim. Archived documents show that one of those
he approached was de Valera himself, then president of the
Dáil. Lynch met de Valera in Leinster House on 1 October
1936, requesting that he would use his position to influence
a favourable decision. In April 1937, de Valera supplied a
letter to support Lynch's application.[41] In it, he included a
statement that said 'in the Spring of 1920 the leaders of the
organisation [FOIF] openly disagreed with the representatives
of the Irish Government'.[42] As National Secretary, Lynch was
one of the disagreeing leaders referred to in the letter, and de
Valera himself was the representative of the Irish government.
Lynch must have deemed that such a letter would have acted
against his interests with the Pensions Board because he did
not present de Valera's letter with his pension claim.[43]

By November 1937, with no resolution forthcoming, Lynch
turned to Frank Aiken again. In a letter to Aiken, Lynch refers
to a recent interview they had had and the lengthy case exposi-
tion he had subsequently supplied to Aiken. In this explanation he quoted a letter he had received from Collins, dated 1
August 1919, in which Collins wrote in military terminology
that Lynch was not available for 'work' in Ireland 'by reason of
enemy action' – a reference to his forced deportation in April

1918. Lynch added that in 1923 he was still classed as an 'enemy alien' because when he and his wife arrived at Tilbury Docks, London, en route to Ireland, they were not permitted to disembark at the official immigration checkpoint because Lynch was blacklisted.

Lynch queried whether a possible factor that may have adversely influenced the Pensions Board was that on being deported to America in 1918 he was employed almost immediately as National Secretary of the FOIF, hence that it would be deemed that he was in gainful employment. Lynch denied that the relevant clause in the 1934 Pensions Act ever stipulated that no pension would be granted to those who were employed during the relevant dates. He ended with a plea to Aiken: 'Perhaps a suggestion from you might hasten a decision.'[44]

In March 1938 there were further written exchanges with the Military Services Pensions Board querying the status of Lynch's claim and Lynch disputing once more whether the Board should count his 'gainful employment' with the FOIF as negating his claim. He was adept at quoting and interpreting clauses in the Pensions Act of 1934 to strengthen and prove his own case.

In a renewed effort during 1938 to find out how his application stood, he contacted an 'insider', Commandant Joe O'Connor, who was frequently employed as a certifying officer at Pension Board hearings. O'Connor replied that a new condition was being demanded by the Board: to establish that Lynch, 'while a deportee in the United States engaged in specific army work for or on behalf of the Forces in Ireland'.[45]

Lynch provided appropriate evidence. The FOIF had supplied funds for armaments and guns during 1919 and 1920 to Liam Pedlar, Seán Nunan and Harry Boland, and Lynch, in his meticulous way, had records and receipts for all donations.[46] He even provided a copy of the original receipt he had presented to a meeting of the FOIF in September 1919, showing that $40,000 had been given by him to Boland and Nunan.[47] He pointed out again that none of the clauses in the Pensions Act specified the nature of duties to be performed by agents of Dáil Éireann while abroad.

By August 1938, Lynch was getting nowhere with his campaign to have his full service recognised and he consulted Dan Breen, TD, about the matter. A letter from the Department of Defence in September 1938 informed him of yet another dismissal of his claim, a decision which Lynch conveyed to Breen by letter from his new address in his native Tracton.

O'Connor, who was then retiring, had turned down his appeal once more. 'The Referee has reviewed his report in the light of the additional evidence submitted by you and has confirmed his findings as set out on your Service Certificate of August, 1935.'[48] Lynch was rueful that O'Connor had not left his case 'open' for a successor to investigate. He added, 'If the Act had not made the Referee the court of last appeal I would have no hesitation in carrying the matter further, even if I had to borrow money to meet the costs. The situation being as it is I am astopped [sic].'[49]

With the retirement of O'Connor and the appointment of a new Referee, Judge O'Donnell, in 1940 Lynch decided to appeal the decision again, this time emphasising that the original decision was based on a perception that his 'active' service finished on 25 April 1918, the day he was deported to Liverpool from Dublin on the first leg of his enforced exile in America. Lynch pointed out that he was continuously under arrest in the ship's hospital on board the SS *New York* until it sailed on 27 April; therefore, the period of his imprisonment should rightly be extended to when he was released from custody for the purpose of deciding the correct pension period.

The response of the new Referee in November 1940 to Lynch's latest attempt was more conciliatory in tone, but was still a refusal, and contained a strong recommendation that Lynch should drop the case and accept the findings as irrevocably final:

> The additional evidence submitted by you in support of your appeal was carefully and sympathetically considered by the Referee who, however, saw no reason to change his findings and made his report accordingly to the Minister. The report of the Referee as shown on the Service Certificate issued to you on 12 September 1935 is, in accordance with the terms of the Act, final and conclusive and binding on you. No further action can be taken in the matter.[50]

Lynch was forced to accept the situation. However, with an amendment to the Pensions Act in 1944, following relevant

Supreme Court cases, Lynch had renewed hopes that his case might be settled to his satisfaction, and he set in motion a new appeal under the guidance of his solicitor, John B. Cottrell of Cork city. Lynch supplied a hefty file of the case history to Cottrell detailing all of his efforts in the pension saga to date. He indicated his intention to have an interview with the Minister for Defence stating that he would ultimately seek justice through the courts should this attempt be refused. It is clear from letters between Lynch and Cottrell concerning engaging a suitable barrister that court was now being seriously considered.

To bolster his case, Lynch sought and received active support from Judge Diarmuid Fawsitt and Liam Tóibín. Fawsitt, a founding member in 1913 of the Cork Volunteers, was well known to the Lynch brothers, Diarmuid and Michael. He had served as Consul for the Irish Government in the USA from 1919. In his submission, Fawsitt wrote:

> After my arrival in New York I contacted Mr Lynch who had been favourably known to me in Ireland; at that time he was national secretary of the Friends of Irish Freedom, an office he continued to fill throughout the period of my stay in the States. This organisation, under the direction of Mr Lynch, did much valuable work in combating the prejudice against our country's efforts to secure national independence, in combating the vicious anti-Irish propaganda of pro-British organisations in the States and in raising funds for political and military purposes at home.

Lynch obtained for me the use rent free of a furnished office as temporary premises for the Irish Consulate … and as free gift, certain articles of furniture for the premises. This aid was timely and valuable as it was urgently necessary in the interests of the home government that I should begin to function as Consul and since the funds at my disposal were limited.[51]

Lynch solicited a supporting letter once again from Taoiseach de Valera. De Valera issued a letter which was almost an exact copy of that issued in 1937. At the time of writing, 3 December 2012, the pensions files are unavailable to public scrutiny because of the long delay in digitisation, so it is not known if Lynch submitted this second letter with his application to the board.[52]

Lynch had prepared a detailed discussion document for the new hearing in 1944, covering his active service from his release from Lewes Prison in 1917 to the critical date in July 1921, adding that it was he who, as Secretary of the FOIF, handed money drafts to a third party who was travelling to Ireland in the autumn of 1919 for delivery to Collins. In total, $115,000 was sent to Collins through Lynch's hands between 1919 and 1921.[53] Lynch concluded his five-page submission:

If through any strained interpretation of the Act, I should now be excluded from the benefits which it purported to afford under certain eventualities it would be tantamount to penalisation; (a) because of the fact that instead of being imprisoned in England

193

in 1918 (and thus rendered helpless as far as the Forces in Ireland were concerned) I happened to be deported to the United States, and (b) notwithstanding the fact that (though the Act lays down no condition whereby a deportee would or could be expected to engage in any pro-Irish national work whatever) I did engage while in the United States in the afore-mentioned important activities in support of the military and political forces in Ireland, by virtue of which the Irish Republican campaign was in large measure pushed forward so aggressively in all its aspects both at home and abroad.[54]

Liam Pedlar of *The Irish Press* was summoned to appear before the Referee and advisory committee on 19 December 1944 as a sworn witness for Lynch. During his testimony, Pedlar explained, 'I met Mr Lynch frequently in the USA. I never knew him to be engaged in anything other than political work. I don't think he would have a "dog's chance" of making a public appearance in Ireland. My impression would be that if a question of his return arose, it would be felt that he would be of more use in the USA.'[55]

To a new suggestion made at the hearing that Lynch should obtain from the British authorities a copy of the order under which he was deported from Dublin in 1918, he replied courteously but firmly to the Referee: 'With regard to the suggestion that I write to the British Home Secretary for the desired information, I feel I should not be required to adopt that course. In view of the positions held by me in the Irish National Movement, you will, I am sure, agree with me in this.'[56]

It is difficult to understand why such a suggestion was made and why such an action on Lynch's part was thought necessary. The details of his deportation were blazoned across the front pages of English, Irish and American newspapers in the final days of April 1918. Conversely, the likely reaction of the British Home Office to such a request from a man whom the British Intelligence Service had variously labelled in confidential reports, 'enemy alien', 'a dangerous agitator' and 'leader of the IRB in America', is not hard to imagine.

Lynch was informed in January 1946 that he had been successful in his long campaign and that he was to be awarded the full service pension for the entire period for which he had claimed in his original application.

Former Republican activists also seeking to establish the legitimacy of their claims to a service pension often appealed to Lynch for assistance. Seán Byrne of Larkfield Grove, Kimmage, in Dublin, wrote a long and impassioned letter to Lynch in 1935, asking that he vouch for him. Byrne had been one of the post-office engineering squad assembled and briefed by Lynch in April 1916. Lynch replied cordially and supplied Byrne with certificates covering the periods in April 1916 and again for a period during 1917 and 1918 when Byrne was given money by Lynch and Collins, both on the Executive Council of the IRB, for the purchase of guns from British soldiers returning from the Great War.

In November 1935, Lynch provided a similar service in relation to pension claims for John Twamley of South Circular

Road, Dublin, another of the post-office employees on the 'manhole committee' who went into action in Bray on Easter Sunday and Monday.

John Reynolds wrote to Lynch from an address in Sutton, County Dublin, in November 1937, seeking written affirmation in support of his claim for a service pension. Lynch replied with detailed confirmation from his own recollections of the occupation of the GPO, and he added information supplied by Éamonn Dore in his witness statement. Dore had recorded that Reynolds was the man in charge at Messrs Williams, Sampson's Lane, Dublin, after the evacuation of the GPO on Friday 28 April.

Thomas Craven of Akron, Ohio, who had been in action at Annesley Bridge, Dublin, during Easter Week 1916, also requested help from Lynch in obtaining his service pension. As in all cases, Lynch responded positively with practical suggestions as to the right procedure for Craven to follow, adding wryly, 'Decisions (by the board) are very arbitrary, as I have reason to know not merely from hearsay but from personal experience, very dear experience at that!'[57]

11

Cork – the Final Decade

Lynch's financial circumstances for those twelve pensionless years were very restricted. His only income between 1935 and 1946 was almost $2,000 in back pay paid by the FOIF in recognition of his increased workload in preparation for several court cases, the sum of $5,000 awarded in recognition of his representation of the FOIF during the court cases and the sum of $2,000 paid in 1935 on the completion of the FOIF draft history.

No further official funds came to Lynch from America. In 1938 he had to be the very model of financial prudence when building his home on a site on the Lynch farm at Granig sold to him by his brother Dan.[1] Records show that every item of expenditure concerning the bungalow was dated and priced and the source of the materials recorded, down to the last pound of cement nails.[2] Consistent with the meticulous nature of Lynch's record-keeping in all matters, domestic and political, was the listed minutiae of the building programme. Yet Lynch could not conceal his joy at the prospect of moving back to his native parish.[3]

Careful budgeting had to be the Lynchs' rule of life. When returning a borrowed copy of Desmond Ryan's book *Seán Treacy and the Third Tipperary Brigade* to Florrie O'Donoghue in November 1945, he remarked, 'Some years ago I ceased to buy books but hope to be able to start again in the near future.'[4] For Lynch, whose library of over 200 volumes on Irish history and culture is still extant in the farmhouse at Granig, this would have been a real hardship.

After the move home, life in Tracton settled into a contented pattern. Lynch was much exercised by his garden, and a family anecdote recalls him taking his gun to rabbits that had the temerity to munch on his newly planted hedges. Local schoolboys teased him with false reports that soccer was being played on the nearby GAA pitch. He was active in his brother's farmyard at harvest time.[5]

Local recognition of his abilities was evident in his employment as auditor of the local Ballyfeard Red Cross branch. He took the salute at the Ballyfeard Local Defence Force Easter Parade in successive years.[6]

Lynch's niece Dolores recalls that he encouraged her greatly in pursuing her education at the agricultural college in Dunmanway and after that as a student at the Munster Institute. Diarmuid would beg a lamb from his brother Dan and sell it to a butcher in Kinsale town to raise funds for her college expenses.[7]

It may have been the Lord Mayor of Cork City, Seán McCarthy, a serving Fianna Fáil TD, who nominated Lynch for the Senate in 1944. He was certainly encouraging and closely involved in the process. There was a flurry of representations made to deputies and committees, with de Valera allegedly in favour to the extent that he proposed Lynch for the industrial and commercial panels. However, it all came to nothing, and Seán McCarthy reflected in a subsequent letter, 'Had you been put on the Educational or Administrative panel your prospects would have been much brighter.'[8] A letter on Dáil Éireann notepaper from Deputy Liam Tóibín hinted at political chicanery:

> You were proposed in fitting words by Dev. After that it was agreed you had a fair sporting chance to get on the panel but even if you had got that far, the chances of being elected were remote. You will understand my reluctance to even attempt to explain the reason for such an opinion (I will when I see you).[9]

Lynch thanked de Valera for proposing his nomination: 'I accept your fine action as an honour and a high compliment conferred, notwithstanding those sharp differences of opinion between us in the USA a quarter of a century ago.'[10] This letter from Lynch to de Valera was cordial, yet colouring all communications between them were the bitter memories of the unseemly and public disunity that occurred during de Valera's fund-raising trip to America.

With the move back to County Cork, Lynch and Florrie O'Donoghue renewed their acquaintance. With active encouragement from O'Donoghue, fresh impetus was given to

Lynch's self-appointed mission of recording accurately what was known about all aspects of the Easter Rising and correcting what he perceived to be erroneous. O'Donoghue recognised the value of what Lynch could contribute to historical records and encouraged him to compile further reports on various aspects of the Easter Rising. Lynch authored several of these, which he informed O'Donoghue were 'ready for transmission' in April 1947.[11] They are archived at the Bureau of Military History at Cathal Brugha Barracks in Dublin.[12]

When Donagh MacDonagh (the son of Thomas Mac-Donagh) prepared scripts for radio talks on the 1916 leaders in 1944, O'Donoghue encouraged him to submit the drafts to Lynch for editing. Lynch returned extensive commentary on each of the articles. However, he was incensed when, in subsequent articles based on the radio talks and published in *An Cosantóir*, MacDonagh repeated Le Roux's discredited story that Clarke had been court-martialled by the IRB. Lynch wrote indignantly to P. S. O'Hegarty:

> I wrote pages of comments to straighten out the story as contained in the scripts. He has taken 'dope' on the IRB from Pollard and put his own construction on it.[13] As men with no personal knowledge of these matters will doubtless continue to write about them it is better to prevent the appearance of errors in print, whenever possible. And there was that damned awful stuff about the Clan-na-Gael. It made me clean mad to think that while I had been working on the radio scripts he was

penning that libel on what I described in a note to the editor as 'the most single-minded, generous and unselfish body of friends Ireland ever had'.[14]

Lynch was acerbic in his comments on MacDonagh's article for *An Costantóir* on Joseph Plunkett:

On reading your article on Joseph Plunkett I was particularly desirous to note the extent to which you edited your manuscript in the light of my comments furnished to the editor. The published article left much to be desired. I repeat queries set out in my commentary of 7 August 1945, and add a few others that now occur to me.[15]

At O'Donoghue's request, Lynch himself prepared an article for publication in the *An Cosantóir* journal on the subject of MacNeill's countermanding orders in Holy Week 1916. O'Donoghue made a private plea to Colonel D. Bryan, editor of *An Cosantóir*, when the publication of Lynch's article was being considered:

The one further point I wish to make to yourself personally is that if it is published you would consider the possibility of sending him a cheque for it. He did not suggest anything of the sort to me and would be offended if he thought I mentioned it.[16]

The article was intended for the April 1945 edition of the

journal, but an editorial decision meant that it never appeared. Lynch was informed on 21 March 1945:

> It was thought undesirable that this article should be published in a semi-official journal at the present time, because it may start a large-scale controversy on a matter of historical importance and a certain gentleman referred to is now a civil servant and thereby precluded from replying at present.[17]

Bulmer Hobson was the civil servant in question, and he objected to how the draft article depicted his role in MacNeill's countermanding orders.[18]

Lynch wrote to O'Donoghue about the editorial decision not to print his article. 'The suggested possibility of a controversy incites me to seek publication in some other medium later on. If ground for controversy there be, better it should come out in the open while some of us who were in touch with developments are alive to meet it.'[19] The article was never published, but a copy is archived at the Bureau of Military History.[20]

When O'Donoghue was appointed as Director of the newly established Bureau of Military History in 1947, further impetus was given to recording and archiving all that could be obtained from witnesses to the epochal events of Easter 1916. O'Donoghue suggested to Geraldine Plunkett, sister of Joseph Plunkett, that she submit a draft of the manuscript she was preparing for publication to Lynch for comment in

1949. Lynch's contribution 'was meticulous in distinguishing between what he asserted as fact and what he stated was merely a matter of opinion'.[21]

During 1945 Lynch was consulted by Lieutenant Rúairí Mac Ionnraic and Colonel T. P. Gallagher of the Military College, Curragh Command, with regard to a planned military tattoo and the construction of a chart or map of Dublin showing the various posts occupied during Easter Week. Lynch's contribution was acknowledged by Mac Ionnraic and Gallagher, Gallagher adding in his letter, 'I am particularly grateful for the trouble to which you have gone to supply us with data for our 1916 chart.'[22]

Lynch wrote testy and scornful critiques of several books published on the Easter Rising during those years, and though, according to O'Donoghue, 'while the comments are often severe and occasionally caustic, they are almost always factual and never offensive', offence was often taken.[23] One example of this meticulous but acerbic approach was his review of *Green Banners* by R. M. Fox in April 1946. Lynch's method was to quote an assertion with which he disagreed and then to demolish its rationale utterly. For Fox's account of the crisis that arose with MacNeill's countermanding orders, Lynch quoted the relevant lines from page 243 of *Green Banners*: 'Connolly had never believed in these wheels within wheels, revolving in different directions ... Now, at the last moment, he exerted himself to create a firm centre of revolt, to save the plan from the wreck.' Lynch then commented:

Well! Well! No one counted but Connolly! All the others – Clarke, Pearse, MacDiarmada, Plunkett, Ceannt, MacDonagh – were mere ciphers! I know the sentiments expressed by Pearse and MacDonagh after midnight Saturday, 22nd April, that the Rising should go ahead notwithstanding MacNeill's cancellation of the Sunday 'Parades.'[24]

Lynch did pay fulsome tribute to Connolly in this critique:

I was the last of the men who fought under Connolly to bid him farewell as he lay on his stretcher on the side walk of the Upper Castle Yard on Saturday, 29th April. I am proud to have known him and to have fought under him. He was a great man and as such I revere his memory. But the over-stressing by mis-eulogists of his part in the preparations and decisions pertaining to the Rising at Easter 1916, and their sneers at the men who comprised the Military Council prior to Connolly's membership thereof, compel me to record the present criticisms.[25]

Desmond Ryan remarked in relation to Lynch's comprehensive shredding of his own book, *The Rising* (1949): 'Mr Diarmuid Lynch criticised that book with a meticulous fury that won my admiration.'[26] In the same column, Ryan acknowledged Lynch's insider knowledge of the years leading up to the Rising: 'Lynch was in closer touch with the Military Council than most.'[27]

Lynch frequently undertook missions to Dublin during this decade to consult documents archived in the National Library in his quest for accurate answers concerning the events of the Easter Rising. On one such trip he met the Minister for Agriculture, James Ryan, to clarify points regarding the actions of the Volunteers in Cork in 1916.[28]

To end speculation as to which flag flew over the GPO during the Rising, Lynch corresponded with Frank Thornton, Seán MacEntee, Joe O'Connor and Patrick O'Connor, all of whom had been in the GPO garrison.[29] In one letter to Patrick O'Connor, he remarked, 'Like yourself, I think nothing should be left undone to arrive at or rather verify the truth of matters such as this.'[30] The research was painstaking, with further correspondence between Lynch and Thornton, Denis McCullough and Gearóid Ó Súilleabháin.[31] Concluding his research and information-gathering, Lynch submitted an article on 'The National Flag' to the Bureau of Military History in December 1947.[32]

Lynch had been in regular correspondence with his American friends and ex-colleagues in the FOIF during the 1930s. The Great Depression of that decade in America had affected his FOIF friends. Judge Cohalan suffered a financial setback. James McGurrin informed Lynch in 1935 that:

> The Cohalans have moved from the old house in Ninety-Fourth Street to an apartment at 21, East Eighty-Second. Of course you know that the Judge is a Referee at $16,000 a year which represents an income away [*sic*] below his average while at the Bar. This change made it necessary to effect some radical adjustments in the mode of living.[33]

Writing to Cohalan in 1941, Lynch referred to a recent visit of James and Nancy McGurrin, and recalled his first meeting with Cohalan: 'A few of us from the Gaelic League interviewed you in the matter of getting the Volunteers out to form a guard of honour for the coffin [of Fr O'Growney]. It's many the smile I had in later years at my naive remark to you in that regard and of your diplomatic reply.'[34]

When Cohalan died in November 1946, Lynch felt compelled to refute accusations made against the judge that appeared in a front-page article in *The Irish Press*. The comments alleged that the Judge 'vehemently opposed' de Valera's bond-cert drive in 1920. The article also asserted that 'the Judge refused to cooperate with Mr de Valera' at the party conventions held in Chicago and San Francisco in June 1920.[35]

Lynch's reply appeared in *The Irish Press* on 26 November, and in a detailed and robust defence of Cohalan he ended with a ringing endorsement of his deceased friend:

> The cleavage between Mr de Valera and Judge Cohalan – one the leader of the Irish at home and the other the outstanding man of our race in America – was most unfortunate. Be our opinions of their respective policies what they may, criticism should be based on authenticated facts. Furthermore, it is not fitting that any nationalist Irishman should assess in a grudging spirit the preeminent services rendered to Ireland's cause, long before 1916 and long after it, by that great American of Irish blood, Daniel F. Cohalan.[36]

Lynch's defence of Cohalan led to a spate of hostile letters to *The Irish Press*, with one correspondent, Mrs Kitty O'Doherty (whose name Lynch judged to be a *nom de plume*) claiming that 'The Devoy–Cohalan group engineered plots to destroy the Irish Republic.'[37] Lynch's measured and detailed reply to Kitty O'Doherty's letter was not published, and the editor of *The Irish Press* responded to his query about the failure to publish by saying, 'The points you now make have already been thrashed out in a newspaper controversy extending over several years and I do not propose to cover that ground again.'[38]

Cohalan's death spurred Dalton to urge Lynch to consider once more re-editing the draft manuscript of the history of the FOIF for publication in the USA.[39] Lynch replied with detailed reasons as to why he could not and would not, at that stage in his life, take up the challenge. He sent Dalton a file of the recent correspondence in *The Irish Press* concerning Cohalan, including a copy of Kitty O'Doherty's letter. He observed in his letter:

> You can appreciate the amount of work and worry which this letter to the I. P. gave me, in my anxiety to make my remarks 'watertight'. And yet that only represents an infinitesimal fraction of what I'd have to go through were I to attempt to edit the entire FOIF material – even as written by myself – and get it into shape for publication. In compiling the record I feel that I have contributed my share towards the establishment of historical truth so far as the FOIF is concerned.[40]

In a letter of condolence to Cohalan's widow, Lynch refers to the visit of her son Fr Florence Cohalan and of her late husband's brother Fr Patrick Cohalan earlier in that year.[41] Dalton also visited from America. He referred to an evening spent 'in the parlour at Tracton' with O'Donoghue, Seán O'Hegarty and Charles T. Rice in the summer of 1948. This memory was shared in a letter to Florrie O'Donoghue in February 1957, before *The I.R.B. and the 1916 Insurrection* was launched.[42] Widow Madge Cohalan and her daughter Kathleen were also the Lynchs' welcome guests, in May 1949.

As the years passed, Lynch became increasingly frail. A lifelong propensity to stomach ulcers, exacerbated by the poor diet in gaol and his participation in hunger strikes while a prisoner, led to recurring bouts of illness throughout his life. Despite a severe heart attack in February 1950, he continued to correspond prolifically from his invalid's bed. A handwritten letter to Piaras Béaslaí in March was unusual, as Lynch's habit was to type all documents, but he explained cheerfully that he was forbidden by his doctor to even press the typewriter keys.[43] He was unfit in June of that year to accompany Dick and Máire Dalton to Skibbereen to a ceremony honouring O'Donovan Rossa.

Lynch wrote to his brother Michael in Dundrum, County Wicklow, on 31 August, with queries put to him by O'Donoghue. Florrie was working on an article about the Cork Volunteers for publication in *An Cosantóir* and wished to know if anyone had travelled with Michael Lynch on the

'Indian' sidecar of his motorbike on the morning of Easter Sunday 1916 when he ferried arms to Macroom and Bweeing, County Cork.

Among the letters written during the last full month of his life, October 1950, was one to the Director of the National Museum regarding the Roll of Honour which Lynch had helped to compile in 1935. Lynch was anxious that no copy of the original roll existed and intended to apply to Taoiseach de Valera, for funding to pay for the copying and archiving of the roll.[44] He had also written to the Director of the Cork Museum in Fitzgerald's Park, expressing his wish that he could personally afford to have a copy of the roll commissioned for presentation to the museum.[45]

Diarmuid still took *The Irish Press* daily and continued to archive columns concerning politics, history and cultural matters. The final cutting filed was dated 1 November 1950 and was a report on the Fianna Fáil Ard-Fheis with the listing of elected officers, headed by 'the President, Mr de Valera'.[46]

Ten days before he died, a letter Lynch received from Denis McCullough provoked his wrath, and he peppered its margins with corrections and acerbic observations. McCullough recounted that he had met up with Bulmer Hobson and P. S. O'Hegarty on the previous evening, and between them they had compiled a sequence which they were satisfied explained the 'disappearance' of Connolly for three days in January 1916. Once more, Lynch jotted down his own version of that disappearance in the margins of McCullough's letter, and his jottings ended with the observation, 'McCullough's statements are be-yond my understanding'.[47]

An account of Diarmuid Lynch's death, which occurred at home on 9 November 1950, was given by his brother Denis in a letter to *The Gaelic American*. 'His death, unexpected, was indeed most happy. For a few days before, he suffered a good deal of pain from his heart, but the end came quickly, just after he had said goodbye to his loving wife, and he faced death as bravely as he had done so many times before.'[48]

The 18 November edition of *The Gaelic American* featured the news of Lynch's death on the front page, and, for the first time, the fact that he had faced a 'firing squad' on Thursday, 18 May 1916, was blazoned across the front page. 'British Firing Squad Had Guns Loaded to Shoot Irish Patriot.'[49]

Lynch was buried in Tracton Abbey churchyard on 11 November 1950 with full military honours. The report in *The Cork Examiner* on the funeral noted that the attendance was very large: 'Many of those present came long distances to pay their respects to the memory of an Irishman who had played such a large part in the fight for Independence.'[50] The report noted that President Seán T. O'Kelly attended and walked behind the coffin to the graveside.

General Tom Barry, Major-General Michael J. Costello, Denis McCullough and Seán O'Hegarty were among the pro-minent nationalists present. O'Hegarty delivered the graveside oration, concluding with the words, 'His great and vital interest and activity was expressed in those years before 1916 when he went through the country doing the spade work in the IRB which made 1916 possible.'[51]

Robert Barton recalled, 'He was a serious, earnest and intense man, whose every waking thought was for the cause of Irish freedom. His quiet sense of humour was never malicious. Our people would be ungrateful if they were to forget what we owe to the sacrifices of such men as Diarmuid Lynch.'[52]

The brief entry in de Valera's diary for 9 November 1950 reads, 'Diarmuid Lynch dead.'[53] In the course of that year Taoiseach de Valera had travelled to Wales, France, Rome, Athens and Israel. Four days after Lynch was buried de Valera travelled to Strasbourg. He did not travel to County Cork to attend the funeral of Diarmuid Lynch.[54]

When Lynch died in 1950 his only income, the service pension granted belatedly in 1946, died with him. Kit found herself in financial distress, so two months later Florrie O'Donoghue and Michael J. Costello set up the 'Diarmuid Lynch Memorial Committee' with a branch in both Cork and Dublin to raise funds for his widow's welfare and to pay for a gravestone. Membership in the Cork branch included the chairman, Seán O'Hegarty, Tom Barry, Seán Ó Muirthile and Professor D. Corcoran of UCC. The inaugural meeting was held at Barry's Auction Rooms in Academy Street. The Dublin branch was established under the chairmanship of Denis McCullough and included Frank Thornton, Dan Breen, Alec McCabe, Liam Deasy, Liam Tóibín and Michael J. Costello. By February, Costello had organised a letter of appeal which was sent to 500 individuals. Lynch was eulogised in the petitioning letter: 'Up to the day of his death he had subordinated all else to his devotion to Ireland. He was the living embodiment of the Fenian tradition. An undeviating and uncompromising Ireland-er, he was a man who counted Ireland everything and himself nothing.'[55]

A bank account was opened at the Munster and Leinster Bank. President Seán T. O'Kelly donated generously, and the total raised between both branches of the committee was £473. This was invested by McCabe in a 5 per cent national loan, the stock being held by the bank. Dalton sought funding from the Irish Palace Board (an Irish-American organisation founded in the late nineteenth century in New York) to purchase some of Diarmuid's papers from Kit. Eventually he managed to secure £500 from the AIHS towards the purchase of the papers, but he observed despondently in a letter to Costello, 'So far as the younger generation now active in the Irish Movement is concerned, Diarmuid Lynch is merely a name in history to them.'[56]

Dalton arranged that Kit be paid £120 per year until the £500 ran out. Ellis & Sons, Stonemasons, erected a headstone over Diarmuid's grave, and by November 1953 the stonemason had not yet been paid, to Kit's distress. O'Donoghue personally settled this account in December of that year and was to be reimbursed by a donation from the Palace Board in America. Dalton raised a further £385 by selling two of Devoy's letters to the AIHS, one from Pearse and one from Clarke.[57]

Kit Lynch died in September 1955, before the American fund ran out. According to the executor of her will, her total assets amounted to £522. Lynch's nephew and godson, Diarmuid, inherited the bungalow home built by the couple in 1938.[58]

No public monument, no bridge, no road, street or building is dedicated to the memory of Diarmuid Lynch, one of the inner circle of IRB men who engineered the 1916 Easter Rising. A commemorative plaque was unveiled in 1966 in the garden of the farmhouse at Granig where Lynch was born and reared. The Cork 1916 Commemorative Committee organised the plaque, and the unveiling took place on 19 June 1966. In attendance were Lynch's brother Denis and other family members. Denis McCullough performed the unveiling ceremony and in his address paid tribute: 'No country to my knowledge was ever better served than Ireland by Diarmuid Lynch. He had courage and determination and loyalty and when he had belief in any cause he did not hesitate to serve it faithfully without ever flinching in his duty.'[59]

12

Lynch's Contribution to Historical Records

On the ninety-ninth anniversary of Lynch's birth, 7 January 1977, Pádraig Ó Maidín, Cork City Librarian, celebrated Lynch's life in his *Cork Examiner* column. 'A Boy from Old Knocknamana' was largely taken from the autobiographical essay written by Lynch and published as Chapter 1 in *The I.R.B. and the 1916 Insurrection* edited by Florence O'Donoghue.[1] The essay had been encouraged by O'Donoghue and other friends, but was undertaken with reluctance as Lynch 'felt that the writing of an autobiography might well lead to the conclusion that I had far too exaggerated an idea of my own importance'.[2]

Shortly after Lynch died, Dr Richard Hayes of the National Library urged O'Donoghue to 'go after' the papers stockpiled in the Lynch home in Cork. O'Donoghue was aware of the historical importance of Lynch's collection of documents and, with Kit's consent, took what he deemed the most significant documents into his own possession. Over the course of the next few years he edited and prepared selected documents in anticipation of publication. Included in the draft were the several reports which Lynch had completed in the 1940s, copies of which O'Donoghue had lodged in the Bureau of Military History in 1947. At Dalton's suggestion, O'Donoghue included in the manuscript the comprehensive address delivered by Lynch to the Clan na Gael rally in New York on 9 April 1921.[3]

Before publication, O'Donoghue consulted Seán Fawsitt at the Law Library about possible libel implications. Fawsitt's advice was that the language in the chapters dealing with R. M. Fox's *History of the Irish Citizen Army* should be modified.[4] Included in Chapter 8 of *The I.R.B. and the 1916 Insurrection* is O'Donoghue's own judgement on Lynch's reports:

> His own intimate personal knowledge of operations in the G.P.O. area, his keen eye for discrepancies or fiction, and his passionate devotion to truth in the record were invaluable. The result of his quiet and persistent labours is a factual report on Easter Week in the G.P.O. area which may be accepted as complete and wholly reliable.[5]

Professor Robert Dudley Edwards of University College Dublin was warm in his praise of the draft which O'Donoghue submitted to him for proof-reading, adding 'Dr Michael Tierney, College President, looked over the proofs. He thought it "a very honest account with content unexceptionable. It is possibly the best account so far put together".[6]

O'Donoghue, Michael J. Costello and Dalton saw the book through to publication. The book was produced on a 'no profit' basis by Captain Seán Feehan, the founder of Mercier Press, and was launched at Easter 1957. One thousand five hundred copies were printed, and there was only one print run. Dalton arranged the shipping of 150 copies to America. O'Donoghue and Costello had borne the printing costs and were refunded when the Irish Palace Board in New York paid for the US copies.

Pádraig Ó Maidín, Cork County Librarian, thanked O'Donoghue for the donation of thirty-five copies which were presented to schools and colleges in Cork.[7]

In deciding to have a book-length publication, O'Donoghue did Lynch no favours by including some of his acerbic and caustic critiques of other writers' work. Professor Tierney had expressed caution about that aspect of the text: 'The arrangement of the book might lead to some criticism by reviewers. Some re-editing of the material might be worthwhile in this connection.'[8]

After publication, Walter McGrath in *The Cork Examiner* condemned the harsh language used by Lynch: 'Running through many of its pages is a querulous peevishness at what Lynch considered to be a slight to the memory of the IRB men perpetrated and perpetuated by earlier writers of the 1916 period.'[9] However, McGrath did not challenge the veracity and accuracy of Lynch's account.

As well as the brief autobiographical essay and extensive criticisms of several books, *The I.R.B. and the 1916 Insurrection* contains Lynch's account of the lead-up to the Easter Rising and the progress of Easter Week as compiled by the survivors of the GPO garrison in 1936–7. In 1977, Ó Maidín wrote:

> With the execution of the leaders after the Rising went the secret history of how the Rising was planned and brought about. The survival of Lynch and his persistent efforts to record the events that led to the Rising and of the Rising itself was to be a vital record for historians of the period.[10]

Ó Maidín expressed his opinion that the subsequent book had 'become a classic source book on the secret history of how the Easter Rising was brought about'.[11] Referring to some of the main works published since 1957 concerning the Rising and the IRB, Ó Maidín's confident assertion regarding the value of Lynch's work to historians seems to be accurate.

The I.R.B. and the 1916 Insurrection is extensively quoted by authors. One publication from 1966 claimed, 'Is foinse thábhachtach é leabhar Dhiarmuid Lynch [Lynch's book is an important source of information].'[12] Its author, Pádraig Ó Snodaigh, quoted extensively from Lynch's book. In the publication *Leaders and Men of the Easter Rising: Dublin 1916*, Edward MacLysaght stated, 'Diarmuid Lynch's book, *The I.R.B. and The 1916 Rising* [*sic*] gives due credit to Connolly's part in the Rising though rightly criticising the tendency of R. M. Fox and others to detract from the IRB's major share.'[13] An account of the Rising produced by W. J. Brennan-Whitmore in 1961 was reissued in 1996, edited by Dr Pauric Travers. Travers referred often to Lynch's testimony.[14]

The editor of several highly regarded works on the Rising, F. X. Martin, came down unequivocally on the side of the veracity and authenticity of Lynch's records. In an essay to commemorate the fiftieth anniversary of the Rising in 1966, Martin quoted Lynch extensively and wrote, 'Lynch is precise in his statements and on the whole, can be relied on for accuracy.'[15] He singled Lynch's book out as one of four that merited 'special attention'.[16] On Lynch's insider position on the Supreme Council of the IRB, Martin concluded, 'One of the real values of Lynch's book is the information he gives, limited though it may be, about the IRB, the body principally responsible for the Easter Rising.'[17]

Charles Townshend implied that Lynch presented a misleading picture of the organisation of men and armaments in the lead-up to and during Easter Week.[18] He also quoted Bulmer Hobson's assertion that Lynch's account of events was Lynch's 'particular distortion'.[19] However, Townshend quoted from Lynch's reports when details were in agreement with his own conclusions.[20]

A recent work by Professor Keith Jeffery dismissed Lynch's testimony completely.[21] Jeffery may have been unaware that the original statements collected and edited painstakingly in 1936–37 by Lynch in consultation with the survivors of the

GPO garrison are archived at the National Library of Ireland (NLI).[22] Not only are the statements collected by Lynch from those who were present in the GPO in this archive but, following the expansion of the witness statement project under the Bureau of Military History, a further 1,300 statements were collected by trained interviewers. The Bureau of Military History in Cathal Brugha Barracks, Dublin, holds these later witness statements. It is difficult to understand how Jeffery or any other researcher could summarily dismiss the combined testaments of over 1,000 witnesses who were participants in the Easter Rising.

A 2010 publication by Fearghal McGarry is based predominantly on the witness statements. However, McGarry did not include Lynch's book in the bibliography of further reading, nor did he credit Lynch with organising the first witness statement programme in 1936, almost a decade before the state-sponsored one came about.[23]

Even more startling was the exclusion of any mention of Lynch in Owen McGee's monumental history of the IRB.[24] The author explained that as his account extended only to 1910, the exclusion of Lynch was understandable as he played no major role until after that date. It ignores the reality that from Lynch's first acquaintance with Devoy and Clarke in New York he was an enthusiastic and committed recruit to the Fenian and Republican tradition which both men espoused and personified. McGee singled out the founding of Sinn Féin in 1905 as a pivotal milestone in the history of the IRB, and though his lengthy concluding chapter extended to the 1918 Sinn Féin election, two IRB men are absent from the book: the executed Seán MacDiarmada, an IRB man and signatory of the 1916 Proclamation, and Supreme Council member Diarmuid Lynch, elected to Dáil Éireann in that 1918 election.

That more recent writers have dismissed, ignored or downgraded the evidence of Lynch in comparison to the prominence accorded to it by earlier historical writers is a factor in his national obscurity. What is more, Lynch's papers are scattered in several locations, and in some instances are misleadingly filed, which does not facilitate research. For example, the only known copy of the draft history of the FOIF is archived with the Florence O'Donoghue papers in the National Library in Dublin. Extensive correspondence between Lynch and O'Donoghue, and Lynch and others, is filed under an *An Cosantóir* reference in the Cork City and County Archives (CCCA).

To the end of his life, Lynch was engaged in establishing the facts and the truth in relation to all aspects of nationalist issues. On several occasions he requested the return of one or other of his reports from the Bureau of Military History. In September 1950 he requested the return of his own manuscript on the draft of Le Roux's book, *Tom Clarke and the Irish Freedom Movement*, as he wished to amend a detail of his critique.[25] Michael McDunphy, Director of the Bureau of Military History, asked for the file on Le Roux's manuscript to be returned in 1952; however, at O'Donoghue's instigation it was retained until he had completed work on *The I.R.B.* book.[26] Unfortunately when the book was published and the Bureau once more sought the return of this file it was discovered to be missing.[27]

The subscription letter sent out by the 'Diarmuid Lynch Memorial Committee' in 1951 – by men who had been intimately involved with Lynch in 1916 and in the subsequent years – was unequivocal in its estimation of the value of his records:

> He had in recent years, devoted much of his time and energy to the self-imposed task of recording some of the invaluable knowledge of the IRB which he possessed. As one of the last surviving members of the Supreme Council which decided on and planned the 1916 Rising, and as a man who had travelled the country on behalf of the organisation and represented it in the United States, his knowledge of its work was unique and comprehensive. With inflexible honesty and regard only for the truth, he had also recorded extensive comments on, and corrections of, the many errors which have appeared in published works dealing with the period.[28]

Conclusion

In March 1924, Diarmuid Lynch, the National Secretary of the FOIF, addressed the IRB Veterans' Banquet at the Hotel Astor in New York. 'Looking back now on the history of Ireland since December 1921, many are tempted to speculate on *what might have been*.'[1] In the twilight years of his own life, did Lynch entertain the same speculation with regard to his own fate?

If the bitter discord between the de Valera camp and Clan na Gael and the FOIF in America had not happened; if Lynch had thrown in his lot with his Dáil colleagues and supported de Valera in opposing Devoy and Cohalan; if he had retained his Dáil seat and returned to Ireland when the signing of the Treaty decriminalised him; if he had not remained in America as National Secretary of the FOIF, fighting court cases on behalf of that organisation; if his public life had developed in Ireland in tandem with the developing state – how would it have affected his life?

Should Lynch have resigned his Dáil seat in July 1920? In the charged atmosphere of those weeks, when trust was destroyed between de Valera and Clan na Gael and the FOIF, he decided to resign to avoid causing divisions at home in

Ireland, particularly in the small rural constituency which he represented. His resignation was also strategic; he hoped to force his Dáil colleagues in Ireland to attend to the crisis unfolding in America. However, as one of Lynch's friends, Liam De Róiste, observed in regard to his own resignation from the Dáil in 1927, 'Politically it was a great mistake on my part to retire from the Dáil. Political representatives do not "come back" in Ireland.'[2]

The Treaty of 6 December 1921 made it possible for Lynch to return to Ireland, as he was no longer a fugitive from English justice. His primary commitment then was to the FOIF which was haemorrhaging members to the rival AARIR, set up by de Valera specifically to bypass the established Irish-American triumvirate, Devoy, Cohalan and Lynch, and to destroy their grip on Irish-American funding. Another reason was that while Lynch remained in America he had an income. There was no immediate prospect of employment in Ireland, and the Lynchs did not have private means.

If Lynch had repatriated in 1923 he could have contributed considerable ability, organisational skills, leadership flair and American experience to the new Irish state. However, there was always the possibility, considering the lifelong antipathy of de Valera towards the Clan na Gael trio, that any career Lynch might have aspired to in Irish political life would have been stymied when de Valera and Fianna Fáil gained political ascendancy in 1932, the year Diarmuid and Kit Lynch returned to live in Ireland.

While Lynch was resident in Dublin there was an apparent willingness to call on him for any public ceremony relating to the Easter Rising.[3] But leaving Dublin in 1938 to live in a quiet corner of rural County Cork removed him from the day-to-day encounters with those in government at Leinster House. If his nomination to the Senate in 1944 had succeeded, perhaps he might have had a place among the publicly honoured patriot dead.

That de Valera never forgot his grievances with the Irish Americans is evident. He obsessively and repeatedly revisited the relevant documentation. 'Throughout the 1950s and 1960s de Valera's thoughts were often on his tour of the USA in 1919 and 1920, and he wanted all the information he could get on that subject.'[4] In 1957 de Valera wrote to John Finerty, who had represented him in his attempts to gain control of the bond-cert funds, seeking documents relating to the period of his American tour.[5] Again in 1963, he wanted to find out all about 'the tactics of Cohalan and Devoy'.[6] He was also anxious to purchase files of *The Gaelic American* for the years 1919–22 if the cost was reasonable.[7]

According to Patrick Murray, de Valera displayed 'a fundamental unease about some aspects of his behaviour between 1920 and 1927 which could only be assuaged by frequent exercises in self-defence and self-justification'.[8] In 1954, when O'Donoghue repeatedly requested the return of a copy of the GPO report which Lynch had sent to de Valera in 1937, the copy could not at first be found, and de Valera's response was dismissive: 'Apart from glancing over it, as I possibly did when I received it, I have not read it since.'[9]

It is clear from correspondence filed at Granig House in Tracton that Lynch retained links with his American associates.[10] Having been conferred, while still a resident in America, with the honorary vice-presidency of the AIHS, he was listed as a member into the 1940s.[11] In the 2012 synopsis of the history of the FOIF archived by the AIHS, tribute is paid to him. 'Diarmuid Lynch, the national secretary, was probably the most influential member of the FOIF. As a result of his day-to-day oversight Lynch became the predominant force within the FOIF.'[12]

In every venture Lynch undertook he showed his leadership capability. The Philo-Celtic Society acknowledged his remarkable contribution to the revival and promotion of Irish culture and language with the presentation of an illuminated scroll, delivered to his Tracton home at Easter 1939 by Eithne Keane, a member of the New York branch of the Philo-Celtic Society. The long eulogy to Lynch recorded on the embellished scroll includes the following sentiments: 'You were unceasing in promoting the culture and history of Ireland. Your Presidency of the Gaelic League of New York State was one of extraordinary success.'

At decisive junctures in the lead-up to the Rising in 1916, Lynch acted to promote the agenda of the IRB. When it was deemed necessary to oust the pacifists from the Gaelic League in 1913, and again in 1915, it was Lynch who threw down the challenge.[13] It was he who proposed setting up the ultra-secret military committee in 1915: 'About the end of May, 1915, at a meeting of the I.R.B. Executive (on which I functioned as Acting-Secretary – MacDiarmada being in prison) Pearse, Plunkett and Cennt [*sic*] were, on my motion, formally appointed a "Military Committee".'[14]

It was Lynch who travelled to Kerry in 1915 to elicit the best landing site for the German armaments, and it was Lynch whom Pearse entrusted with the oral final orders for the southern commandants of the Volunteers in January 1916. With Collins, Lynch was central to the revival of the IRB programme in 1917–18 until his deportation to America.

Lynch's unfaltering loyalty to Devoy was typical. He wrote a glowing commendation of the book *Devoy's Post Bag* to one of its compilers, William O'Brien, when a complimentary copy was sent to him in May 1948. 'My chief delight in the "Post Bag" lies in the fact that the correspondence constitutes a splendid monument to the status and stature of Devoy, and furnishes proof that Pearse's encomium, "Devoy was the greatest of the Fenians", was fully justified.'[15]

Lynch's loyalty to Devoy and Cohalan did not preclude his asserting strong opinions to both. Boland's allegation that Lynch was the 'puppet' of Cohalan, or Maloney's description of Lynch as a 'dupe' of the judge,[16] is contradicted by the tone of Lynch's frequent letters to Cohalan in times of crisis. 'J.D., Dalton and myself think it very advisable that you come down at once to talk over the situation.'[17] With firmness he further pressed, 'I believe you promised Flood that this would be attended to. Please let me know what has been done in the matter.'[18] Another letter stated, 'I am thinking of sending McHugh to Detroit and feel that he should go straight to Bishop G[allagher]. McHugh said that you are desirous that he go to Westport for a further talk but in my opinion he should go straight to Detroit.'[19]

With regard to Devoy, when Devoy accused de Valera in *The Gaelic American* of appropriating bond-cert money to pay for his Chicago Convention expenses, Lynch resigned from the directorship of that publication in protest at the scurrilous nature of Devoy's attacks.[20]

Lynch's obituary in *The Gaelic American* on 18 November 1950 described him as 'honest and incorruptible'. This was an apt choice of words. Filed in the papers of the FOIF is the record of the National Secretary's modest expenditure of approximately $3,000 for the ten years from 1921 to 1931. It is noteworthy that the greatest single expense was incurred in 1929 when it cost $950 to accompany Devoy's body back to Ireland for burial at Glasnevin and to make arrangements for the upkeep of his grave.[21]

Ironically, in the last decade of his life, Lynch gave his political allegiance to de Valera's Fianna Fáil, because it was the republican party. He canvassed for Fianna Fáil candidates in elections and 'presided at meetings during the 1943 and 1944 General Elections at the invitation of the Fianna Fáil Coiste Ceanntair'.[22]

In an exchange of letters with Professor Liam Ó Bríain of University College Galway, discussing R. M. Fox's book *Green Banners*, the professor asked whimsically, 'How is it de Valera didn't make you something?'[23]

Though he had good friends and loyal supporters in the party, Lynch remained an outsider with the Fianna Fáil elite and had no public platform, no position of significance from which to promote his political philosophy.

Financially, he was a poor man. All of the research and writing he completed were at his own expense; there was no grant on which to draw. This constant shortage of money probably curtailed the amount of research he would have liked to complete. Lack of funding was worrying him a few months before he died when he expressed his regret to the Director of the Cork Museum that he could not afford to provide a copy of the Roll of Honour compiled in 1935 for the museum's archives.

Lynch professed that he was a reluctant contributor to the letters pages of newspapers.[24] Only an attack on the FOIF, Devoy or Cohalan would compel him to appear in print in a spirited response.[25] Newspaper columns do not provide a convincing or sustainable public platform, and his work was about the past, correcting what he claimed were errors, checking and rechecking facts.

In his graveside eulogy, O'Hegarty's summary of Lynch's work for Ireland ignored his energetic and positive contribution in America to the Gaelic Revival in the years 1896–1907. Nor did his extraordinary work from 1918 to 1932, as National Secretary of the FOIF, the organisation which had a powerful impact on American–Irish relationships at a crucial time in Ireland's history, merit so much as a mention.[26]

Tellingly, Lynch introduced his draft history of the FOIF with a quote from the radical Fenian John Boyle O'Reilly: 'We can do Ireland more good by our American-ism than by our Irish-ism.'[27] However, his agenda while resident in America was always Ireland and the furtherance of Irish independence.[28] Aware that the efforts and contribution of the FOIF, Clan na Gael and Irish Americans in general might well be overlooked in the future, Lynch observed to O'Donoghue, 'If and when the history of the FOIF in America comes to be written, a fitting title might be, "A Hidden Phase of Irish History".'[29]

Some weeks after Lynch's death, his colleague on the Supreme Council of the IRB, Denis McCullough, summed up the motivation of this true Irish patriot: 'up to the day of his death he had subordinated all else to his devotion to Ireland'.[30]

Appendix I

Witness statements by Diarmuid Lynch archived at the Bureau of Military History

WS 4, Part 1: The I.R.B.: Some Recollections and Comments

WS 4, Part 2: Distribution of the Casement Pamphlet

WS 4, Part 3: Supplementary Statement on 'Easter Week', 1916

WS 120: The National Flag, 1916

WS 121: Comments on a talk by P. H. Pearse to G/Coy. 2nd Bn. I.V. on 6.2.1916

WS 364: Provisional Committee of Irish Volunteers

WS 651: The Countermanding Orders of Holy Week, 1916

BMH CD 88/6: the forty-four-page report of the survivors of the GPO garrison with a foreword written by Diarmuid Lynch, compiled in 1936–37 and submitted to the Bureau of Military History in 1947

Appendix II

Sources of materials relating to the life of Diarmuid Lynch

List of Diarmuid Lynch material in Cork Public Museum

L.1946.85.1–5, Uniform used by Lynch in the GPO in 1916 (tunic, shirt, collar, tie, trousers).

L.1946.28, Copy of charges put to Diarmuid Lynch at his court-martial, 18 May 1916, including a covering letter from Lynch.

L.1965.24, Ten-shilling note received by Lynch the day after he was sentenced to death.

L.1965.27, *The New York Times* cutting re death sentence passed on Lynch.

L.1965.29, Newspaper cutting, 27 May 1916: 'How Lynch's Life Was Saved'.

L.1965.30.04, Photograph of D. Lynch and other Volunteer leaders at the Manchester Martyrs commemoration in Cork.

L.1965.58, Typescript of Lynch's speech at his trial on 8 March 1918.

L.1965.59, Newspaper cutting: 'Lynch Is Deported'.

L.1965.78, Photograph of Diarmuid Lynch.

L.1965.79, Photograph of Diarmuid Lynch wearing a soft hat.

L.1965.80, Photograph of Michael Lynch with beard.

List of material donated by Diarmuid Lynch and family to Cork Museum, 1965

L1965.1, Typewritten account of the Siege at Clonmult, 20 February 1921, by Marjorie Aherne.

L.1965.2, Framed photograph of Seán Hurley (Ó Muirthile).

L.1965.3, Charcoal drawing of Seán Hurley (Ó Muirthile).

L.1965.4, Copy of letter from Fr Augustine to Seán Hurley's mother.

L.1965.17.1–7, Suit with kilt including cap, sporran and stockings.

L.1965.19, Satchel, Michael Lynch, Frongoch.

L.1965.20, Lee-Enfield rifle.

L.1965.21, Double-barrelled revolver.

L.1965.22, Book of cuttings from American newspapers, 1916.

L.1965.23, Book of cuttings from *An Phoblacht*, *Irish Press* and *Irish Independent*.

L.1965.25, Newspaper, *The Gaelic American*, 29 April 1916.

L.1965.26, Newspaper, *New York American*, 1917.

L.1965.28, Album, *Dublin and the Sinn Féin Rising*.

L.1965.30, Booklet, *The Rebellion in Dublin*.

L.1965.31, Book, *Catechism of Irish History* by the Christian Brothers.

L.1965.32, Souvenir of O'Donovan Rossa's funeral.

L.1965.33, Pamphlet, *Irish Bishops on English Rule*.

L.1965.34, Leaflet, 'German Catholic Leader Raises Irish Question'.

L.1965.35/36, Leaflet, 'Strike in Lewes Jail'.

L.1965.37, Leaflet, 'Pronouncement of the Most Rev. Dr O'Dwyer'.

L.1965.38, Typescript, 'Ireland and the American Civil War' by Erskine Childers.

L.1965.39, Pamphlet, *To Rebuild the Nation* by Arthur Griffith (two copies).

L.1965.39.01, Envelope addressed to Mr Michael Lynch, Frongoch Camp, North Wales.

L.1965.40.1, Booklet, *A Fragment of 1916 History*.

L.1965.40.2, Notice of internment at Frongoch to Michael Lynch.

L.1965.41.1–2, Newspaper, *Free State*, 30 August 1922 (two copies).

L.1965.42, Newspaper, *Free State*, 2 September 1922.

L.1965.43, Newspaper, *Free State*, 9 September 1922.

L.1965.44, Pamphlet, *A Page from 1916 History*.

L.1965.45, Booklet, *The Rescue of the Fenians from Australia*.

L.1965.46, Pamphlet, *John Redmond Accuses England*, 1919.

L.1965.47, Letter to Michael Lynch (Frongoch) from his sister.

L.1965.48.1–3, Letters (3) to Michael Lynch (Frongoch) from Kit.

L.1965.49, Letter to Michael Lynch (Frongoch) from 'Molly Bawn'.

L.1965.50, Letter to Michael Lynch (Frongoch) from 'Belle Bar'.

L.1965.51, Pamphlet, *The Authority of Dáil Éireann*.

L.1965.52, Pamphlet, *The Authority of Dáil Éireann* [second copy].

L.1965.53, Pamphlet, *England Dilemma*.

L.1965.54, Pamphlet, *Presidential Statement of Policy 10/4/1919*.

L.1965.55.1–2, Booklet on Dáil Éireann Session (two copies).

L.1965.56, Booklet, *Two Years of English Atrocities in Ireland*.

L.1965.57, Leaflet, 'War!! England, Germany and Ireland'.

L.1965.60, Booklet, *Religious Intolerance under Home Rule*.

L.1965.61, 'Tales of the Hillsides of Ireland no. 4'.

L.1965.62, Pamphlet, *Irish in the Schools*.

L.1965.63, Pamphlet, *Purchase of the Railways* (Sinn Féin).

L.1965.64, Pamphlet, *Arguments for the Treaty* by Arthur Griffith.

L.1965.65, Typescript, 'What Ireland Is' by Arthur Griffith.

L.1965.66, Pamphlet, *Constitution of the Irish Volunteers, 1917*.

L.1965.67, Verses, 'The Irish Volunteers' by Phil O'Neill.

L.1965.68, Correspondence re H. C. Tracton, Fr McCarthy and the National Aid Fund (three letters).

L.1965.69, Letter to all GAA clubs re National Aid Fund.

L.1965.70, Manuscript, 'The Landlord's Ten Commandments'.

L.1965.71, Copy of messages from internees re Sinn Féin tactics, etc.

L.1965.72, Receipt for 2/1 to Seán Ó Núalláin, Tracton, signed by The O'Rahilly.

L.1965.73, Receipt to M. F. Lynch for 3/–.

L.1965.74, Receipt to M. F. Lynch for 6/6 signed by Bulmer Hobson.

L.1965.75, Irish Volunteer subscription card for M. Lynch.

L.1965.76, Reply form to M. Lynch at Wakefield Prison from the YMCA.

L.1965.77, Photograph of M. Lynch in Volunteer uniform.

L.1965.81, Photograph of the 'Cuba Five'.

L.1965.82, Photograph of O'Donovan Rossa.

L.1965.83, Photograph of first Dáil meeting.

Notes

INTRODUCTION

1 Diarmuid Ó Murchadha, *Liam de Róiste*, Dublin: An Clóchomhar, 1976, p. 339.

2 Peter Hart, *Mick: The Real Michael Collins*, London: Pan Books, 2006, p. 157.

3 Gabriel Doherty and Dermot Keogh, *Michael Collins and the Making of the Irish State*, Cork: Mercier Press, 1998, p. 12.

4 Mary Lynch, personal communication, June 2012.

5   Diarmuid Lynch, *The I.R.B. and the 1916 Insurrection*, edited by Florence O'Donoghue, Cork: Mercier Press, 1957.

6   *The Gaelic American*, 18 November 1950.

1. 'THE CHILD IS FATHER OF THE MAN'

1   William Wordsworth, 'The Rainbow', 1804.

2   Richard Griffith, *General Valuation of Rateable Property in Ireland, County of Cork, Barony of Kinalea*, Dublin: G. & J. Grierson, 1851.

3   Lynch (1957), p. 2.

4   Lynch (1957), p. 2.

5   Lynch (1957), p. 3.

6   Lynch (1957), p. 4.

7   Lynch (1957), p. 3.

8   Lynch (1957), p. 4.

9   LFA, Letter from Michael McCarthy to Diarmuid Lynch, 19 December 1895.

10 LFA, Letter from Michael McCarthy to Diarmuid Lynch, 19 December 1895.

11 LFA.

12 *Dun's Review*, Vol. 3, No. 1, March 1904.

13 LFA, Letter from Maurice Fitzmahony to Diarmuid Lynch, 5 October 1950.

14 Lynch (1957), p. 4.

15 Lynch (1957), p. 4. *The American Commonwealth* was written by James Bryce and published in two volumes in 1888.

16 Lynch (1957), p. 18.

17 Lynch (1957), p. 5.

18 Lynch (1957), p. 5.

19 LFA, Letter from Diarmuid Lynch to Dan, Tim, Denis and Michael Lynch, 4 April 1899.

20 LFA, Letter from Diarmuid Lynch to Dan, Tim, Denis and Michael Lynch, 4 April 1899.

21 LFA, Letter from Diarmuid Lynch to Dan, Tim, Denis and Michael Lynch, 4 April 1899.

22 Lynch (1957), p. 8.

23 Lynch (1957), p. 6.

24 *The New York Times*, 28 March 1903; Lynch (1957), p. 6.

25 Lynch (1957), p. 5.

26 Lynch (1957), p. 8.

27 Lynch (1957), p. 10. The I.V. here is short for Irish Volunteers, the name given to the uniformed men of Clan na Gael according to Lynch.

28 'We're Buying Back Ireland', *Pittsburg Post-Gazette*, 9 June 1912.

29 NLI, MS 32,597, unpublished draft history of the Friends of Irish Freedom (FOIF) by Diarmuid Lynch, p. 257.

30 NLI, MS 32,597, FOIF history, Lynch on Daniel F. Cohalan.

31 Lynch (1957), p. 11.

32 Lynch (1957), p. 12.

33 Lynch (1957), p. 12.

34 CCCA, U271, Liam De Róiste Diaries, 30 August 1904.

35 LFA.

36 LFA.

37 LFA.

38 LFA.

39 LFA, Play programme, *An Pósadh* at Lexington Opera House, 28 April 1906, p. 7.

40 Lynch (1957), p. 17.

41 LFA, Letter from Arthur Farquhar to Diarmuid Lynch, 13 March 1907.

42 Lynch (1957), p. 18.

43 *The Cork Examiner*, 22 July 1907.

44 LFA, Letter from John W. Lynch, written on *New York Herald* notepaper, to Diarmuid Lynch, 17 July 1907.

2. IRELAND, 1907–1915

1 Kathleen Clarke, *Revolutionary Woman*, ed. Helen Litton, Dublin: O'Brien Press, 2008.

2 Clarke (2008), p. 48.

3 Clarke (2008), p. 50.

4 Charles Callan Tansill, *America and the Fight for Irish Freedom, 1866–1922: An Old Story Based Upon New Data*, New York: Devin-Adair, 1957, p. 133.

5 Lynch (1957), p. 21.

6 LFA, Letter from Richard Dalton to Diarmuid Lynch, 14 December 1907.

7 LFA, Letter from A. B. Farquhar to Diarmuid Lynch, 27 December 1907.

8 Lynch (1957), p. 20.

9 Lynch (1957), p. 21.

10 BMH WS 4, Part 1: *The I.R.B.: Some Recollections and Comments*, by Diarmuid Lynch, p. 14. Lodged with the Bureau of Military History in 1947 by Florence O'Donoghue on behalf of Diarmuid Lynch.

11 LFA, Pension Files, sworn statement presented by Diarmuid Lynch, 19 December 1944, to Military Pensions Board hearing.

12 NLI, MS 31,409, correspondence of Diarmuid Lynch (1936–1950), Letter from Lynch to O'Donoghue, 21 April 1945.

13 William O'Brien and Desmond Ryan (eds), *Devoy's Post Bag, 1871–1928*, 2 vols., Dublin: C. J. Fallon, 1948–53, vol. II, p. 396.

14 Lynch (1957), p. 26.

15 BMH, WS 4, Part 1, *The I.R.B.*, pp. 12–13.

16 List of active Volunteers (1915) supplied by Captain James Cotter, 9th Battalion, Cork No. 1 Brigade, to Department of Defence, Military Service Pensions, 1934.

17 Florence O'Donoghue, *Tomás MacCurtain*, Tralee: Kerryman, 1958, p. 55.

18 Breandán MacGiolla Choille, 'Review of Intelligence Notes, 1913–16, Preserved in the State Paper Office', *Irish Historical Studies*, 16 (61) (1968): 99–102.

19 Lynch (1957), p. 27.

20 Lynch (1957), p. 24.

21 LFA, Letter from Diarmuid Lynch to Michael Lynch, 4 March 1914.

22 Pearse speech, delivered in New York on 9 March 1914, published by the Kilmainham Gaol Historical Museum in 1975.

23 LFA, Newspaper cutting, 'Heard in Knighthood', *The Columbiad*, 1914.

24 *Irish-American*, 9 April 1914.

25 LFA, *Boston Globe* newspaper cutting, 18 May 1914.

26 John Devoy, *Recollections of an Irish Rebel; the Fenian Movement; personalities of the organization; the Clan-Na-Gael and the Rising of Easter Week, 1916: A Personal Narrative*, New York: Charles Young, 1929, p. 393.

27 *The Gaelic American*, 3 October 1914, p. 1.

28 AIHS, FOIF Papers, Letter from Gaelic League of Ireland to Diarmuid Lynch, 7 October 1914.

29 Lynch (1957), pp. 24–5.

30 Lynch (1957), p. 25.

31 Letter from Tomás Ághas to John Devoy, 27 April 1914, in O'Brien and Ryan (1948–53), vol. II, p. 427.

32 Lynch (1957), p. 27.

33 Lynch (1957), p. 28.

34 Charles Townshend, *Easter 1916*, London: Penguin, 2006, p. 94.

35 BMH, WS 4, Part 1: *The I.R.B.*, p. 4.

36 Louis N. Le Roux, *Tom Clarke and the Irish Freedom Movement*, Dublin: Talbot Press, 1936, p. 170: 'Tom Clarke and Diarmuid Lynch may be said to comprise the Executive of the IRB at this time, for Seán Mac Diarmada was in prison.'

37 BMH, WS 4, Part 1: *The I.R.B.*, p. 4.

38 Lynch (1957), p. 28.

39 BMH, WS 4, Part 3: *Supplementary Statement on 'Easter Week' 1916*, pp. 1–2.

40 BMH, WS 4, Part 2: *Distribution of the Casement Pamphlet*, p. 1.

41 NLI, LO 1530, Main Reading Room, *Casement Pamphlet*.

42 NLI, LO 1530, Main Reading Room, *Casement Pamphlet*.

43 Lynch (1957), pp. 39–40.

44 Lynch (1957), p. 40.

45 Lynch (1957), p. 41.

46 Lynch (1957), p. 43.

47 Lynch (1957), p. 42.

48 *Irish Independent*, 20 September 1915.

49 Kevin Girvin, *Seán O'Hegarty: Officer Commanding, First Cork Brigade, Irish Republican Army*, Aubane: Aubane Historical Society, 2007, p. 156.

3. 1916

1 Lynch (1957), p. 30.

2 BMH, WS 4, Part 3: *Supplementary Statement on 'Easter Week' 1916*.

3 Terry Golway, *Irish Rebel: John Devoy and America's Fight for Ireland's Freedom*, New York: St Martin's Press, 1998, p. 226.

4 BMH, WS 4, Part 3: *Supplementary Statement on 'Easter Week' 1916*, p. 2.

5   Lynch (1957), pp. 183–4.

6   BMH, WS 121, p. 2.

7   T. Desmond Williams, 'Eoin MacNeill and the Irish Volunteers', in F. X. Martin (ed.), *Leaders and Men of the Easter Rising: Dublin 1916*, London: Methuen & Co., 1967, p. 144.

8   BMH, WS 651, *The Countermanding Orders of Holy Week, 1916*, p. 6.

9   Lynch (1957), p. 184.

10   Lynch (1957), p. 53.

11   Lynch (1957), p. 185.

12   Desmond Ryan, *The Rising: The Complete Story of Easter Week*, Dublin: Golden Eagle Books, 1949, p. 153.

13   Max Caulfield, *The Easter Rebellion*, Dublin: Gill & Macmillan, 1995, p. 256.

14   LFA, copy of record sheet designed by Diarmuid Lynch, 1935.

15   BMH, CD88/6, *Report on Operation Easter Week with foreword by Diarmuid Lynch, 1937.*

16   BMH, WS 4, Part 3: *Supplementary Statement on 'Easter Week' 1916.*

17   CCCA, U179, *An Cosantóir* Files, Letter from Diarmuid Lynch to Donagh MacDonagh, 14 December 1944.

18   BMH, WS 4, Part 3: *Supplementary Statement on 'Easter Week' 1916*, p. 4.

19   BMH, WS 4, Part 3: *Supplementary Statement on 'Easter Week' 1916*, pp. 4–5.

20   BMH, WS 4, Part 3: *Supplementary Statement on 'Easter Week' 1916*, p. 5.

21   Seán MacEntee, *Episode at Easter*, Dublin: Gill and Son, 1966, pp. 146–7.

22   BMH, WS 4, Part 3: *Supplementary Statement on 'Easter Week' 1916*, p. 5.

23 BMH, WS 4, Part 3: *Supplementary Statement on 'Easter Week' 1916*, p. 6.

24 Lynch (1957), p. 167.

25 BMH, WS 4, Part 3: *Supplementary Statement on 'Easter Week' 1916*, p. 6.

26 BMH, WS 4, Part 3: *Supplementary Statement on 'Easter Week' 1916*, p. 6.

27 MacEntee (1966).

28 BMH, WS 4, Part 3: *Supplementary Statement on 'Easter Week' 1916*, p. 7.

29 David Fitzpatrick, *Harry Boland's Irish Revolution*, Cork: Cork University Press, 2003, pp. 42–3.

30 Ryan (1949), p. 153.

31 Ryan (1949), p. 143.

32 Lynch (1957), p. 148 – a thorough dissection of Desmond Ryan's book *The Rising* is given in pp. 110–49.

33 Lynch (1957), p. 148.

34 Lynch (1957), p. 179.

35 LFA, Letter to Florence O'Donoghue from Lynch, May 1945.

36 BMH, WS 4, Part 3: *Supplementary Statement on 'Easter Week' 1916*, note on p. 1.

37 BMH, WS 4, Part 3: *Supplementary Statement on 'Easter Week' 1916*, p. 8.

38 Lynch (1957), p. 107.

39 BMH, WS 4, Part 3: *Supplementary Statement on 'Easter Week' 1916*, p. 8.

40 BMH, WS 4, Part 3: *Supplementary Statement on 'Easter Week' 1916*, p. 8.

41 BMH, WS 4, Part 3: *Supplementary Statement on 'Easter Week' 1916*, p. 8.

42 Lynch (1957), p. 180.

43 BMH, CD88/6.

44 *Sinn Féin Rebellion Handbook*, compiled by the *Weekly Irish Times*, Dublin: Fred Hanna, 1917, p. 13.

45 *Sinn Féin Rebellion Handbook*, p. 14.

46 LFA, Letter from Diarmuid Lynch to Edward L. Adams, via Denis Lynch, May 1916.

47 BMH, WS 4, Part 3: *Supplementary Statement on 'Easter Week' 1916*, p. 7.

48 BMH, WS 4, Part 3: *Supplementary Statement on 'Easter Week' 1916*, p. 11.

49 Ryan (1949), p. 125.

50 Lynch (1957), p. 141.

51 Desmond Fitzgerald, *Desmond's Rising: Memoirs, 1913 to Easter 1916*, Dublin: Liberties Press, 2006, pp. 135–7. Originally published in 1986 under the title *Memoirs of Desmond FitzGerald, 1913–1916*.

52 BMH, WS 4, Part 3: *Supplementary Statement on 'Easter Week' 1916*, p. 12.

4. COURT MARTIAL AND IMPRISONMENT

1 Cork Museum, Gift No. 102 (original charge slip on permanent loan to museum from Diarmuid Lynch, 17 July 1946).

2 BMH, WS 4, Part 3: *Supplementary Statement on 'Easter Week' 1916*, p. 12

3 *Daily Telegraph*, New York, Saturday, 20 May 1916.

4 Bríd Duggan Archives, Letter from Diarmuid Lynch to his brother Denis, Sunday 21 May 1916.

5 Consul Edward L. Adams' report to Secretary Robert Lansing, December 1916, 'Matters relating to internal affairs of Great Britain, 1910–29', 841.00/5–85, microcopy 580, Roll 6.

6 Owen Dudley Edwards, 'American Aspects of the Rising', in

Owen Dudley Edwards and Fergus Pyle (eds), *1916: The Easter Rising*, London: MacGibbon & Kee, 1968, p. 162.

7   LFA, Letter from a law officer at Dublin Castle to Sir John Maxwell, 18 May 1916.

8   LFA, Letter from a law officer at Dublin Castle to Sir John Maxwell, 18 May 1916.

9   LFA, Letter from Alice Lynch to Diarmuid Lynch, 12 January 1917.

10 LFA, List and letter of acknowledgement from Séamus Ó Coigligh, Curator, to Diarmuid Lynch (nephew), 3 December 1965.

11 Brian Barton, *From Behind a Closed Door: Secret Court Martial Records of the 1916 Easter Rising*, Belfast: Blackstaff Press, 2002, p. 70.

12 Bríd Duggan Archives, Letter from HM Prison Dartmoor to Denis Lynch, 25 August 1916.

13 LFA, Letter from Jeremiah (Diarmuid) Lynch, Prisoner No. 30, Dartmoor, to Mary Lynch, 29 May 1916.

14 LFA, Letter dated 8 November 1916 from Diarmuid to Denis referring to the October visit of Mary and the two Murphy ladies to Dartmoor.

15 LFA, Letter from Mary Lynch to the Right Honourable H. Samuel, October 1916.

16 LFA, Letter from the Home Office to Mary Lynch, 14 November 1916.

17 LFA, Letter from Dr Thomas J. Murphy, Grand Parade, Cork city, to Diarmuid Lynch, undated.

18 LFA, Letter dated 16 November 1916 to Mary Lynch from the Home Office, Whitehall (Whitehall ref, 314, 159/2).

19 LFA, Letter from Denis Lynch to Diarmuid Lynch, 20 November 1916.

20 LFA, Letter from Diarmuid Lynch to Herbert Samuel, British Home Secretary, 30 October 1916.

21 LFA, Letter from Richard Dalton to Denis Lynch, 5 December 1916.

22 Robert Brennan, *Allegiance: An Account of the Author's Experiences in the Struggle for Irish Independence*, Dublin: Browne and Nolan, 1950, pp. 110–11.

23 Brennan (1950), p. 109.

24 LFA, Letter from Denis Lynch to Richard Dalton, 20 December 1916.

25 LFA, Letter from Diarmuid Lynch to Dan Lynch, 18 December 1916.

26 LFA, Letter from Diarmuid Lynch to Dan Lynch, 18 December 1916.

27 LFA.

28 Fitzpatrick (2003), p. 63.

29 Brennan (1950), Chapter 12.

30 LFA, postcard dated 17 March 1917.

31 UCLA, Madge Daly Papers, Folder 14, Letter from Diarmuid Lynch to Madge Daly, 24 April 1917.

32 Piaras Béaslaí, *Michael Collins and the Making of a New Ireland*, 2 vols., Dublin: Phoenix, 1926, vol. 1, pp. 157–8.

33 Michael Doorley, *Irish-American Diaspora Nationalism: The Friends of Irish Freedom, 1916–35*, Dublin: Four Courts Press, 2005, pp. 66–7.

5. 'THE MOST SENIOR IRB LEADER'

1 John Borgonovo, 'Evolution of a Revolution, Cork City, 1916–1918', PhD thesis, UCC, 2009, p. 27.

2 John Borgonovo, '"Thoughtless young people" and "The battle of Patrick Street": Cork City Riots of June 1917', *Journal of the Cork Historical and Archaeological Society*, 114 (2009), pp. 13–14.

3 *Cork Constitution*, 26 June 1917.

4   LFA, Election notification and data.

5   Béaslaí (1926), vol. 1, p. 161.

6   *Sunday Independent*, 26 August 1945.

7   NLI, MS 33,930, Piaras Béaslaí Papers, Folders 4–6, Letter from Diarmuid Lynch to Piaras Béaslaí, 7 August 1925.

8   Andrew Brasier and John Kelly, *Harry Boland: A Man Divided*, Dublin: New Century Publishing, 2000, p. 57.

9   Thomas J. Morrissey, SJ, *William O'Brien, 1881–1968*, Dublin: Four Courts Press, 2007, p. 131.

10 J. Bowyer Bell, *The Secret Army: A History of the IRA, 1916–1970*, London: Blond, 1970, p. 142.

11 CCCA, U179, *An Cosantóir*, File 6.

12 CCCA, U179, File 2, Letter from Diarmuid Lynch to Florence O'Donoghue, 7 January 1945.

13 CCCA, U179, File 2, Letter from Diarmuid Lynch to Florence O'Donoghue, 7 January 1945.

14 O'Donoghue (1958), p. 205.

15 Tim Pat Coogan, *De Valera: Long Fellow, Long Shadow*, London: Hutchinson, 1993, p. 98.

16 Dorothy Macardle, *The Irish Republic: A Documented Chronicle of the Anglo-Irish Conflict and the Partitioning of Ireland, with a Detailed Account of the Period 1916–1923*, 4th edn, Dublin: Irish Press, 1951, p. 242.

17 *The Gaelic American*, 23 February 1918.

18 Charles Dalton, *With the Dublin Brigade (1917–1921)*, London: Peter Davies, 1929.

19 Darrell Figgis, *Recollections of the Irish War*, London: Ernest Benn, 1927, p. 177.

20 LFA, newspaper cuttings from *The Irish Times* and *The Cork Examiner*.

21 Cork Museum, Diarmuid Lynch Collection, L.1965.58, original

typescript of Lynch's speech at his trial on 8 March 1918.

22 *The Irish Times* reported on this event under the heading 'Lawlessness in Dublin' on 22 February 1918.

23 LFA, Letter from Diarmuid Lynch to Mary Lynch, 11 March 1918.

24 LFA, Letter from Diarmuid Lynch to Mary Lynch, 11 March 1918.

25 LFA, Letter from Diarmuid Lynch to Mary Lynch, 11 March 1918.

26 Bríd Duggan, personal communication, April 2012.

27 Cork Museum, Diarmuid Lynch Collection, L.1965.75. The note is one of over 100 items of historical interest relating to the Lynch brothers, Diarmuid and Michael, most of which were donated to the Cork Museum in 1965 by Michael's son, Diarmuid, as part of the 1966 Commemoration Exhibition.

28 BMH, WS 821, p. 30.

29 Michael Brennan, *The War in Clare, 1911–1921: Personal Memoirs of the Irish War of Independence*, Dublin: Four Courts Press and Irish Academic Press, 1980, p. 34.

30 Earnán De Blaghad, *Gaeil Á Múscailt*, Dublin: Sáirséal agus Dill, 1973, pp. 169–70.

31 LFA, Pension files.

32 *The Gaelic American*, 22 June 1918.

33 LFA, Letter from Kit Quinn to Mary Lynch, 30 April 1918.

34 Bríd Duggan, personal communication, February 2012.

35 LFA, Letter from T. J. Gill to Mary Lynch, 2 July 1918.

36 Bríd Duggan Archives, Letter to Denis Lynch from Diarmuid Lynch, 2 July 1918.

37 Bríd Duggan Archives, Letter from Kit Lynch to Alice Lynch, 23 June 1918.

38 LFA, Letter from Diarmuid and Kit Lynch to Mary Lynch, 3 October 1918.

39 LFA, Letter from Diarmuid and Kit Lynch to Mary Lynch, 3 October 1918.

40 LFA, Letter from Diarmuid and Kit Lynch to Mary Lynch, 3 October 1918.

6. AMERICA: SETTING THE SCENE

1 LFA, Pension files, Ref: 497.

2 Mark Hennessy, 'US Envoys Plot to Deport "Dangerous Agitator"', *The Irish Times*, 6 July 2011.

3 National Archives, Kew, London, War Cabinet Memorandum, GT 8227, 25 September 1918.

4 President Woodrow Wilson stated this in his address to Congress on 2 April 1917.

5 NLI, MS 32,597, FOIF history.

6 Doorley (2005), p. 74.

7 NLI, MS 49,415, Autograph letter from Liam Mellows to his brother Barney Mellows, 4 November 1917.

8 NLI, MS 32,597, FOIF history, Convention Minutes, pp. 317–18.

9 LFA, Telegram from Diarmuid Lynch to Kit Lynch, 14 May 1918.

10 *The Gaelic American*, 25 May 1918.

11 *The Gaelic American*, 9 June 1918.

12 NLI, MS 13,141, Peter Golden Papers, Letter from Liam Mellows to Peter Golden, 26 August 1918.

13 Patrick McCartan, *With De Valera in America: An Account of Irish Republican Propaganda in the United States, 1918–21*, Dublin: Fitzpatrick, 1932, pp. 68–9.

14 Doorley (2005), p. 196.

15 NLI, MS 32,597, FOIF history.

16 NLI, MS 32,597, FOIF history.

17 NLI, MS 32,597, FOIF history.

18 Tansill (1957), p. 280.

19 AIHS, FOIF Papers, *Report on Congressional Hearing*.

20 Doorley (2005), p. 116.

21 Doorley (2005), p. 93.

22 USA Congressional Records, LV11, 5057, 4 March 1919.

23 AIHS, FOIF Papers, Treasurer's reports.

24 NLI, MS 32,597, FOIF history.

25 Lawrence Ginnell, *The Irish Republic, Why?* New York: The Friends of Irish Freedom, 1919.

26 AIHS, Daniel F. Cohalan Papers.

27 Tansill (1957), p. 302.

28 LFA, Magazine report on banquet.

29 AIHS, FOIF Papers, Incorporation files.

30 AIHS, FOIF Papers, Letter from Richard Wolfe to Diarmuid Lynch, 28 September 1919.

31 LFA, Letter from Robert Brennan to Diarmuid Lynch, 13 November 1918.

32 Lynch (1957) plates 10 and 13 are copies of letters sent from Collins, Griffith and Cathal Brugha to Diarmuid Lynch, 15 February and 6 March 1919.

33 NLI, MS 32,597, FOIF history.

34 Tansill (1957), p. 336.

35 AIHS, FOIF Papers, Washington Bureau files.

36 AIHS, FOIF Papers, Washington Bureau files, Document, 7 May 1919.

37 Daniel O'Connell, 'Irish Influence on American Policy', in William G. Fitzgerald (ed.), *The Voice of Ireland: A Survey of the Race and Nation from All Angles by the Foremost Leaders at Home and Abroad*, Dublin: Virtue & Co., 1923, p. 237.

38 LFA, Letters from Diarmuid and Kit Lynch to Mary Lynch, January–July 1919.

39 Lynch (1957), p. 198.

40 Lynch (1957), p. 198.

41 J. J. Splain, 'The Irish Movement in the United States since 1911', in Fitzgerald (1923), p. 231.

7. THE SLIDE TOWARDS DESTRUCTION

1 NLI, MS 13,141, Peter Golden Papers, Letter from Liam Mellows to Peter Golden, 8 August 1919.

2 BMH, WS 1207, Biographical note on Liam Mellows by Alfred White.

3 Lynch (1957), p. 209.

4 Doorley (2005), p. 108; the laws prohibited the sale of bonds of a country which had no official international recognition.

5 AIHS, FOIF Papers, Minutes of FOIF meeting, 25 June 1919.

6 NLI, MS 32,597, FOIF history, p. 270.

7 NLI, MS 32,597, FOIF history.

8 NLI, MS 32,597, FOIF history.

9 AIHS, FOIF Papers, Newsletter.

10 *Irish Press*, 9 October 1919.

11 NLI, MS 32,597, FOIF history.

12 *Chicago Daily Tribune*, 13 July 1919.

13 UCDA, Éamon de Valera Papers.

14 UCDA, Éamon de Valera Papers.

15 AIHS, Colahan Papers, Letter from John Devoy to Harry Boland, 6 September 1919.

16 AIHS, FOIF Papers, Minutes of National Council meeting, 3 October 1919.

17 AIHS, FOIF Papers, Minutes of meeting, 9 February 1920.

18 AIHS, FOIF Papers, Minutes of meeting, 9 February 1920.

19 Dave Hannigan, *De Valera in America: The Rebel President's 1919 Campaign*, Dublin: The O'Brien Press, 2008, p. 131.

20 LFA, Letter from Terence MacSwiney to Diarmuid Lynch, 6 December 1919.

21 Fitzpatrick (2003), p. 149.

22 AIHS, National Council FOIF minutes, 10 December 1919.

23 Department of Irish Foreign Policy, 30, NAI DE 2/245.

24 UCDA, Éamon de Valera Papers, P150/1125.

25 Letter from John Devoy to John McGarry, 26 February 1920. In McCartan (1932), p. 165.

26 LFA, Letter from Joe McGuinness to Diarmuid Lynch, 7 February 1920.

27 *Westminster Gazette*, 7 February 1920.

28 LFA, 15 April 1920.

29 Doorley (2005), p. 127

30 NLI, MS 32,597, FOIF history. Letter from James O'Mara to Diarmuid Lynch, 10 April 1920.

31 *Irish Independent*, 19 October 1920.

32 Katherine O'Doherty, *Assignment America*, New York: De Tanko Publishers, 1957, pp. 142.

33 Doorley (2005), p. 127.

34 AIHS, FOIF Papers, Meeting at Washington Bureau, 22 May 1920.

35 NLI, MS 32,597, FOIF history.

36 McCartan (1932), p. 191.

37 Doorley (2005), p. 129.

38 Coogan (1993), p. 180.

39 *Irish Press*, 26 June 1920.

40 NLI, Dáil Éireann Report on Foreign Affairs, Section 2, June 1920.

41 Hannigan (2008), p. 224.

42 *Philadelphia Public Ledger*, 12 July 1920.

43 NLI, MS 31,403, Florence O'Donoghue Papers, newspaper articles on seized letters.

44 NLI, MS 31,403, Florence O'Donoghue Papers, newspaper articles on seized letters.

45 NLI, MS 31,405, Diarmuid Lynch Papers, Letter from Peter MacSwiney to Terence MacSwiney.

46 UCDA, Éamon de Valera Papers, P150/728, Letter from Arthur Griffith to Daniel F. Cohalan and John Devoy, 23 June 1920.

47 AIHS, FOIF Papers, Letter from Diarmuid Lynch to Daniel F. Cohalan, 13 July 1920.

48 Dáil Éireann, Parliamentary Debates, vol. I, 6 August 1920.

49 NLI, MS 33,930, Piaras Béaslaí Papers.

50 Lynch (1957), pp. 211–13.

51 UCDA, Éamon de Valera Papers, P150, Letter from Diarmuid Lynch to Éamon de Valera, 19 July 1920.

52 LFA, Letter from Kit Lynch to Lynch family members, 28 July 1920.

53 NLI, MS 32,597, FOIF history, p. 412.

54 UCDA, Éamon de Valera Papers, P150, Cablegram from Arthur Griffith to Éamon de Valera, 1 July 1920.

55 UCDA, Éamon de Valera Papers, P150, Cablegram from Michael Collins to Harry Boland, 14 August 1920.

56 State Papers, D/E series, Michael Collins to Arthur Griffith, 20 July 1920; Diarmuid Lynch told Florence O'Donoghue in 1947 that the *Bulletin* got to him anyway, through 'underground' means; CCCA, U179, Letter from Diarmuid Lynch to Florence O'Donoghue, 17 May 1947.

57 *The Cork Examiner*, 2 August 1920.

58 Béaslaí (1926), vol. II, p. 15.

59 *Irish Press*, 4 July 1920.

60 *Irish Press*, 17 July 1920.

61 *Irish Press*, 28 August 1920.

62 *Irish Press*, 25 July 1920.

63 *Irish Press*, 4 August 1920.

64 *Irish Press*, 7 August 1920.

65 AIHS, FOIF Papers.

66 AIHS, Daniel F. Cohalan Papers, Letter from Diarmuid Lynch to Daniel F. Cohalan, 20 August 1920.

67 AIHS, Daniel F. Cohalan Papers, Letter from Diarmuid Lynch to Daniel F. Cohalan, 20 August 1920.

68 AIHS, Daniel F. Cohalan Papers, Letter from Diarmuid Lynch to Daniel F. Cohalan, 20 August 1920.

8. THE FALL-OUT CONTINUES

1 AIHS, FOIF Papers.

2 AIHS, FOIF Papers.

3 AIHS, Daniel F. Cohalan Papers, Letter from Diarmuid Lynch to Daniel F. Cohalan, 7 August 1920.

4 *Irish World*, Editorial, 3 July 1920.

5 *The Gaelic American*, 4 September 1920.

6 *New York American*, 3 August 1920.

7 AIHS, FOIF Papers, Letter from Edward Dunne to John Devoy, 7 September 1920.

8 AIHS, FOIF Papers, Minutes of National Council meeting, 17 September 1920.

9 AIHS, FOIF Papers, Minutes of National Council meeting, 17 September 1920.

10 AIHS, FOIF Papers, Minutes of National Council meeting, 17 September 1920.

11 Golway (1998), p. 282.

12 AIHS, FOIF Papers, Minutes of meeting, 20 October 1920.

13 McCartan (1932), pp. 216–17.

14 Lynch (1957), p. 198.

15 Béaslaí (1926), vol. II, p. 18.

16 NLI, MS 32,597, FOIF history.

17 Lynch (1957), p. 214.

18 *Irish Independent*, 19 October 1920.

19 NLI, MS 32,597, FOIF history, p. 315.

20 *The Freeman's Journal*, 2 December 1920.

21 *Irish Independent*, 21 January 1921.

22 *The Freeman's Journal*, 23 December 1920, p. 3.

23 *The Gaelic American*, 20 December 1920.

24 AIHS, FOIF Papers, 19 November 1920 Newsletter.

25 AIHS, FOIF Papers, 19 November 1920 Newsletter.

26 AIHS, FOIF Papers, from Bishop's Residence, Detroit, Mich., 9 April 1921.

27 *Irish World*, 9 December 1921.

28 *The New York Times*, 9 December 1921.

29 LFA, Letter from Muriel MacSwiney to Diarmuid and Kit Lynch, October 1920.

30 AIHS, FOIF Papers, Western Union telegram, 26 August.

31 LFA, Letters from Diarmuid Lynch to Muriel MacSwiney, 15 December 1920.

32 LFA, Photograph, taken 20 November 1920 in Rathgar, Dublin.

33 *New York American*, 20 August 1921.

34 *New York American*, 20 August 1921.

35 AIHS, Daniel F. Cohalan Papers, Letter from John Devoy to Daniel F. Cohalan, 17 August 1921.

36 Golway (1998), p. 298.

37 *The New York Times*, 8 December 1921.

38 *The Freeman's Journal*, 29 December 1921.

39 *The New York Times*, 8 January 1922.

40 AIHS, FOIF Papers, Letter from John Devoy to Michael Collins, February 1922.

41 Letter from Michael Collins to John Devoy, February 1922; quoted in Golway (1998), p. 302.

42 Doorley (2005), p. 145.

43 *The Cork Examiner*, 25 August 1922.

44 The *Irish Independent*, *The Cork Examiner*, the *Belfast News* and *The Freeman's Journal*.

45 AIHS, FOIF Papers, Box 4, 'Publicity Campaigns'.

46 *Irish World*, 26 October 1922.

47 *The Gaelic American*, 18 November 1950.

48 NLI, MS 32,597, FOIF history.

49 AIHS, FOIF Papers, Minutes of meeting, 7 January 1923.

50 LFA, Lynch couple's passport, stamped 13 March 1923.

51 Bríd Duggan, *Diarmuid Lynch Tells of Trip to Ireland*, New York: Allied Printers, 31 December 1923, pp. 1–2.

9. THE NATIONAL SECRETARY SOLDIERS ON

1 AIHS, FOIF Papers, Minutes of meeting, 29 October 1923.

2 *The Gaelic American*, 22 March 1924.

3 *The Gaelic American*, 28 June 1924.

4 *The Gaelic American*, 28 June 1924.

5 AIHS, FOIF Papers, Secretary's report, 10 July 1924.

6 LFA, Seating arrangement for testimonial dinner, 17 July 1924.

7 AIHS, FOIF Papers, Letter to members from Diarmuid Lynch, 21 October 1924.

8 AIHS, FOIF Papers, Minutes of meeting, 26 November 1926.

9 AIHS, FOIF Papers, Minutes of meeting, 26 November 1926.

10 NLI, MS 33,930, Piaras Béaslaí Papers, Folders 4–6.

11 NLI, MS 33,930, Piaras Béaslaí Papers, Folders 4–6.

12 NLI, MS 33,930, Piaras Béaslaí Papers, Folders 4–6.

13 LFA, Copy of Diarmuid Lynch's address, 29 September 1925.

14 LFA.

15 AIHS, FOIF Papers, 1925.

16 Bríd Duggan Archives, Letter from Diarmuid Lynch to Denis Lynch, 21 June 1927.

17 AIHS, Daniel F. Cohalan Papers, Letter from Diarmuid Lynch to Daniel F. Cohalan, 14 September 1927.

18 LFA, Script for Radio Athlone, *A Talk on Devoy* by Diarmuid Lynch, May 1936.

19 Lynch (1957), p. 10.

20 Address delivered at Westminster Hotel, Boston, Mass., on 8 March 1921.

21 AIHS, Daniel F. Cohalan Papers, Letter from Pádraig Pearse to John Devoy, 28 December 1914.

22 Pádraig Pearse, 'Oration of P. H. Pearse over the Grave of O'Donovan Rossa, August 1915', in Eleanor Hull, *A History of Ireland and Her People*, 2 vols, Dublin: The Phoenix Publishing Company Limited, 1926–31. Pearse's speech is quoted in full in vol. 2, appendix 2.

23 NLI, MS 32,597, FOIF history.

24 AIHS, FOIF Papers, Letter from National Secretary Lynch to approximately twenty people, 23 February 1925.

25 Seán Ó Lúing, *John Devoy*, Dublin: Cló Morainn, 1961, pp. 188–9.

26 AIHS, FOIF Papers.

27 AIHS, FOIF Papers, Letter from Diarmuid Lynch to Peter Devoy, December 1928.

28 AIHS, FOIF Papers, Minutes of meeting, 27 November 1931.

29 F. M. Carroll, *Money for Ireland: Finance, Diplomacy, Politics and the First Dáil Éireann Loans, 1919–1936*, Westport, Conn.: Praeger, 2002, p. 35.

30 Carroll (2002), p. 50.

31 Hannigan (2008), p. 281.

32 Carroll (2002), appendix V.

33 NLI, MS 32,597, FOIF history, p. 367, Lynch's italics.

34 NLI, MS 32,597, FOIF history, p. 244.

35 NLI, MS 32,597, FOIF history, p. 595.

36 AIHS, FOIF Papers, Minutes, 5 April 1929.

37 AIHS, FOIF Papers, Box 2. (Typescript manuscript is archived.)

38 NLI, MS 32,597, FOIF history, p. 119.

39 NLI, MS 32,597, FOIF history, p. 119.

40 NLI, MS 32,597, FOIF history, p. 119.

41 Florence O'Donoghue, 'Diarmuid Lynch as National Secretary, Friends of Irish Freedom, Part 1', in Lynch (1957), p. 218.

42 AIHS, FOIF Papers, Letter from Michael Collins to Diarmuid Lynch, 28 July 1919.

43 AIHS, FOIF Papers, File St Enda's, Folder 4.

44 NLI, MS 32,597, FOIF history, Report on court proceedings.

45 NLI, MS 32,597, FOIF history, p. 547.

46 NLI, MS 32,597, FOIF history, p. 245.

47 NLI, MS 32,597, FOIF history, p. 245.

48 LFA, Letter from Frank Fahy to Diarmuid Lynch, 22 July 1927.

49 AIHS, FOIF Papers, Minutes of meetings.

50 LFA, Minutes of meeting of FOIF Executive, 16 July 1930.

51 AIHS, FOIF Papers, Minutes of meeting of FOIF National Executive, 27 November 1931.

52 AIHS, FOIF Papers, Minutes of meeting, 21 December 1931.

10. 'WE'RE HOME FOR GOOD'

1 LFA, Letter from Diarmuid Lynch to Mary Lynch, 11 August 1918.

2 LFA, Letter from Kit Lynch to Mary Lynch, 23 January 1919.

3 NLI, Piaras Béaslaí Papers, Letter from Diarmuid Lynch to Piaras Béaslaí, 7 August 1925.

4 AIHS, FOIF Papers, Minutes, 27 July 1932.

5 LFA, Minutes of FOIF meeting held at 280 Broadway, Wednesday 27 July 1932.

6   LFA, Letter from Diarmuid Lynch to Michael McGreal, 29 November 1932.

7   LFA, Telegram from Diarmuid Lynch to Richard Dalton, 20 December 1932, 'We're home for good.'

8   NLI, MS 32,597, FOIF history.

9   NLI, MS 32,597, FOIF history, Introduction.

10 LFA, The Mallow Book.

11 LFA, The Mallow Book, Letter from Diarmuid Lynch to Seán O'Hegarty, 10 October 1934.

12 LFA, Letter from John Lynch to Kit Lynch, 26 October 1932.

13 NLI, MS 32,597, FOIF history, Proposed Preface.

14 LFA, Letter from Diarmuid Lynch to Richard Dalton, 27 September 1934.

15 LFA, Letter from Diarmuid Lynch to Richard Dalton, 27 September 1934.

16 NLI, MS 31,405, Florence O'Donoghue Papers, Scrapbooks compiled by Diarmuid Lynch.

17 LFA, Letter from Diarmuid Lynch to Richard Dalton, 15 May 1935.

18 LFA, Letter from James McGurrin to Diarmuid Lynch, 21 August 1935.

19 LFA, Letter from Richard Dalton to Diarmuid Lynch, 5 February 1936.

20 LFA, Letter from Richard Dalton to Diarmuid Lynch, 12 February 1936.

21 LFA, Letter from Diarmuid Lynch to Richard Dalton, 4 March 1936.

22 Lynch (1957), Plate 7.

23 *Irish Independent*, Report on Diarmuid Lynch's talk in the GPO, 22 April 1935.

24 NLI, MS 11,131, Boxed witness statements.

25 CCCA U179, Letters arranging meeting 'at the corner of Henry Street and Henry Place on 22 May'. Correspondents included Liam Cullen, Liam Daly, Jim Ryan and John Twamley.

26 BMH, CD88/6.

27 LFA, Letter from Easter Week Commemoration Committee to Diarmuid Lynch, 22 April 1936.

28 NLI, MS 31,409, Florence O'Donoghue Papers.

29 Le Roux (1936).

30 LFA, Letter from Diarmuid Lynch to James McGurrin, 3 June 1946.

31 NLI, MS 11,126.

32 NLI, MS 31,409, Florence O'Donoghue Papers, Diarmuid Lynch correspondence.

33 See, for example, *Irish Press*, December 1937, sequence of letters concerning the Fenian James Stephens.

34 LFA, Pension files.

35 Military Service Pension Act, Army Pensions Board, 1934, p. 2, clause (a).

36 Information provided by the Army Pensions Board on the official application form.

37 LFA, Pension files.

38 Lynch (1957), Plates 10 and 13.

39 Carroll (2002), p. 16.

40 Lynch (1957), p. 197 and Plate 11.

41 UCDA, Éamon de Valera Papers, P150, Letter from Éamon de Valera to the Military Pensions Board, 19 April 1937.

42 UCDA, Éamon de Valera Papers, P150, Letter from Éamon de Valera to the Military Pensions Board, 19 April 1937.

43 LFA, Pension files.

44 LFA, Pension files, Letter from Diarmuid Lynch to Frank Aiken, 8 November 1937.

45 LFA, Pension files.

46 AIHS, FOIF Papers, Record Book, p. 2; 'Record of all money sent directly or indirectly to Ireland from the Victory Fund'.

47 AIHS, FOIF Papers, Minutes of meeting, 24 September 1919.

48 LFA, Pension files, Letter from Pensions Board to Diarmuid Lynch, 12 September 1938.

49 LFA, Pension files, Letter from Diarmuid Lynch to Dan Breen, 15 September 1938.

50 LFA, Pension files, Letter from Military Pensions Board to Diarmuid Lynch, 6 November 1940.

51 LFA, Pension files, Letter from Diarmuid Fawsitt to Pensions Board, 27 October 1944.

52 According to the administrator, Pensions Section, Department of Defence, 3 December 2012.

53 NLI, MS 32,597, FOIF history.

54 LFA, Pension files, 497, Document prepared for 19 December 1944 hearing.

55 LFA, Pension files.

56 LFA, Pension files, Letter from Diarmuid Lynch to the Referee of Pensions Board, 28 December 1944.

57 LFA, Pension files, Letter from Thomas Craven to Diarmuid Lynch, 19 August 1940. Reply from Diarmuid Lynch to Thomas Craven, 23 September 1940. The LFA pension files contain letters from Byrne, Twamley, Reynolds and Craven seeking Lynch's help. The files also contain Lynch's replies to these men and copies of his supportive letters to the Pensions Board.

11. CORK – THE FINAL DECADE

1 LFA, Deed signed 1 March 1939.

2 LFA, Accounts booklet.

3 NLI, MS 11,126, Letter from Diarmuid Lynch to Éamonn Dore,

24 July 1938. 'I leave Dublin next Thursday to take up residence in County Cork, so slán agus beannacht.'

4 LFA, Letter from Diarmuid Lynch to Florence O'Donoghue, November 1945.

5 Mikey Barry (local ex-postman), aged ninety-five, personal communication, 2010.

6 LFA, Letter from Diarmuid Lynch to Éamonn Kissane, TD, 15 June 1944.

7 Dolores Lynch, personal communication, May 2012.

8 LFA, Letter from Seán McCarthy to Diarmuid Lynch, 23 June 1944.

9 LFA, Letter from Liam Tóibín to Diarmuid Lynch, 22 June 1944.

10 LFA, Letter from Diarmuid Lynch to Éamon de Valera, 27 June 1944.

11 LFA, Letter from Diarmuid Lynch to Florence O'Donoghue, 25 April 1947.

12 See Appendix I.

13 H. B. C. Pollard, *The Secret Societies of Ireland: Their Rise and Progress*, London: Philip Allan & Co., 1922.

14 CCCA, U179, *An Cosantóir* files, Letter to P. S. O'Hegarty, 14 February 1945.

15 CCCA, U179, *An Cosantóir* files, Letter from Diarmuid Lynch to Donagh MacDonagh, 26 January 1946.

16 NLI, MS 31,407–9, Letter from Florence O'Donoghue to Colonel D. Bryan, 5 March 1945.

17 CCCA, U179, *An Cosantóir* files, Letter from Editorial Offices, Collins Barracks, Cork, to Diarmuid Lynch, 21 March 1945.

18 CCCA, U179, *An Cosantóir* files, Letter from Florence O'Donoghue to *An Cosantóir*, 19 September 1945.

19 CCCA, U179, *An Cosantóir* files, Letter from Diarmuid Lynch to Florence O'Donoghue, 6 April 1945.

20 BMH, WS 651.

21 NLI, MS 31,409, Florence O'Donoghue Papers, Letter from Geraldine Plunkett to Florence O'Donoghue, 4 February 1952.

22 BMH, WS 1686, Letters from Rúairí Mac Ionnraic to Diarmuid Lynch and from Colonel T. P. Gallagher to Diarmuid Lynch, May–August 1945.

23 NLI, MS 31,493–31,514, Florence O'Donoghue Papers, Letter from Florence O'Donoghue to General Michael J. Costello, 18 December 1953.

24 LFA, Document of twenty-six foolscap pages, original of 'Quotations and Comments by Diarmuid Lynch' on R. M. Fox, *Green Banners*. The critique was reproduced in Lynch (1957), p. 103.

25 Lynch (1957), p. 94.

26 *Sunday Press*, 21 May 1961.

27 *Sunday Press*, 21 May 1961.

28 CCCA, U179, *An Cosantóir* files, Series of letters between Joe O'Connor, National Library and Diarmuid Lynch, September and October 1946.

29 BMH, WS 120, *The National Flag*.

30 CCCA, U179, Letter from Diarmuid Lynch to Patrick O'Connor.

31 NLI, MS 31,409 (5).

32 BMH, WS 120.

33 LFA, Letter from James McGurrin to Diarmuid Lynch, 21 August 1935.

34 AIHS, Daniel F. Cohalan Papers, Letter from Diarmuid Lynch to Daniel Cohalan, 28 November 1941.

35 *The Irish Press*, 14 November 1946.

36 *The Irish Press*, 26 November 1946.

37 *The Irish Press*, 29 November 1946.

38 LFA, Letter from William Sweetman to Diarmuid Lynch, 15 January 1947.

39 LFA, Letter from Richard Dalton to Diarmuid Lynch, 26 November 1946.

40 LFA, Letter from Diarmuid Lynch to Richard Dalton, 7 December 1946.

41 LFA, Letter from Diarmuid Lynch to Madge Cohalan, November 1946.

42 NLI, MS 31,412, Florence O'Donoghue Papers.

43 NLI, 33,930, Piaras Béaslaí Papers, Letter from Diarmuid Lynch to Piaras Béaslaí, 21 March 1950.

44 LFA, Letter from Diarmuid Lynch to G. A. Hayes-McCoy, 27 October 1950.

45 LFA, Letter from Diarmuid Lynch to Curator of Cork Museum, Mr M. J. Kelly, 17 July 1950.

46 *The Irish Press*, 1 November 1950, LFA cutting.

47 LFA, Letter from Denis McCullough to Diarmuid Lynch, 30 October 1950.

48 *The Gaelic American*, 2 December 1950, Letter from Denis Lynch.

49 *The Gaelic American*, 18 November 1950, p. 1.

50 *The Cork Examiner*, 13 November 1950.

51 *The Cork Examiner*, 13 November 1950.

52 *Sunday Press*, 12 November 1950.

53 UCDA, Éamon de Valera Papers, P150, Diaries.

54 UCDA, P150/342.

55 LFA, Diarmuid Lynch Memorial Committee data.

56 NLI, MS 31,493, Florence O'Donoghue Papers, Letter from Richard Dalton to Michael J. Costello, 12 December 1951.

57 AIHS, FOIF Papers.

58 LFA, Executor's account, December 1955.

59 *The Cork Examiner*, 20 June 1966.

12. LYNCH'S CONTRIBUTION TO HISTORICAL RECORDS

1   Lynch (1957), Chapter 1.

2   Lynch (1957), Preface.

3   Lynch (1957), pp. 181–6.

4   NLI, MS 31,412 (2), Florence O'Donoghue Papers.

5   Lynch (1957), p. 155 (comment by O'Donoghue).

6   NLI, MS 31,412, Letter from Robert Dudley Edwards to Florence O'Donoghue, 19 February 1957.

7   NLI, MS 31,412 (2), Florence O'Donoghue Papers.

8   NLI, MS 31,412 (2), Florence O'Donoghue Papers, Letter from Robert Dudley Edwards to Florence O'Donoghue, 19 February 1957.

9   Review of *The I.R.B. and the 1916 Insurrection*, by Walter McGrath; 'The Plans Which Led to Easter Week', *The Cork Examiner*, 16 May 1957, p. 4.

10 Pádraig Ó Maidín, 'A Boy from Old Knocknamana', *The Cork Examiner*, 7 January 1977.

11 Pádraig Ó Maidín, 'A Boy from Old Knocknamana', *The Cork Examiner*, 7 January 1977.

12 Pádraig Ó Snodaigh, *Comhghuaillithe na Réabhlóide, 1913–1916*, Dublin: Coiscéim, 1966.

13 Edward MacLysaght, 'Larkin, Connolly, and the Labour Movement', in F. X. Martin (ed.), *Leaders and Men of the Easter Rising: Dublin 1916*, London: Methuen & Co., 1967, p. 129.

14 W. J. Brennan-Whitmore, *Dublin Burning: The Easter Rising from behind the Barricades*, edited by Pauric Travers, Dublin: Gill & Macmillan, 1996.

15 F. X. Martin, '1916: Myth, Fact, and Mystery', *Studia Hibernica*, 7 (1967): 7–126.

16 Martin (1967), p. 34.

17 Martin (1967), p. 34.

18 Townshend (2006), p. 157.

19 Townshend (2006), p. xvi.

20 Townshend (2006), p. 158.

21 Keith Jeffery, *The GPO and the Easter Rising*, Dublin: Irish Academic Press, 2006.

22 NLI, MS 11,128, Boxed and labelled GPO Garrison, 1936 Reports.

23 Fearghal McGarry, *The Rising: Ireland, Easter 1916*, Oxford: Oxford University Press, 2010.

24 Owen McGee, *The IRB: The Irish Republican Brotherhood from the Land League to Sinn Féin*, Dublin: Four Courts, 2005.

25 LFA, Letter from Diarmuid Lynch to the Bureau of Military History, 11 September 1950.

26 LFA, Letter from Florence O'Donoghue to Kit Lynch, 20 June 1952.

27 LFA, Letter from P. J. Brennan, of the BMH, to Diarmuid Lynch (nephew), 28 June 1957.

28 LFA, Diarmuid Lynch Memorial Committee Circular.

CONCLUSION

1 *The Gaelic American*, 22 March 1924, Report on banquet held in the Hotel Astor on 9 March 1924. Italics speaker's own.

2 Ó Murchadha (1976), p. 335.

3 LFA, Letter from Liam Cullen and Liam Tannan of the Easter Week Memorial Committee to Diarmuid Lynch, 19 June 1936.

4 Patrick Murray, 'Obsessive Historian: Éamon De Valera and the Policing of his Reputation', *Proceedings of the Royal Irish Academy*, 101C (2) (2001), p. 44.

5 Murray (2001), p. 44.

6 Murray (2001), p. 44.

7 Murray (2001), p. 44.

8 Murray (2001), p. 39.

9   NLI, MS 31,412, Florence O'Donoghue Papers, Letter from de Valera to Florence O'Donoghue, 9 July 1954.

10 LFA.

11 For example, he was listed as a member in the *Journal of the American-Irish Society*, vol. 34, 1940.

12 AIHS, FOIF Papers, History Summary.

13 BMH, WS 4, Part 1: *The I.R.B.*, pp. 5–6.

14 BMH, WS 4, Part 1: *The I.R.B.*, p. 4.

15 LFA, Letter from Diarmuid Lynch to William O'Brien, 2 June 1948.

16 UCDA, Éamon de Valera Papers, P150/1011.

17 AIHS, Daniel F. Cohalan Papers, Letter from Diarmuid Lynch to Daniel F. Cohalan, 12 July 1920.

18 AIHS, Daniel F. Cohalan Papers, Letter from Diarmuid Lynch to Daniel F. Cohalan, 12 July 1921.

19 AIHS, Daniel F. Cohalan Papers, Letter from Diarmuid Lynch to Daniel F. Cohalan, 10 August 1921.

20 Lynch (1957), p. 210.

21 AIHS, FOIF Papers, Record of expenses of National Secretary, 1921–31.

22 LFA, Letter from Diarmuid Lynch to Éamon Kissane, TD, 15 June 1944.

23 LFA, Letter from Liam Ó Bríain to Diarmuid Lynch, 15 April 1946.

24 LFA, Letters from Diarmuid Lynch to Florence O'Donoghue and to Richard Dalton, 1937–48.

25 CCCA, U179, Letter from Diarmuid Lynch to editor of *An Cosantóir*, 19 September 1945, defending Clan na Gael; see also AIHS, Cohalan Papers, copy of letter by Diarmuid Lynch which appeared in *The Irish Press*, Dublin, on 26 November 1946 defending Devoy and Cohalan.

26 'It is clear to me however ... that his great and vital interest and activity was expressed in those years before 1916 when he went through the country doing the spade work in the IRB which made 1916 possible.' From the eulogy by O'Hegarty at Lynch's funeral.

27 Included in an essay on O'Reilly written by George MacNamara, published in the *Notre Dame Scholastic*, 19 November 1904, p. 151.

28 NLI, MS 32,597, FOIF history; see also AIHS FOIF Papers.

29 CCCA, U179, Letter from Diarmuid Lynch to Florence O'Donoghue, 28 June 1947.

30 NLI, 31,409, Letters from Denis McCullough to Kit Lynch and Richard Dalton, January 1951.

Manuscript Sources
and Official Publications

IRELAND

GRANIG HOUSE, CORK COUNTY, LYNCH FAMILY ARCHIVES
Chronological Files, 1–7
Box of thirty-five folders of loose documents, organised chronologically, 1–35
Library of Diarmuid Lynch (1878–1950)

ARCHIVE OF BRÍD DUGGAN, INNISHANNON, COUNTY CORK, NIECE OF DIARMUID LYNCH

ARCHIVE OF DUIBHNE DALY, COUNTY WEXFORD, GRAND-NIECE OF DIARMUID LYNCH

NLI, DUBLIN
Diarmuid Lynch Papers
Florence O'Donoghue Papers
John Devoy Papers
Daniel F. Cohalan Papers
Peter Golden Papers
Piaras Béaslaí Papers

UCDA SPECIAL COLLECTIONS
Éamon de Valera Papers

UNIVERSITY COLLEGE LIMERICK GLUCKSMAN LIBRARY, SPECIAL COLLECTIONS

Madge Daly Papers

CORK CITY AND COUNTY ARCHIVES

U271, Liam De Róiste Papers

U179, *An Cosantóir* Files

BRITAIN

THE NATIONAL ARCHIVES, KEW, LONDON

British Intelligence Files

UNITED STATES OF AMERICA

AIHS ARCHIVES, NEW YORK

FOIF Papers

Judge Daniel F. Cohalan Papers

Newspapers, Periodicals and Journals

An Cosantóir

Chicago Daily Tribune

Cork Constitution

Cork Examiner, The

Freeman's Journal, The

FOIF Newsletters

Gaelic American, The

Irish-American

Irish Historical Studies

Irish Independent

Irish Press (Dublin), The

Irish Press (Philadelphia)

Irish Times, The

Irish World (New York)

Journal of the Cork Historical and Archaeological Society

National Bureau of Information, Washington, Bulletins

New York Times, The

Philadelphia Ledger

Studia Hibernica

Sunday Press

Westminster Gazette

Bibliography

Barry, Tom, *Guerilla Days in Ireland*, 2nd edn, Cork: Mercier Press, 1955

Barton, Brian, *From Behind a Closed Door: Secret Court Martial Records of the 1916 Easter Rising*, Belfast: Blackstaff Press, 2002

Béaslaí, Piaras, *Michael Collins and the Making of a New Ireland*, 2 vols, Dublin: Phoenix, 1926

Bell, J. Bowyer, *The Secret Army: A History of the IRA, 1916–1970*, London: Blond, 1970

Borgonovo, John, *Spies, Informers and the 'Anti-Sinn Féin Society': The Intelligence War in Cork City, 1920–1921*, Dublin: Irish Academic Press, 2007

— 'Cork City Riots of June 1917', *Journal of the Cork Historical and Archaeological Society*, 114 (2009): 10–20

— 'Evolution of a Revolution, Cork City, 1916–1918', PhD thesis, University College Cork, 2009

Brasier, Andrew and John Kelly, *Harry Boland: A Man Divided*, Dublin: New Century Publishing, 2000

Breen, Dan, *My Fight for Irish Freedom*, Cork: Mercier Press, 2007

Brennan, Michael, *The War in Clare, 1911–1921: Personal Memoirs of the Irish War of Independence*, Dublin: Four Courts Press and Irish Academic Press, 1980

Brennan, Robert, *Allegiance: An Account of the Author's Experiences in the Struggle for Irish Independence*, Dublin: Browne and Nolan, 1950

Brennan-Whitmore, W. J., *With the Irish in Frongoch*, Dublin: Talbot Press, 1917

— *Dublin Burning: The Easter Rising from behind the Barricades*, edited by Pauric Travers, Dublin: Gill and Macmillan, 1996

Brown, Thomas N., *Irish-American Nationalism, 1870–1890*, Philadelphia, Pa.: Lippincott, 1966

Carroll, F. M., *American Opinion and the Irish Question, 1910–1923: A Study in Opinion and Policy*, Dublin and New York: Gill & Macmillan and St Martin's Press, 1978

— *Money for Ireland: Finance, Diplomacy, Politics and the First Dáil Éireann Loans, 1919–1936*, Westport, Conn.: Praeger, 2002

Caulfield, Max, *The Easter Rebellion*, Dublin: Gill & Macmillan, 1995

Clarke, Kathleen, *Revolutionary Woman: Kathleen Clarke*, edited by Helen Litton, Dublin: O'Brien Press, 2008

Coffey, Thomas M., *Agony at Easter: The 1916 Irish Uprising*, London: Harrap, 1970

Collins, Michael, *The Path to Freedom*, Cork: Mercier Press, 2011

Coogan, Tim Pat, *De Valera: Long Fellow, Long Shadow*, London: Hutchinson, 1993

Cosgrave, W. T., *With the President in America: The Authorised Record of President Cosgrave's Tour in the United States and Canada*, Dublin: O'Kennedy-Brindley Ltd, 1928

Cowell, John, *A Noontide Blazing: Brigid Lyons Thornton, Rebel, Soldier, Doctor*, Blackrock: Currach Press, 2005

Cullen, Finbar (ed.), *The 1916 Rising: Then and Now*, Dublin: Ireland Institute, 2008

Dalton, Charles, *With the Dublin Brigade (1917–1921)*, London: Peter Davies, 1929

Daly, Mary E. and Margaret O'Callaghan (eds), *1916 in 1966: Com-*

memorating the Easter Rising, Dublin: Royal Irish Academy, 2007

De Blaghad, Earnán, *Gaeil Á Múscailt*, Dublin: Sáirséal agus Dill, 1973

Denieffe, Joseph, *A Personal Narrative of the Irish Revolutionary Brotherhood*, London: Irish University Press, 1969

Devoy, John, *Recollections of an Irish Rebel; the Fenian Movement; personalities of the organization; the Clan-Na-Gael and the Rising of Easter Week, 1916: A Personal Narrative*, New York: Charles Young, 1929

Doherty, Gabriel and Dermot Keogh, *Michael Collins and the Making of the Irish State*, Cork: Mercier Press, 1998

Dooley, Terence A. M., *The Greatest of the Fenians: John Devoy and Ireland*, Dublin: Wolfhound Press, 2003

Doorley, Michael, *Irish-American Diaspora Nationalism: The Friends of Irish Freedom, 1916–35*, Dublin: Four Courts Press, 2005

Dudley Edwards, Owen and Fergus Pyle (eds), *1916: The Easter Rising*, London: MacGibbon & Kee, 1968

Dudley Edwards, Ruth, *Patrick Pearse: The Triumph of Failure*, London: Gollancz, 1977

Duggan, Bríd, *Diarmuid Lynch Tells of Trip to Ireland*, New York: Allied Printers, 1923

English, Richard, *Irish Freedom: The History of Nationalism in Ireland*, London: Macmillan, 2006

Ferguson, Stephen, *Business as Usual: GPO Staff During the 1916 Rising*, Cork: Mercier Press, 2012

Ferriter, Diarmaid, *Judging Dev: A Reassessment of the Life and Legacy of Eamon De Valera*, Dublin: Royal Irish Academy, 2007

Figgis, Darrell, *Recollections of the Irish War*, London: Ernest Benn, 1927

Fitzgerald, Desmond, *Desmond's Rising: Memoirs, 1913 to Easter 1916*, Dublin: Liberties Press, 2006

Fitzgerald, William G. (ed.), *The Voice of Ireland: A Survey of the Race and Nation from All Angles by the Foremost Leaders at Home and Abroad*, Dublin: Virtue & Co., 1923

Fitzpatrick, David, *Harry Boland's Irish Revolution*, Cork: Cork University Press, 2003

Fox, R. M., *Green Banners: The Story of the Irish Struggle*, London: Secker & Warburg, 1938

Gallagher, Frank, *Days of Fear: Diary of a 1920s Hunger Striker*, Cork: Mercier Press, 2008

Garvin, Tom, *1922: The Birth of Irish Democracy*, Dublin: Gill and Macmillan, 1996

Ginnell, Lawrence, *The Irish Republic, Why?*, New York: The Friends of Irish Freedom, 1919

Girvin, Kevin, *Seán O'Hegarty: Officer Commanding, First Cork Brigade, Irish Republican Army*, Aubane: Aubane Historical Society, 2007

Golway, Terry, *Irish Rebel: John Devoy and America's Fight for Ireland's Freedom*, New York: St Martin's Press, 1998

Greaves, C. Desmond, *Liam Mellows and the Irish Revolution*, London: Lawrence & Wishart, 1971

Griffith, Richard, *General Valuation of Rateable Property in Ireland, County of Cork, Barony of Kinalea*, Dublin: G. & J. Grierson, 1851

Gwynn, Denis, *The History of Partition, 1912–1925*, Dublin: Browne and Nolan, 1950

Hannigan, Dave, *De Valera in America: The Rebel President's 1919 Campaign*, Dublin: The O'Brien Press, 2008

Hart, Peter, *Mick: The Real Michael Collins*, London: Pan Books, 2006

Hennessy, Mark, 'US Envoys Plot to Deport "Dangerous Agitator"', *The Irish Times*, 6 July 2011

Hobson, Bulmer, *Ireland Yesterday and Tomorrow*, Tralee: Anvil Books, 1968

Holt, Edgar, *Protest in Arms: The Irish Troubles, 1916–1923*, London: Putnam, 1960

Hull, Eleanor, *A History of Ireland and Her People*, 2 vols, Dublin: The Phoenix Publishing Company Limited, 1926–31

Hyde, Douglas, *Mo thurus go hAmerice: no, Imeasg na nGaedheal ins an Oileán Úr*, Dublin: Oifig Díolta Foillseacháin Rialtais, 1937

Jeffery, Keith, *The GPO and the Easter Rising*, Dublin: Irish Academic Press, 2006

Lavelle, Patricia, *James O'Mara: A Staunch Sinn-Féiner, 1873–1948*, Dublin: Clonmore & Reynolds, 1961

Le Roux, Louis N., *Tom Clarke and the Irish Freedom Movement*, Dublin: Talbot Press, 1936

Lee, J. J. and Marion R. Casey (eds), *Making the Irish American: History and Heritage of the Irish in the United States*, New York: New York University Press, 2006

Longford, Earl of and Thomas P. O'Neill, *Eamon de Valera*, London: Hutchinson, 1970

Lynch, Diarmuid, *The I.R.B. and the 1916 Insurrection*, edited by Florence O'Donoghue, Cork: Mercier Press, 1957

Mac an Bheatha, Proinsías, *Tart na Córa: Saol agus Saothar Shéamais Uí Chonghaile*, Dublin: Foilseacháin Náisiúnta Teóranta, 1962

Macardle, Dorothy, *The Irish Republic: A Documented Chronicle of the Anglo-Irish Conflict and the Partitioning of Ireland, with a Detailed Account of the Period 1916–1923*, 4th edn, Dublin: Irish Press, 1951

MacCurtain, Fionnuala, *Remember ... It's for Ireland: A Family*

Memoir of Tomás Mac Curtain, Cork: Mercier Press, 2006

MacEntee, Seán, *Episode at Easter*, Dublin: Gill and Son, 1966

MacGiolla Choille, Breandán, 'Review of Intelligence Notes, 1913–16, Preserved in the State Paper Office', *Irish Historical Studies*, 16 (61), 1968, pp. 99–102

MacLysaght, Edward, 'Larkin, Connolly, and the Labour Movement', in F. X. Martin (ed.), *Leaders and Men of the Easter Rising: Dublin 1916*, London: Methuen & Co., 1967, pp. 122–33

Maher, Jim, *Harry Boland*, Cork: Mercier Press, 1998

Martin, F. X., *The Irish Volunteers, 1913–1915: Recollections and Documents*, Dublin: James Duffy, 1963

— '1916: Myth, Fact, and Mystery', *Studia Hibernica*, 7, 1967, pp. 7–126

— (ed.), *Leaders and Men of the Easter Rising: Dublin 1916*, London: Methuen & Co., 1967

Matthews, Ann, *Renegades: Irish Republican Women, 1900–1922*, Cork: Mercier Press, 2010

McCaffrey, Lawrence J. (ed.), *Irish Nationalism and the American Contribution*, New York: Arno Press, 1976

McCartan, Patrick, *With De Valera in America: An Account of Irish Republican Propaganda in the United States, 1918–21*, Dublin: Fitzpatrick, 1932

McGarry, Fearghal, *The Rising: Ireland, Easter 1916*, Oxford: Oxford University Press, 2010

McGee, Owen, *The IRB: The Irish Republican Brotherhood from the Land League to Sinn Féin*, Dublin: Four Courts, 2005

McHugh, Roger, *Dublin 1916*, London: Arlington Books, 1966

Moran, James, *Staging the Easter Rising: 1916 as Theatre*, Cork: Cork University Press, 2005

Morrissey, Thomas J., SJ, *William O'Brien, 1881–1968*, Dublin: Four Courts Press, 2007

Murray, Patrick, 'Obsessive Historian: Éamon De Valera and the Policing of his Reputation', *Proceedings of the Royal Irish Academy*, 101C (2), 2001, pp. 2–65

Nevin, Donal, *James Connolly: 'A Full Life'*, Manchester: Manchester University Press, 2005

Ní Bhroiméil, Úna, *Building Irish Identity in America 1870–1915: The Gaelic Revival*, Dublin: Four Courts Press, 2003

Norstedt, Johann A., *Thomas MacDonagh: A Critical Biography*, Charlottesville, Va.: University Press of Virginia, 1980

Norway, Mary Louisa and Arthur Hamilton Norway, *The Sinn Féin Rebellion as They Saw It*, London: Smith, Elder & Co., 1932

O'Brien, Paul, *Blood on the Streets: 1916 and the Battle for Mount Street Bridge*, Cork: Mercier Press, 2008

O'Brien, William and Desmond Ryan (eds), *Devoy's Post Bag, 1871–1928*, 2 vols, Dublin: C. J. Fallon, 1948–53

Ó Broin, Leon, *Na Sasanaigh agus Éirí Amach na Cásca: Scéal Nathan*, Sairséal agus Dill, 1967

— *Fenian Fever: An Anglo-American Dilemma*, London: Chatto & Windus, 1971

— *Revolutionary Underground: The Story of the Irish Republican Brotherhood, 1858–1924*, Dublin: Gill & Macmillan, 1976

O'Carroll, John P. and John A. Murphy (eds), *De Valera and His Times*, Cork: Cork University Press, 1983

O'Connor, John, *The 1916 Proclamation*, Cork: Mercier Press, 2001

O'Doherty, Katherine, *Assignment America*, New York: De Tanko Publishers, 1957

O'Donoghue, Florence, *Tomás MacCurtain*, Tralee: Kerryman, 1958

O'Farrell, Mick, *A Walk through Rebel Dublin, 1916*, Cork: Mercier Press, 1999

O'Hegarty, P. S., *The Victory of Sinn Féin: How It Won It and How It Used It*, Dublin: Talbot Press, 1924

— *A History of Ireland under the Union, 1801–1922: with an Epilogue Carrying the Story Down to the Acceptance, in 1927*, London: Methuen, 1952

Ó Lúing, Seán, *John Devoy*, Dublin: Cló Morainn, 1961

O'Mahony, Seán, *Frongoch: University of Revolution*, Killiney: FDR Teóranta, 1987

Ó Maidín, Pádraig, 'A Boy from Old Knocknamana', *The Cork Examiner*, 7 January 1977

O'Malley, Ernie, *The Singing Flame*, Cork: Mercier Press, 2012

Ó Murchadha, Diarmuid, *Liam de Róiste*, Dublin: An Clóchomhar, 1976

Ó Siadhail, Pádraig, *An Béaslaoích: Beatha agus Saothair Phiarais Béaslaí*, Dublin: Coiscéim, 2007

Ó Snodaigh, Pádraig, *Comhghuaillithe na Réabhlóide, 1913–1916*, Dublin: Coiscéim, 1966

Pearse, Patrick, *The Coming Revolution: the political writings and speeches of Patrick Pearse*, Cork: Mercier Press, 2012

Pollard, H. B. C., *The Secret Societies of Ireland: Their Rise and Progress*, London: Philip Allan & Co., 1922

Rafter, Kevin, *Sinn Féin, 1905–2005: In the Shadow of Gunmen*, Dublin: Gill & Macmillan, 2005

Ryan, Annie, *Witnesses Inside the Easter Rising*, Dublin: Liberties Press, 2005

Ryan, Desmond, *Unique Dictator: A Study of Eamon de Valera*, London: Arthur Barker Ltd, 1936

— *The Phoenix Flame: A Study of Fenianism and John Devoy*, London: Arthur Barker Ltd, 1937

— *The Rising: The Complete Story of Easter Week,* Dublin: Golden Eagle Books, 1949

Sinn Féin Rebellion Handbook, compiled by the *Weekly Irish Times*, Dublin: Fred Hanna, 1917

Stephens, James, *The Insurrection in Dublin*, Dublin and London: Maunsel & Co., 1916

Tansill, Charles Callan, *America and the Fight for Irish Freedom, 1866–1922: An Old Story Based Upon New Data*, New York: Devin-Adair, 1957

Tarpey, Marie Veronica, *The Role of Joseph McGarrity in the Struggle for Irish Independence*, New York: Arno Press, 1976

Thompson, William Irwin, *The Imagination of an Insurrection: Dublin, Easter 1916 – A Study of an Ideological Movement*, Oxford: Oxford University Press, 1967

Townshend, Charles, *Easter 1916*, London: Penguin, 2006

Uí Fhlannagáin, Fionnuala, *Fíníní Mheiriceá agus an Ghaeilge*, Dublin: Coiscéim, 2008

Valiulis, Maryann Gialanella, *Portrait of a Revolutionary: General Richard Mulcahy and the Founding of the Irish Free State*, Dublin: Irish Academic Press, 1992

Ward, Alan J., *Ireland and Anglo-American Relations, 1899–1921*, London: Weidenfeld & Nicholson, 1969

Whelan, Bernadette, *United States Foreign Policy and Ireland: From Empire to Independence, 1913–29*, Dublin: Four Courts Press, 2006

White, Gerry and Brendan O'Shea, *'Baptised in Blood': The Formation of the Cork Brigade of Irish Volunteers, 1913–1916*, Cork: Mercier Press, 2005

— *The Burning of Cork*, Cork: Mercier Press, 2006

Williams, T. Desmond, 'Eoin MacNeill and the Irish Volunteers', in F. X. Martin (ed.), *Leaders and Men of the Easter Rising: Dublin 1916*, London: Methuen & Co., 1967

Wills, Clair, *Dublin 1916: The Siege of the GPO*, London: Profile Books, 2009

Index